# TWICE ARMED

# TWICE ARMED

## An American Soldier's Battle for Hearts and Minds in Iraq

### R. ALAN KING
LIEUTENANT COLONEL, USAR

ZENITH PRESS

First published in 2006 by Zenith Press, an imprint of MBI Publishing Company, Galtier Plaza, Suite 200, 380 Jackson Street, St. Paul, MN 55101-3885 USA

Zenith Press titles are also available at discounts in bulk quantity for industrial or sales-promotional use. For details write to Special Sales Manager at MBI Publishing Company, Galtier Plaza, Suite 200, 380 Jackson Street, St. Paul, MN 55101-3885 USA.

ISBN-13: 978-0-7603-2386-1
ISBN-10: 0-7603-2386-0

*On the front cover:* "Here I pose with villagers outside An Najaf, April 2, 2003. I had removed my gun holster when in the village as a show of trust, which was reciprocated by the villagers." *Spc. James Allen*

*On the spine:* "Sheik Hussein Ali al-Shaalan and I greet each other." *Annia Ciezadlo*

*On the back cover:* "Village elders near An Najaf declared me to be a believer and brought me into a mosque for afternoon prayers, March 2003." *Staff Sgt. Kevin Bell*

Library of Congress Cataloging-in-Publication Data

King, R. Alan, 1963-
    Twice armed : an American soldier's battle for hearts and minds in Iraq / R. Alan King.
        p. cm.
    Includes index.
    ISBN-13: 978-0-7603-2386-1 (hardbound w/ jacket)
    ISBN-10: 0-7603-2386-0 (hardbound w/ jacket) 1. Iraq War, 2003—Personal narratives, American. 2. King, R. Alan, 1963- 3. Soldiers—United States—Biography. I. Title.
    DS79.76.K55 2006
    956.7044'3092—dc22
    [B]
                                        2006019679

Printed in the United States of America

*Could we see when and where we are to meet again,*
*we would be more tender when we bid our friends goodbye.*
—Marie Louise de la Ramée

To Capt. John Smathers, Cpl. Mark Bibby, Omar, Fallah,
and the courageous American and Iraqi men and women who
have given their lives in pursuit of freedom and democracy.

*May we succeed so you did not die in vain!*

*We are twice armed if we fight with faith.*
—Plato

# Contents

# Introduction

*God sells knowledge for labor, honor for risk.*
*—Arab proverb*

Through experience and study, I have gained an appreciation and understanding of the rich history of Iraq. I could not have dreamed of the splendor of the country and the people I would meet. Iraq might not have Egypt's pyramids and mummies, but it is second only to Israel in the number of Bible references. Babylon, Nineveh, and other great biblical cities of antiquity once lay within its borders, and many people believe the Garden of Eden lies somewhere in the fertile lands between the Tigris and Euphrates Rivers.

The people of Iraq have ageless traditions. Their tight family units and community social structures have survived numerous occupations through the centuries. Iraqis deeply cherish their traditions and in the rural areas the tribal aspect of life is ever present. Whether traveling north, south, east, or west, Iraqis are prone to come across a relative they did not know they had, guaranteeing room and board for the evening.

Iraq's major cities are unlike those of Middle Eastern countries. Baghdad, for instance, with its five-and-a-half million inhabitants, more closely resembles a large village than a major city like Beirut or Cairo. Though most of the area of Iraq is rural or desert, especially in the west and south, it is nevertheless a modern country whose society and culture has been evolving over five millennia.

Exporting freedom and democracy by way of our military to the birthplace of mankind on the other side of the globe creates unique challenges, particularly for a young upstart nation like the United States. It requires answering the fundamental questions as to how and why all this became necessary.

Iraq has been occupied since 579 B.C., and generations have learned to survive under an occupier's law. This history gives the Iraqis a worldview different from that of the Westernized world. We can make all the assurances in the world, but to many Iraqis, the United States is just another occupier. It will only be possible to overcome deeply rooted cultural beliefs by recognizing and fully acknowledging their existence. Herein lies the great challenge in Iraq.

Today's Iraq is populated by more than twenty-five million people who have lived for over three decades as prisoners in a country isolated from the rest of the world. Under Saddam Hussein, one could be imprisoned for six months merely for possessing a satellite dish (one dares not imagine the punishment for actually using it). In Iraq, the government told citizens what to think, when to think, and how to respond to what they thought. Independent thought was reserved for Saddam and his closest followers. Because of the oppression of thought, Iraqis have a minimal grasp of the true meaning of liberty. A quaint notion such as "freedom ends when it transgresses the freedom of others" would sound like something from another world to many Iraqis.

Having met and listened to so many of the former Iraqi elites, sheiks, and average citizens, there is no doubt in my mind that the war in Iraq was necessary and justified. Saddam was a tyrant and a criminal. His sons were even worse, and simply had to go. Even though no weapons of mass destruction (WMD) were found in Iraq, there is little doubt that one day a future Iraqi government, led by Saddam's sons, would have created or acquired them. It is undeniable that Saddam had developed and prolifically used WMD against the Iranians and the Kurds in the 1980s. It is apparent now that the search and removal efforts by the United States and the United Nations after the first Gulf War had removed all of Saddam's existing WMDs. What still remained were the knowledge and the will to reacquire them in the future.

Saddam's government continued covertly researching weapons that were not sanctioned under the UN. Several members of the Iraqi military industry told me they had personally researched and designed plans for long-range missiles even while the country was under UN sanctions. Former scientists who had worked on Iraq's nuclear program explained with a degree of smugness that by 1991, they were only a few years away from developing nuclear weapons. Although their research was halted, the knowledge that came from their research had been retained. That there were unscrupulous individuals and governments in the intervening years who would have sold Saddam their souls (or the materials to make WMDs) for the right price should go without saying.

Saddam's regime left countless horrors in its wake. I sat with many victims and individuals whose family members had been killed and tortured. The brutality was incomprehensible, even with the physical evidence right before my eyes. One individual had literally been nailed to a table with stakes driven through his legs, leaving horrible scars. Others had been severely beaten. In a sense, they were the lucky ones. Others had their ears amputated or eyes gouged out. I will refrain from describing the most horrid stories I heard. Simply put, Saddam was a terrorist. He was not just a threat to the people of Iraq, but to his neighbors and to the United States. He had made plans to assassinate former presidents George H. W. Bush and Bill Clinton. He terrorized his own people and he paid the families of suicide bombers in Palestine.

Our presence in Iraq has become less and less popular with each passing day, week, and month. It is easy for those not faced with decision-making responsibility to play amateur politician, questioning those who voted in favor of going to war. The simple truth is that the United States should have gone into Iraq, did go into Iraq, and now has a responsibility to stay in Iraq and finish what it started.

This war is not about oil, race, or religion, as many antiwar pundits try to argue. This war is not Vietnam, which was a regional conflict. In fact, the fighting in Iraq is only one battle in a global threat. This war toppled a dictator who was ruthless and evil. He and his sons needed to be removed, for the safety of Iraq, the Middle East, and the rest of the world.

When I arrived in Baghdad, my first frustration was the inability to communicate. The Iraqi dialect is unlike any other Arab dialect. While the Iraqis might have been able to understand American translators, the American translators I worked with did not, for the most part, understand what the Iraqis were saying to them.

My frustration with communicating was insignificant compared to the frustration of the Iraqis over their shortage of electricity. It is perhaps the most immediate problem that Iraq faces on a day-to-day basis. The country's system, old and decrepit as it was, had the added strain of new appliances and air conditioners that flooded the market after the Coalition's arrival. To this day, Iraq contends with hours, sometimes days, without electricity. Tempers reach a boiling point from the lack of sleep in temperatures that hover at 70 to 80 degrees at night and more than 140 degrees during the day. Most Iraqis I spoke with said that if the Coalition were able to fix this one problem, it would cool many a temper and gain a measure of devotion from the people of Iraq.

Though I was told the night I arrived in Baghdad that there was no plan for the reconstruction of Baghdad, I learned almost a year later that there was a plan for the reconstruction of Iraq. The "Future of Iraq Project" was to be headed by Tom Warrick from the State Department, and technocrats had been identified to fill positions within the various ministries. But it was never implemented. The reasons for this are a mystery, but the fact is that it was not, and now it is important to make the best of what is available.

I have been fortunate to meet some of our country's most intelligent and worldly experts on the Middle East and Islam. For example, Ambassadors Ron Schlicher, Chris Ross, Dick Jones, and Ron Neuman; Drs. Mike Izady and Brad McGuinn; Tom Warrick; Bob Kitrinos; and countless others. The United States has plenty of scholars and regional experts, along with a broader grouping of Iraqi exiles, to advise on the ongoing Middle Eastern issues. These people would have been invaluable resources for the Coalition in planning Iraq's future.

But that didn't happen. Instead, our leadership relied on select individuals in the government here and in Iraq, many of whom carried their own personal agendas. Had we focused more on Iraq's future after the war, we could have significantly lessened both the alienation between the Sunnis and the former military and the resistance to our occupation throughout the country.

# CHAPTER 1

# Reflections of War

*Tell the truth, but keep one foot in the stirrup.*
*—Arab proverb*

On June 27, 2004, I prepared to leave the Green Zone—the heavily protected American sector—for the last time. After seventeen months in the Middle East, sixteen of them in Iraq, it was time to go home and see my family. I should have been in high spirits, but instead, I was full of regrets.

I had served as a battalion commander during the initial combat phase of the operation and then performed duties as the Coalition's tribal and Sunni outreach coordinator. My service in these positions allowed me to leave a mark on the war in Iraq in a way that I could never have imagined. Since March 21, 2003, I met more than 3,300 of the 7,380 Arab sheiks recognized by the former Iraqi regime, along with countless clerics and other dignitaries. I had the honor of sitting with the top sheiks in the country, listening to their advice and drawing from their wisdom. It was through these relationships that I was able to make a positive contribution to the Iraqi endeavor to achieve freedom and democracy. But as I prepared to go back home, I had an empty feeling that my work was unfinished.

Zumurudeh (a translator) came by my apartment as I packed the last of my bags. My driver, Hasan, and my office coordinators, Baseem and his wife Mary, helped carry my bags to the car, but Zumurudeh stayed back as if she had something she wanted to say.

She sat across from me and spoke in a soft voice, asking, "May I tell you something?"

I laughed because she had always spoken her mind. "Of course, haven't you always? What is it?"

She looked down at the table, searching for the words. She was not normally at such a loss.

"What is it?" I probed again. "Go ahead."

"When you first came here," she explained, "we all, I mean all of the translators, saw you as a liberator, even though your government said it was an occupier. You respected us, our culture and our religion."

"Thank you," I replied, feeling a little embarrassed.

She looked up as if to say be quiet and then she continued. "After Omar and Corporal Bibby were killed, we all believed you were an occupier, too."

"Me," I thought, "an *occupier?*"

Taken aback, I sat there with Zumurudeh, thinking about what her words meant. I realized that a lot had changed since I arrived in Baghdad on April 8, 2003. It had been more than four months since the last suspected terrorist had surrendered to me. Prior to this, it had been at least one a month. The failure of the Coalition to comply with the approved agreement for a surrender that I accepted had rippled through the country. There were those who simply lost their trust in me over this incident. Many suspected insurgent leaders who would otherwise be willing to surrender decided it was better to take their chances rather than be deceived, so they thought, as the others had been.

I am referring to Rasheed Sallou, a suspected terrorist cell leader with a $50,000 bounty on his head by the time he surrendered to me on February 4, 2004. An intermediary delivered Rasheed's message of surrender to one of my closest associates, Robert. Rasheed's only request was that his son, Oday, be released from Abu Ghraib Prison.

I checked around and learned that Oday had been detained as part of a raid in the northern area of Iraq a few weeks before, had been in Abu Ghraib Prison since his arrest, and his processing was nearly complete. His release and Rasheed's surrender could not have been better timed. I coordinated Oday's expedited release with the prison officials and other interested units assuming Rasheed did, in fact, follow through on his surrender. The prison agreed to rush the release once Rasheed was in custody.

A week later, a man in his late fifties wearing traditional Arab dress walked into my office. It was Rasheed. He presented me a handwritten note thanking me for my honor and for helping him keep his. He had heard I was an honorable man and that I was known to keep my word. Rasheed went on to explain that there were others wanted by the Coalition who would present themselves to me once Oday had been released. In a separate communiqué through an intermediary, I learned that other suspected cell leaders were prepared to surrender once the agreement with Rasheed was fulfilled.

Shortly after Rasheed arrived, the unit that would be escorting Rasheed to prison called my office from the lobby asking if I was ready for them. The time had come for Rasheed to go, so I shook his hand and walked with him to the awaiting vehicle. I assured him that his son would be released within the next few days.

I later went to my office, located in what was once Saddam's Presidential Palace, sat down at my desk, and drafted a message to the key personnel who were involved in the presurrender discussions. "Rasheed Sallou is in custody. He surrendered at 1530 hours this afternoon. Confirmed capture. Request Oday Rasheed be released from Abu Ghraib Prison immediately as previously coordinated."

That evening I briefed my boss, Ron Schlicher, about the surrender. He in turn briefed Ambassadors Richard Jones, deputy country administrator, and Paul Bremer, country administrator, Iraq. Schlicher was an accomplished career diplomat, and while I felt he appreciated the results my acquaintances produced, I always sensed that he was not entirely comfortable about my contact with the suspected insurgency.

In the days following Rasheed's surrender, his family began to send messengers to my office to inquire about Oday's release date. On February 16, I received a handwritten note from another suspected terrorist cell leader, one who also had a $50,000 bounty on his head: "Dear Mr. King, I have seen what you did for Mr. Rasheed, I will take my own chances."

I continued daily inquiries about the release of Oday and finally, at about 8 p.m. on March 4, 2004, my phone rang. The voice on the other end spoke excitedly in broken English, "Colonel King, thank you, thank you, he is home, we cannot thank you enough!"

"Wonderful," I replied. "I am glad Oday has finally been released."

There was a pause. "What do you mean?"

"I mean I am glad that Oday is back with his family."

"No," the surprised voice retorted, "we are calling to see when Oday will be home."

"Didn't you just say that Oday was home with you?"

The response almost made me flip over in my chair. "No, Mr. Rasheed just arrived. He wants to know when Oday will be released. You told Mr. Rasheed that Oday would be out weeks ago."

I asked for a phone number and said that I needed to check, and that I would call the family in the morning. I sat for a while at my desk in silence, and it began to dawn on me that the mother of all screw-ups had just occurred. Already angry that we had not, as agreed, expedited Oday's release, I walked into Schlicher's office. He was sitting with Ambassador Chris Ross, Tom Warrick, and Col. Dale Shirasago. "Excuse me, may I interrupt?"

Schlicher looked up. "Sure," he said. "Come on in and sit down."

Everyone in the room could tell I was livid, my boiling blood turning my fair complexion red. Ambassador Ross made a comment about the color of my face that went right past me.

"You will not believe the phone call I just received," I continued. "It was from Rasheed Sallou's family, the suspected terrorist that surrendered to me a month ago, and they said that he was at home. Rasheed had been released!"

Schlicher and Ambassador Ross looked at each other and exchanged some words in Arabic. Schlicher asked me a few more questions for clarification, and looked again to Ambassador Ross. Then he shook his head, stood up, and told me to come with him to Ambassador Jones's office. Schlicher knocked on the door and explained to Ambassador Jones what I had told him. Ambassador Jones immediately went to let Ambassador Bremer know what was going on.

That evening, Ross, Schlicher, Tom Warrick, Colonel Shirasago, and I met to discuss how this inconceivable situation came about. None of us imagined the lingering effect this event would have on our regional outreach programs.

The next afternoon I received an e-mail message from Abu Ghraib Prison that asked me why I had started a "shit storm" without getting my facts straight. My first reaction was to write a knee-jerk response, which I knew better than to send. I deleted it and drafted another, more tactful message. I assured the officer that I had received a message from Rasheed's family the night before and felt confident that the shit storm I had stirred up was warranted and based on accurate information.

Two days went by without a word. Then came an e-mail that had copied practically the entire Coalition leadership in the cc line: "Rasheed Sallou is in custody, we have had eyes on, verified his presence, and here is his tag [identification] number. Get your facts straight in the future."

It turned out they did have Rasheed Sallou in custody, but it was Oday Rasheed Sallou. The tag number they gave me was for Rasheed's son, who was supposed to have been released a month ago. My response was straightforward; I assured them that in the future, my facts would be just as accurate as they were this time, and they should check the facts before making rash assumptions. Meanwhile, Oday remained in custody. I never received another message about Rasheed, but a few days later saw his name back on the wanted list with the same bounty as before—$50,000.

Prior to this incident, I traveled extensively throughout Iraq without the slightest concern that I would be the direct target of an attack. It is an ancient Iraqi custom to provide security for guests, even if it means sacrificing one's own life. Though I was never so naïve to believe every Iraqi host would protect me to the death if I were threatened in their home, there were many devout adherents to tradition who would do so for the sake of preserving their honor. Yet, after the surrender debacle with Rasheed, I learned there were plans to bait me into a meeting, during which I would be kidnapped or assassinated. These reports increased in frequency between March and June 2004.

After verifying the credibility of these reports, I was forced to cancel a number of meetings with sheiks and other individuals I previously trusted, and Ambassadors Jones and Ross discussed sending me home after one location was mortared at the time I was scheduled to arrive.

I have always believed that the only way criminals win is when we back down from them, so I was unhappy about canceling these meetings. Feeling my disappointment, Ambassador Ross had a heart-to-heart talk with me. He explained that while I was willing to risk attending these meetings, he was worried, not only about my safety, but also that of the people who were providing my security.

Ambassador Ross made a convincing argument, but the situation left me conflicted. Since arriving with the first forces to Baghdad, I had been in so many dangerous situations that it felt normal to be under constant threat. I had been in the middle of several ambushes and firefights, but never before was I the specified target, at least not of an attack that had been carried out. I had, however, been threatened. For example, in May and July

2003, criminals I had arrested took out contracts for my murder, hoping to impress me by their sphere of influence.

These new threats were especially disturbing because they were not threats of reprisal. They were signs that the Iraqis I had been working with no longer accepted me as someone who respected them and their culture. Because of this one mix-up, I went from a trusted guest to a targeted enemy.

I endured this situation for the last four months of my tour. Then at 5 p.m., June 27, 2004, the time came for me to run "the gauntlet," the six-mile road to the airport, for the last time. My driver, Hasan, who had been prepared to give his life for me, wept. I would miss him, along with my translators and advisors Faisal, Zumurudeh, Mary, and her husband Baseem.

They had all been with me since April 2003. I developed the deepest respect and admiration for them as they worked so hard to rebuild their country. They were like family. My heart went out to them for what lay ahead. I arrived at the palace near the airport by six o'clock. Hasan carried my bags for me and gave me a hug. He insisted that he would stay with me until my plane left.

Lt. Col. Rick Welch had arrived a few months earlier as the civil-military coordinator for the 1st Cavalry Division, and I handed off my work to him. I knew Rick was a good man for the job. We had been close friends for more than fourteen years. He is my son's godfather. That night as I sat in his room, the thought of finally going home settled in. Having escaped my closest brushes with death, in a bizarre coincidence, on both my sons' and sister's birthdays during my tour, I realized how lucky I was to be able to share future celebrations with them.

I walked outside, sat out front of Welch's trailer, and looked up at the stars; it was such a beautiful clear night. A slight breeze stirred up the sand, and my thoughts drifted back over my tour in Iraq. I had been fortunate, both in combat and in creating deep relationships among the Iraqi people in my endeavor to do my part to advance democracy in Iraq. According to Schlicher and Ambassador Ross, the relationships proved invaluable to the Coalition during some of the tensest periods since the fall of Saddam's regime.

I began to think about what brought me here, how fortunate I was to have been involved in so many different aspects of the Coalition's operations, the people that I was leaving behind and those that never made it home. I was fortunate to have known the Iraqis with whom I worked. And I was fortunate to simply be alive.

My work was so successful thanks to the Iraqis with whom I worked. Because of their efforts, I was able to communicate and develop relationships throughout the country. Faisal, Zumurudeh, and Hasan had survived an ambush with me and there was a special, indescribable bond that had formed between us.

Faisal, for instance, had been an exceptional advisor and translator to me. I use the term "translator" loosely; to the Iraqis I worked with, it was a derogatory term. The work they did went far beyond mere translation. Faisal's father had been an Iraqi diplomat in Britain. Faisal had become fluent in proper British English, in addition to speaking eloquent Arabic, as acknowledged by others who knew the language well. Beginning as a private in the Iraqi Army, Faisal had by now, at age fifty, become quite learned and worldly. His impeccable translation from English to Arabic gave me additional credibility with the sheiks. His counsel on the culture and attitudes of the Iraqis was invaluable. I came to trust his advice and counsel instinctively.

Zumurudeh, another advisor and translator, was also worldly beyond her years. She was well educated and able to speak five languages. Her father, like Faisal's, had been an Iraqi diplomat. She managed my office with great efficiency. I depended on her to both keep me organized and advise me on Iraqi culture. Because of her age, she had a different perspective than Faisal on the Iraqi society. Having lived her entire life under Saddam's regime, she was able to advise me on the attitudes and opinions of younger Iraqis in addition to those of the average Iraqi citizen. She was like a younger sister to me, cautioning me to avoid all missions she perceived as dangerous. She was more persistent in this respect than even Ambassador Ross.

Then there were Mary and Beseem, two of the first people I met upon my arrival in Baghdad. They were so genuine and kind, and I felt discouraged to be leaving with their country in such turmoil and with such uncertainty about its future.

I was reminded of the night Cpl. Mark Bibby and Omar were killed, when I also sat staring up at the night sky. As I scanned the stars, I began to consider the fortunate aspects of my time in Iraq. I had met and helped capture so many of the former elites from Saddam's regime, including Mizban Khadr Hadi, number 23 on the most wanted Iraqis list (and the infamous "nine of hearts" in the U.S. government–issued deck of cards featuring the most wanted former regime officials); Huda Salih Mahdi Amash, number 39/five of hearts; Sa'd Abdul-Majid Al-Faisal Al-Tikriti, number 55/three of spades; Muhammad Saeed al-Sahaf (a.k.a. "Baghdad Bob"), former minister of information; the former chairman of Iraq's atomic energy agency; and countless former ambassadors, general officers, former cabinet ministers, parliament members, and other deposed elites.

Never could I have imagined how my understanding of Iraqi traditions would inform my role in capturing terrorists and members of Saddam's inner circle. During my time in Iraq, I served as the senior advisor for the immediate reconstruction of Baghdad, stopped bank robberies, and arrested counterfeiters and art thieves. I was made an honorary sheik, and served as a member of the cease-fire negotiations in Fallujah. My tour had been long and uncertain, but the people and events that I encountered along the way changed my life forever. Now, it was all about to end.

My June 27, 2004, journal entry reads:

OUR TEAM OF AMERICAN SOLDIERS AND IRAQIS HAD BEEN THROUGH SO MUCH TOGETHER, BOTH HIGHS AND LOWS. WE SURVIVED AMBUSHES, EARNED THE TRUST OF MANY WHO HAD INITIALLY DISTRUSTED OUR MOTIVES; WE HAD SAVED LIVES, AND WERE SOMETIMES FORCED TO TAKE LIVES TOO. OUR FRIENDS HAD BEEN KILLED, WE MOURNED THEM AND CRIED TOGETHER. WE LAUGHED AND CELEBRATED SUCCESSES TOGETHER. NOW, TODAY, THE DAY I AM LEAVING TO START MY JOURNEY HOME, I LEARNED THAT THESE PEOPLE I CALLED FRIENDS, PEOPLE THAT HAD BEEN FAMILY TO ME FOR ALMOST A YEAR AND A HALF, LOOKED AT ME AS THE ENEMY. I WAS CONFUSED AND DUMBFOUNDED. AS I REFLECT ON THE EVENTS THAT CHANGED THEIR PERCEPTIONS, I REALIZE MORE THAN EVER HOW WHAT ARE SEEMINGLY INSIGNIFICANT EVENTS CAN BE MISCONSTRUED AND LEAD PEOPLE TO HATE ONE ANOTHER AND TAKE NATIONS TO WAR.

# CHAPTER 2

# The Journey

*He who has his hand in the water is not*
*like him who has his hand in the fire.*
—*Arab proverb*

I developed a deep respect for and interest in the Middle East after a visit to Egypt in 1989. While earning my master's degree in International Relations, I began to see why historians and scholars identified Iraq (under its ancient name Mesopotamia) as the "Cradle of Civilization." During my studies, I immersed myself in the rich, five-thousand-year-old culture and norms of the area. So when I was selected to command a civil affairs battalion that was regionally oriented to the Middle East, it seemed like an ideal fit.

I assumed command of the 422nd Civil Affairs Battalion in July 2001. Civil affairs (CA) units are responsible for liaison between military forces, civil authorities, and the local population in a foreign country to coordinate with and develop local infrastructures. They work to obtain local acceptance of, and support for, U.S. forces. In my first days of command, I laid out the training plan of my expected peacetime tenure to my staff. I wanted to leave the unit in better shape than when I arrived, as would any incoming commander worth his rank.

Soon after the events of September 11, I knew my battalion would be called upon to serve. Moreover, I was sure that every unit in my command would eventually be called upon to help the United States and its allies rid the world of the fanatics responsible for these terrorist acts.

The battalion was aligned to the 3rd Infantry Division (Mechanized) at Fort Stewart, Georgia, for war contingencies in the Middle East. I realized that if the battalion was going to support the division in combat, we had to know its battle staff procedures and to develop personal relationships with the staff officers. Despite the opposition of the staff officers at my higher command, I was able to take my subordinate commanders and my staff to Fort Stewart several times before we mobilized. By the time the battalion left the conflict, we would learn the value of this pre-coordination and what it added to our credibility with the division.

As tensions grew between the United States and Iraq, my battalion received its warning order in November 2002 for a mobilization date in January 2003. It seemed obvious that we were going to learn firsthand the Iraqi culture and the psyche of its society. From my assessment of the battalion's strengths and weaknesses, I was confident that the soldiers could accomplish any mission. However, this war would stretch to the limit the talents of everyone assigned.

When the unit arrived at Fort Bragg, North Carolina, for mobilization processing, the commanding general met the battalion as we disembarked from the buses. It was cold and had snowed the day before. He asked me to rally the soldiers so he could address them. In response to the notion that the equipment and uniforms we were issued might be inadequate, he announced, "You are not infantry platoon leaders and you will not be on the front lines. You will go in your BDUs [green battle uniforms] and you will have flack vests [non-armored vests that make you sweat, but serve little additional purpose]."

As it turned out, his words could not have been less prophetic. Every team in the battalion would be involved in direct action. Some of them were among the first to cross over into Iraq. I would personally end up firing every round from my weapon at an enemy that was shooting back at me. During the presentation to the battalion of five Purple Hearts, twenty-one awards for valor, and more than 90 percent receiving the Combat Action badge— the highest in the history of the United States Army for a civil affairs unit—the general's words would come back to remind me of how wrong he was, time and time again.

My primary concern during the mobilization process was acquiring the necessary equipment to allow for force protection, communication, and mobility. We were seriously short on radios. The only vehicles we had were unarmored canvas humvees. Every team wanted every piece of equipment it was authorized and then some. While I understood and empathized with them, it simply was not possible. I respected the subordinate commanders and the team leaders for their persistence and concern for the soldiers in their charge. The truth was, we were going to war, ready or not, and would have to make the most of our no-frills supplies and equipment. The battalion staff's efforts were remarkable and, in spite of the shortages in the logistic system, the battalion deployed in desert uniforms—tan battle uniforms—with more radios than any other battalion, and with equipment that was authorized but not readily available to most units. The unit validated in record time. All that was left to do was wait for our flight to Kuwait.

The wait lasted sixteen days. The day of our flight out of Fort Bragg turned out to be my youngest son's birthday. Wesley was turning seven. Little did I know how birthdays in my family were to become omens of significant events during my tour in Iraq. Some of the soldiers were thoughtful enough to sing happy birthday to Wesley. We gave him a few presents that he quickly tore open and played with while we waited. We learned the flight was being delayed, giving me time to walk with my kids to the car. I could feel my heart sink. My daughter Kaitlyn was not yet two and had just been released from the hospital after being admitted for a week with an upper respiratory infection. My youngest son had just turned seven, and my oldest son Brandon was twelve. I was sure I would see them again, but I was not certain when.

When the unit arrived in Kuwait, the battalion moved to Camp New York, approximately twenty kilometers from the Iraqi border, arriving just before dark. I reported to Col. John Sterling, Chief of Staff, 3rd Infantry Division (Mechanized). For the next month, the battalion civil affairs teams integrated into the combat brigades and the battalion headquarters integrated into the division's battle rhythm. The conditions in the desert at Camp New York were tolerable. We had showers and toilets, but at each step along the journey we learned to appreciate the last place we had been. Accommodations and facilities declined with each leg of the trip and would continue that way until we reached Baghdad. We were required to take our protective masks everywhere. The soldiers spent their days planning and preparing for the eventual movement north, and for the most likely scenarios we might face along the way.

We had been at Camp New York for about two weeks when we received orders to move to Assembly Area Spartan, about ten kilometers southeast of our current location. We loaded out the day before and staged our vehicles in their movement order. That night, there was a terrible sandstorm. We would experience these storms all along the way to Baghdad. There were no tents or campsites, so we slept in our vehicles. The five-days supply of food and water along with all of our gear made the humvee very cramped and forced us to sleep sitting up in an extremely confined area. The designers of these vehicles clearly did not make overnight accommodations their top priority.

The next morning we awoke stiff and sluggish from our restless sleep. We shaved and went to the mess hall in a tent that had been set up for breakfast. When we returned to our staging area, a convoy briefing had just begun. With the variety of objects tied to and packed in our vehicles so tightly, there was barely room for the passengers. Our seemingly endless convoy looked like that of a traveling band of gypsies. But to me, it was a testament to resourcefulness, and I was proud of the soldiers and their preparations.

The day before we positioned ourselves for the move north, Col. Timothy Regan, the civil affairs officer from Corps headquarters, had come to see me. He explained that my job was to get to the Iraqi people and show the human side of war. He told me that there would be a combat camera crew assigned to my teams and they would be responsible for taking the pictures and getting them back to Central Command.

On our movement to Assembly Area Appling near the Iraqi border, the passenger in the front vehicle of the convoy jumped out. We were so far back that we could barely see the soldier, and couldn't see exactly what he was doing. Staff Sgt. Bob Laverick was driving and I asked him if he could make out what was going on.

"I think he is giving the hand and arm signal for [a poison] gas [attack]," he replied.

Four vehicles in front of me, a soldier jumped out of his vehicle and he, too, began giving the signal for a gas attack. Neither of these soldiers had their own gas masks on, making their actions seem ridiculous.

"Damn," I thought to myself, "war is no time to play these stupid games." I had been involved in many low-intensity environments over the previous twenty years, and had been deployed in Honduras with Joint Task Force Bravo to Panama with the 7th Special Forces Group. For some reason, my gut told me that this might not be for real. My gut was right. For the next four weeks, it seemed that every time the wind blew sand in an unusual direction, someone would yell, "Gas!"

But I followed procedure, donning my protective gear, as did everyone else. The first rule for nuclear, biological, or chemical (NBC) environments is to get your mask on, and everyone did that. As you place your protective mask on you are supposed to hold your breath. The soldiers did that so well that we had to go and tell some of them to breathe again. The second rule has two parts: One, find shelter, and two, put on your gear. But we were in the middle of the desert, and the only shelter was the humvee, so we broke that part of the rule. We had a hard time with the second part of the rule, being that there was barely enough space to sit in the humvee, let alone to put on your gear. Somehow, we managed.

The alarm really shook up a few of the soldiers; some were crying, causing their gas masks to fog up, and at least one wet herself. I tried to comfort them, reassure them that they had done everything right and they were going to be okay. But the fear of the unknown was overwhelming for all of us.

My March 21, 2003, journal entry reads:

THE WAR HAS STARTED. DURING THE DAY WE SAT AT ASSEMBLY AREA APPLING AND TRIED TO PASS THE TIME AS THE CLOCK TICKED OFF THE MINUTES FOR US TO BEGIN OUR JOURNEY NORTH. EVERYONE APPEARED TO BE UNCONCERNED, YET EAGER, ABOUT THE INEVITABLE CONFRONTATION THAT IS ABOUT TO BEGIN. THE TRUTH IS THAT WE WERE TRYING TO IGNORE OUR EMOTIONS BY FINDING HUMOR AROUND US, OR SIMPLY LOUNGING AWAY THE DAY IN THE SUN.

The responsibility for my soldiers weighed heavier on me this day than ever before. A fear that not all of us would be going home perpetuated in me. I thought about everything that had brought us to this point in time. I thought about my family, my soldiers, the training we had undergone in preparing for this day. I went through a mental checklist of all the contingencies the soldiers might face. Had everything been done to prepare them? It was too late to do anything about it now. They were at war, and I could only pray that we had prepared them enough to survive it.

At approximately nine o'clock that night, artillery began to take out observation posts across the border. It was a spectacular sound and light show, a clear sign that diplomacy had failed. It was time to exert our military power and bring an end to the threat presented against the United States. I hoped that the Iraqis, realizing the inevitability of war, would soon decide to desert. But for now, as the artillery continued to pound border positions, I crawled up on top of my vehicle, laid down, and went to sleep, certain that I would not have an opportunity to sleep again for a long while.

We arrived about eight kilometers west of An Najaf in the very early morning of March 24. As we drove into our positions, we could see and hear helicopters over the city and antiaircraft rounds shooting into the air. Surprisingly, the lights of the city were still on. The next morning, some of my soldiers found fighting positions, Iraqi equipment, and two dead Iraqi soldiers within seventy-five meters of our position. For any soldier who wondered if we were at war, this erased any doubt.

The 11th Air Calvary Regiment (ACR) had been located a few kilometers to our south. Several civilian families had been displaced from their homes, and we were directed to relocate them away from the operational area.

The civil affairs team located nearby relatives and moved the families in with them. This was an easy task except for the livestock. The sheep, chickens, and other small animals were loaded into the vehicles, and the goat was tied to the back of the humvee. Not exactly what you would expect to see in twenty-first-century warfare.

One slight problem—the vehicles spooked the donkey and he ran off. The team was unable to catch him, but we promised the family that we would come by the next day to try again.

As promised, I accompanied the team on what we now fondly refer to as "Operation Donkey Pull." The donkey had ventured about three kilometers into the 11th ACR area. As the team took turns walking the donkey out, word spread among the soldiers' tents like wildfire. They came out laughing and pointing at the comical sight of us slowly making our way toward the donkey's owners, our heads bowed in embarrassment. We hoped no one would recognize us. But when we finally reached the family, they were more than grateful.

The battalion was directed to locate a water supply for the division. A horrific sandstorm caused a "tactical pause" that lasted for days. Thousands of villagers from the operational area, who were running out of supplies, carried white flags into the division's area asking for help. I went to Colonel Sterling and explained that these people had been cooperating when we directed them to stay in their homes, but now they were running out of water and other necessities. I proposed using "water buffalos" (small water tanks pulled on the back of vehicles) to distribute water. Colonel Sterling agreed to let us use two of the five available at division headquarters. We put the local villages on a distribution plan that allowed us to provide water every other day. It was a schedule similar to that which the villagers were used to before the war.

The Iraqis were mostly welcoming, but concerned about their future. Many of them asked if we were committed to the war. They shared stories about their family members who were killed after the Shi'a intifada throughout Southern Iraq in 1991. One of the village elders asked if Saddam was going to poison the water. When I told him no, he asked me why then was I wearing a gas mask and chemical suit. I told him it was part of my uniform. He and the other villagers gazed at me in disbelief. Clearly they were not getting the message we wanted them to receive.

That evening I went to Colonel Sterling and recounted the conversation with the village elder. I requested that I be allowed to remove my chemical suit and wear a patrol cap, rather than all the combat gear, when I went into the villages. I assured him that I would be safe, that the villagers were thankful for us, not resentful. But I knew the request concerned Colonel Sterling, and when he said yes, it was with great reluctance.

But what a difference it made with the Iraqis. When they saw us without all the combat gear, they had a renewed appreciation for us, and overwhelming sense of gratitude and trust. Because we weren't concerned about being poisoned, they were not concerned about being poisoned, either.

At the village, I was invited into the diwan (meeting room) of the village elder. As I entered, I told him that I felt I was among friends and there was no reason for me to wear a gun. I removed my holster and handed it to Capt. Kevin Guidry, head of my security team.

The elder looked at me in total surprise. He smiled, grabbed me by the shoulders and said, "Yes, yes, you are right. You do not need a gun while you are here." This was a turning point for me, and bolstered my understanding of the culture. I knew the rules of hospitality for the Middle East, but the look in the eyes of the elder was one that assured me I had earned his total trust and acceptance.

At another village close by, the local school had been damaged during the battle of An Najaf. The villagers assured us that the Iraqi Army had not used the school during the battle, but the fighting positions and shell casings on the roof told me otherwise. I asked the village elder who the teacher was. He told me the teacher was a man who had been sent from the city, but had not been around for many months.

We determined from inspecting the school that all but one classroom was reparable. I told the villagers that we would do so in preparation for students to return to class, but the men of the village were not interested in this proposal. Many were themselves illiterate, and did not see why this was important. We continued our discussion with the sights and sounds of war raging less then five kilometers away. Understandably, their primary concerns were electricity and water. I could help with the water, I told them; electricity was another issue. I emphasized that I still needed their help in repairing the school.

That evening at headquarters, many on the staff came up to congratulate me. I was tired and unsure of what the fuss was about. Then I learned that a photo of me sitting with one of the village elders had been used in briefing the President. The photo would be used to demonstrate to the world that the Iraqi people were openly accepting the U.S. presence in Iraq.

That evening I received a phone call from one of the civil affairs staff at Marine Corps headquarters. Apparently, they had also seen the briefing, because the individual asked me why I was running around like a cowboy in a combat zone. He rambled on and on, not making much sense.

"Excuse me," I said, and the officer became silent. "I was ordered by Colonel Regan to show the human side of the war. I did that. If there is a problem, take it up with him or the chief of staff here at the division."

No response. I thought we might have been disconnected. "Hello," I exclaimed. "*Hello?*"

After a long pause, the officer replied, "Yes, I am here."

"Okay, so go and talk to Colonel Regan."

"Well," he said, dumbfounded, "he is the one who made the comment."

I hung up the phone, thinking to myself, "Such is the fog of war."

The next morning, March 31, 2003, I brought the battalion into the village and put the soldiers to work. Within hours, the school looked like new. I was so proud of their effort. One of the most memorable moments of the war was when a young child asked if we would lift him up to remove Saddam's picture from the wall. The moment was priceless—a seven-year-old pulling Saddam's picture down. Such an act of defiance assured me that we were doing the right thing. A huge lunch was prepared to honor my soldiers and me. For us, there was no doubt we would win the war. The question was whether we could continue to win the trust of the people.

Lunch was winding down, and I saw the men of the village start to move toward the mosque. I told the elder of the village he should go ahead, that I would wait until he returned. He said no, he would pray later. But then, a few of the villagers asked me to come and pray with them in the mosque. I felt this was taboo and something I needed to avoid.

"I do not think that is wise," I explained to the elder. "You see, while we pray to the same God of Abraham, I pray on my knees and you pray on your hands and knees. This is a visible difference."

He shook his head, took my hand, and said, "Nonsense—come with me."

He led me to the mosque, where I washed myself in the customary Islamic way before going inside. Mindful to keep near the back, I knelt down and prayed. One man came up to me and quietly explained the significance of the various gestures and movements by the men who came to pray. They each touched my shoulder upon leaving; to me, this meant, "You are welcomed here." I felt honored, and knew that only by respecting Islam could we win the hearts and gain the trust of Iraqis.

Later, as I sat in the village diwan sipping hot tea, some of the same men were discussing an Iraqi news broadcast from the night before. They had watched it on a portable television connected to a car battery. They had seen my picture sitting with the elder from the nearby village. A man I would later meet, Mohammed Saeed al-Sahaf, more famously known as "Baghdad Bob," the Iraqi Minister of Information, had discredited the account stating that it was propaganda and a staged event, that the photograph did not show real Iraqis.

The men who were in the photograph found it particularly amusing, asking each other if they were real Iraqis. One of the men joked that when I got to Baghdad I should find al-Sahaf and tell him that they were Iraqis. Everyone laughed as we finished our tea.

On the way back to the headquarters, we passed seven men in their early twenties. To see this group of fighting-age men walking together was a little suspicious, so I told my driver to turn around and go back. When we approached, the men stopped and explained that they had deserted from the army in An Najaf. It seemed to me they wanted to surrender.

I asked my translator if I had understood their words correctly.

"Yes, sir, they want to surrender."

Surprised, I told them to stand on the side of the road. A security team patted them down as I radioed back to the division headquarters and explained that we had seven enemy prisoners of war (EPWs). They didn't believe it, and a demanded explanation. Finally, I was told to standby.

Several minutes passed before I received the reply: "Bring the EPWs to the division entrance, but do not come into the area with them."

A nearby special forces unit was notified upon our arrival. They came to speak to the prisoners, who provided locations of Iraqi units and a sense of what the attitude was inside the city.

We fed the prisoners meals, ready to eat (MREs). One of the translators showed the prisoners how to use the heat pack to warm up the food. The translator had one of them hold it and then poured water into the bag. The bag heated up almost instantaneously and the man threw it to the ground.

He slowly and cautiously picked it back up and looked at the translator. "You Americans are amazing," he said, adding, to our amusement, "Saddam does not have a chance."

We soon learned that a military police unit had been dispatched to pick up the prisoners. They arrived a couple of hours later. The prisoners were tired but happy that they were no longer in the fight.

My translator and I drove with some fellow Americans into the village the next morning. When we arrived to the repaired school, children ran up to us with schoolbooks in hand. We accompanied them to their classroom. Their smiles and enthusiasm filled the room with breathtaking energy. Here stood the U.S. Army in an Iraqi classroom as sounds of the war could be heard in the distance. We taught the children how to count in English, and they taught us how to count in Arabic. The village elder came in and thanked us for all we had done for them. He then asked to take my photograph so that they could put it where Saddam's picture had been. I was initially humbled by the honor, then considered what it really meant. Saddam's ouster created a vacuum, and the Iraqi's would be eager to replace their fallen figurehead with another one as quickly as possible.

The elder brought me to his diwan where I met a man I immediately recognized. I had seen him the day before on the road, driving a donkey cart. The elder pointed to the man. "He went to town to pick up provisions for us," he said. "He saw the Fedayeen using women and children to carry weapons to different parts of the city."

I thanked him for his information and cautioned him that going to town was very dangerous. He looked at me unconcerned and said nothing. I saw him again the next day on his cart, again riding towards the city.

Later that evening, I was called to the operations section. I was told that an Iraqi officer had surrendered and brought his wife and three daughters to the prison camp. The camp was not prepared to handle civilians, but they did not want to turn the family out either. I was directed to find a place to take the family. I wondered where was I going to take a woman and three young children.

The next morning I went to one of the villages and met with the village elder. I explained that I needed to provide a safe place for the woman and children for a couple of weeks. He agreed to help me, but on two conditions. The first condition was that I was not to tell anyone in the village. This was to insure that he could guarantee their safety.

The second request would be more challenging. Before he told me what it was, he took me to the village diwan where we were met by a larger group of elders. I was ushered to the front of the room and lunch was brought out. It was a lunch fit for a king—no pun intended. We ate lamb, rice, soup, and other things that I am still unsure of to this day.

After lunch, a group of children were brought in and we took photos with them. I then went with the senior elder to his home, where he explained how pleased the Iraqis were that we were there, and that they hoped we were committed to the cause. He told me that although the young men from his village were forced to serve in the military, no one in the village supported Saddam. He then told me the second condition for safeguarding the Iraqi officer's wife and young daughters.

One of his sons had been drafted into the Iraqi army, but he had deserted and made his way back to the village. The elder, of course, did not want him to be arrested. He wanted my help. I asked him to bring his son to me. At first his eyes expressed doubt and fear, but then turned to trust. He waved for one of the men to go and get his son. After a few moments, his son came into the room. He was scared, and looked at his father as if to ask, "Have you sold me out?" I shook the young man's hand and the father motioned for him to sit down next to him.

I asked the son what he had done in the army. He said that he had been a logistics soldier. He had deserted days ago and made his way at night to the village. He told me what unit he was in, what they did, and where it was located. This was going to be challenging, and I did not hide this fact from the village elder. I told him that as long as his son stayed in the village, and did not leave for the duration of the war, he would not be taken prisoner. Essentially, the son would be under house arrest and the father was responsible for him.

The senior elder was beyond grateful, hugging and assuring me that his son would not go anywhere. I told him if I found him outside the village, I would have to arrest him and could not guarantee his safety. The elder looked over at his son, but spoke to me: his son would remain in the village under his watch. The elder expressed his indebtedness to me for my compassion.

We were to bring the mother and children with us later that night when the village was asleep and under a shroud of darkness. I said that was fine and told him that I would see him at around 2 a.m.

Captains Guidry and Damone Garner planned what was classified as a noncombatant evacuation mission. The prison camp was approximately thirty-two kilometers to the north, but we had to travel through no man's land. While our combat units had fought through the area, there were still remnants of the Iraqi Army present and we were going within a few kilometers of the current battle. We would cross the line of departure about eight kilometers from the division headquarters and then we would drive in blackout conditions until we reached the prison camp. We took two vehicles and moved north. We stopped at the designated location and turned off our lights. The drivers adjusted their night vision goggles and we started our movement to the pickup. It was eerie. Through my night vision goggles, I could see the burned out hulls of vehicles as we moved along the deserted road.

We approached the prison camp, which looked like a scene from the movie *Apocalypse Now*. The lights from the prison lit up the sky. We could see the multi-launch rockets being fired to the north approximately eight kilometers away. We could see the flashes of light and hear the sound of fighting in the distance. We turned left off the main road and drove up the service road toward the lights of the prison. It was so bright that we had to remove our night vision goggles.

The camp commander and a special forces officer who met us were pleased to see us arrive. The Iraqi officer whose family we were protecting was brought out to talk to us. I assured him that we would do everything we could to protect his family. He was grateful, but his head remained bowed in embarrassment. Then we began to explain the plan to his wife. When he entered the small room where the wife and children were located, she began to cry and shout in Arabic. The translator told me that she was telling the officer that she did not want to leave. He understood and tried to reassure her that it would be okay.

It took almost an hour for the major to calm his wife enough so we could leave. The children were crying as we loaded them into the back of the troop carrier humvee. It was cold and we had brought blankets for the family. The mother held the youngest in her arms and the two oldest children clung to her for dear life. I felt so sorry for them, but we had to move on and get them to the village.

We loaded up, and as we approached the gate to the prison camp we stopped to put on our night vision goggles, then proceeded onward. The woman and children faced back out of the troop carrier in front of me, looking around and listening to the raging battle and rockets launching in the distance. The fear they felt at being driven to an undisclosed location by an invading army, leaving their husband and father behind in a prison camp, must have been unbearable. I thought about what I could do to take care of them, and about what I would do if my own family were in the same situation.

Approximately eight kilometers away from the village, we stopped and removed our night vision goggles and turned on our lights. When we arrived at the village, there was a downward slope on the road leading to the village elder's residence. We turned off our engines and let the vehicles roll down to within a few meters of his home. As directed, I went and knocked on the metal door once. Nothing. I knocked again. Still nothing.

A dog came near and began to bark. I picked up a rock and threw it in the dog's direction as I had seen the Iraqis do to get the dogs to stop. He just continued barking. I picked up another rock, and must have hit him because he began to yelp and now every dog in the village was barking. Candles began to be lit and were visible in the windows. This mission now had the stealth of a dinosaur moving across the ground. I beat on the door and finally, a half-awakened man opened the door rubbing his eyes. He apologized and explained that he must have fallen asleep. The mother was clearly scared but controlled her emotions enough to allay her children's fears. By now they were clinging to their mother as if they had become her natural appendages. The children began to cry as we helped them from the vehicle. We quickly escorted them into the home and to the women's quarters in the back.

I sat with the village elder a few minutes in the candlelight of the diwan. He offered us tea. I explained that we needed to leave, but that I would come by in the morning to check on the family and talk to him more.

Our departure might as well have been announced over loud speakers. Anyone who was not awakened by the barking dogs was certain to be once we started the engines of the humvees. Nothing to do about it now. I would have to figure out what to tell the others in the village in the morning. When we returned to the division headquarters, I reported that the mission was a success, and went to find myself a bed.

I was awakened early the next morning and informed that there were hundreds of camels running through the division area. They seemed to know where they were going, despite no sign of people. I was told to find the owners and set out to do just that.

We loaded up, headed out to where the camels were coming from, and before long came across a Bedouin and his sons. They were cooperative and seemed relaxed and unconcerned with our presence. The father explained that once a year they move their camels through this area to new watering holes near An Najaf. I explained that for his own safety he would have to go another way this year. He agreed and motioned towards his sons. They scurried off and started pushing the camels in a direction to the south. There were only a few of them and hundreds of camels, so it seemed like an impossible task.

I noticed a blood-soaked cloth wrapped around the Bedouin's finger. When I pointed to it and asked what had happened, he explained that he had cut his finger and asked if we had a doctor. Staff Sergeant Laverick, the battalion medic, was not with us and I went back to my vehicle and retrieved my first aid bag. When I unwrapped the piece of cloth from his finger, I could see that it had been severed at the tip. I did as much as I could do for him and explained that he needed to see a doctor. He was grateful and invited us to have lunch with him. I had to regretfully decline, explaining that we had a lot to do. In the distance, I saw that the camels were moving away from our forces in a surprisingly orderly fashion.

On April 4 we were informed that we were moving north in the morning. We made our rounds to the villages and said goodbye. My last stop was the home of a small boy by the name of Mathan who was the same age as my son Wesley. His father had been very helpful to us. I gave Mathan a "King Lion Heart" toy that Wesley had given me for my trip to Iraq. Mathan's face lit up. He hugged me and smiled, and I tried hard to hold back my tears. Mathan's reaction made me realize how much I missed my family.

When we met the civil affairs team from the 101st Airborne Division to hand over our projects. The team leader told me that they had no intention of continuing the water distribution, and their commander was angry that we had started it in the first place. I explained that the villagers' need to find water had been interfering with combat operations. Distribution was out of necessity and had been directed by the division. If they did not get water to the villages, the villagers would once again come looking for it. For some reason, I could not get the officer to understand the consequences; I decided he would just have to learn it for himself.

That afternoon we lined up vehicles to prepare for the convoy north the next day. That night, I took the team out and we distributed food to the villages. At the first village, we left bags of sugar, beans, and rice on the steps of the schoolhouse. We put small American flags in them and moved on to the next village. It was late and we unfortunately scared some of the villagers. We were departing when a small boy ran up to us and said goodbye. I gave him a handful of American flags and he began to run from door to door in the village giving one to whoever answered.

At the second village, all the men were sitting in the village diwan drinking tea. The elder came out and shook my hand. I told him that we had some food for them, and he called for some of the younger men to come and unload the bags. I gave him an American flag. He hugged me and thanked me for liberating them and their country. We said our last goodbyes and returned to the division to prepare for our move.

On the morning of April 5, we convoyed north. The children from the villages ran to the side of the road waving and cheering us. From a distance I could see the men from the village. They stayed near the school and waved occasionally. As usual, an 80-kilometer movement took a whole day. Along the way we saw blown-up vehicles, tanks, dead bodies, and other evidence of the battles that had taken place. One military installation we passed through had been abandoned, and was like a ghost town. We arrived to our stopping point after dark, and slept next to our vehicles.

# CHAPTER 3

# Twenty-four Hours

*On the day of victory, no one is tired.*
*—Arab proverb*

The drive to Baghdad on April 8, 2003, was sorrowful, foreboding and exhilarating all at the same time. During our delay in An Najaf, we made a lot of friends in the villages. We repaired a school, established water distribution, and captured more than thirty-five enemy prisoners of war. On this day, we drove from the mid-Euphrates about eighty miles to Baghdad at ten miles an hour in the middle of a three-hundred-vehicle convoy. The temperature was unbearably high. With our Kevlar helmet, flak vest, chemical suit, other gear, and the sun beating down on our vehicle, it made you feel as if you were in a broiler. It made for a very miserable trip, to say the least.

The Iraqis we encountered along the way were surprisingly unconcerned with our presence as they went about their daily lives. They drove their cars, farmed their fields, and kept their markets open, where merchants and customers watched us drive by, paying little heed. Young Iraqi men, most likely soldiers the day before, walked along the roads with no apparent concern for the hundreds of vehicles loaded with American soldiers driving past. They simply walked with their heads down. Any attempts to speak to them were met with looks of disgust and contempt. I reached out to hand a bottle of water to a young man; he never looked up, simply shaking his head to signal "no", and continued to walk.

Burned and destroyed vehicles and bodies lined the road. The landscape and homes blended together in a single color of sand. For the most part, homes were made with tan-colored brick, not with the dried mud we saw in the villages in the south. The homes became larger and more modern the closer we got to Baghdad. There was an obvious income and standard of living gap. Several houses were made from marble, and the diwans were large and extravagant. For the first time I saw women wearing something other than black. While most were wearing the hijab (the traditional headscarf), their dresses were more modern and colorful.

We arrived at the newly designated Baghdad International Airport (formerly the Saddam International Airport) in the late afternoon. Exploding artillery and the percussion of bombs being dropped could be felt as we unloaded our gear and began to look through our new headquarters at the catering building for Iraqi Airways. A 727 jetliner that had been blown up was lying on the runway and vehicles were strewn haphazardly across the airport grounds, probably abandoned in place as the occupants fled for their lives. There were pictures of Saddam everywhere, on the buildings, street corners, and billboards. It was more like a cult atmosphere than a country with a government.

That evening Colonel Sterling told me he had just gotten off the phone with the chief of staff at Fifth Corps. They had discussed the civil-military plan for Baghdad. Because no such plan existed, Colonel Sterling told me I would have twenty-four hours to come up with something.

My unit's prewar planning was spent preparing for civilian evacuations from the battlefield and to move them to refugee camps. We had been assured that the reconstruction of governmental functions would be taken care of, so I never anticipated nor planned for the extent of postwar chaos in Baghdad. The 3rd Infantry Division was supposed to have continued north, but because of the speed of our advance, it was decided that we would stay in Baghdad.

The Iraqi people had expected a quick transition to the American way of life, but the rapid and total collapse of the government left an almost euphoric anarchy in its wake. Until the security vacuum could be filled, the American way of life would have to wait.

I was fortunate that my mentors, who had been military governors in Europe after World War II, had shared a great deal of their experiences with me over the last decade. I told Colonel Sterling that in the next ninety-six hours we needed to focus our efforts on getting the public utilities (water, electricity, sewer), public health (hospitals and clinics), public administration (governmental offices), and public safety (police and fire) up and running.

We discussed how to reestablish governmental functions and infrastructure. The suggestion that units of the capitulated Iraqi military under U.S. control could provide security was discarded as unrealistic. Instead, we would tell the Ba'athists and others to return to their offices. My opinion was that if they returned to work, we would know where they were. If it ended up that some of them were on the most-wanted list, we could go and arrest them. In the meantime, we needed all the help we could get in reestablishing governmental functions for their city.

To this end, the Psychological Operations section would drop leaflets over the city with my picture on them telling the citizens of Baghdad to return to their jobs. Colonel Sterling agreed with the recommendation and directed my staff to start a target assessment of the ninety-seven hospitals, twenty-five fire stations, dozens of water and electricity facilities, and police stations.

The follow-on plan, as I understood it, was to have the Office of Reconstruction and Humanitarian Assistance (ORHA) arrive with its staff, then Ahmed Chalabi (the Iraqi National Congress leader, and one of the most controversial politicians in post-Saddam Iraq) would enter and take over the efforts. This would happen in about three weeks.

Meanwhile, the Marines were going to pull out of Baghdad to secure the southern half of Iraq, and the 3rd Infantry Division would assume responsibility for security and stability operations (SASO)—including Baghdad reconstruction efforts—until ORHA arrived. The division's twenty thousand troops were going to be responsible for a city with a population estimated at between five-and-a-half and seven million people. As the senior civil affairs officer in the division, I was responsible for advising the general on our efforts.

That night as I prepared my recommended targeting lists for assessments, I wondered how we intended to accomplish the mission with so few people. In 1920, there were 5 million people in all Iraq and the British found it difficult to secure the country with their 80,000 troops. Today, we had approximately 150,000 soldiers in a country with 25 million people, 5.5 million of them living in Baghdad. We were going to attempt security operations with only twice the number of soldiers the British had eighty years before. I could only hope the euphoria of Saddam's fall carried with it a desire for peace.

The civil affairs teams from my battalion, along with the rest of the 3rd Infantry Division, were out conducting assessments of electric plants, water facilities, hospitals, police and fire stations, and other critical infrastructure on the morning of April 9. I accompanied a team on April 10, and was taken aback by the condition of the city. While evidence of battles was everywhere, there was little battle damage to the infrastructure. For most of the areas that I observed, great care by the combat soldiers and precision munitions had kept much of the infrastructure intact. But the city was falling apart, a condition mostly due to years of neglect.

We left the security of the airport and traveled along the route to the city, where engineers were clearing mines that had been placed to slow the army's advance. It was clear that Baghdad was still a very dangerous place. My team turned off the first ramp from the airport and approached a group of men standing at a street corner. The men complained about the lack of water, and we assured them that we were working to restart the utilities.

When we asked them for directions to the power substation, they warned us of a Fedayeen squad a few blocks away. They then showed us a truck loaded with rocket launchers, mortars, and various other weapons. It had likely been abandoned as the U.S. Army approached. There were rifles and unexploded mortars scattered in the road, on the sidewalk, and in front yards. Bunkers lined every street corner, each having several rocket-propelled grenades, AK-47 assault rifles, and a rocket launcher. A person could walk along, jump into the bunker, fire off a few rounds, and then blend into the crowd or take cover in a nearby building.

The team and I walked several blocks as the men described the demographics of the area called Jihad. They explained that the people were pleased that we had come, but that they really wanted their basic services started again—immediately! The men again warned us about the Fedayeen squad in the area. We stood in front of a building that had obvious scars from battle, and the men became quite nervous.

While the rest of us returned to the vehicles, Master Sgt. Danny Catching paused to pick a rocket launcher up off the sidewalk. He bent down, and a stream of bullets rattled off the wall next to him, right where his head had been just a second before. The team took up security positions, but we could not locate the shooter. Sgt. Carl Meyers said that he thought the shooter had shot from a room in one of the several multistory buildings that surrounded us to conceal his position. We got in our vehicles and sped off to the division area to regroup, plan, and brief the team on our route to the power station.

About two hours later, we drove to find the substation. I would later hear about the media outrage over our failure to control the looters, who were everywhere. We may have been able to secure more sites in the city with an additional thirty thousand soldiers, but there was no way to stop the looting without killing civilians and causing immediate contempt for the U.S. military.

In the aftermath of the first days following the fall of Baghdad, the United States had incredible momentum and, from what news we had, the press was giving us impartial coverage. The euphoria of the people as we drove through town was indescribable. People ran to the vehicles and hugged and kissed us. Looters would lay their stolen booty down and cheer, "Yeah, America," in thick broken accents. There were men pushing a vehicle with no tires and others carrying huge air conditioning units. They would stop, cheer us, then return to looting. One man dragged a huge couch on his back, slumped over from the weight. He turned towards us, and with great effort, strained to shout, "America is great!"

There was still shooting throughout the city, but a lot if it was celebratory gunfire, men standing in their front yards firing their AK-47 rifles towards the sky. Upon seeing this, we remarked to one another, "Don't they realize that shit has to come down?" I would later see dozens of people in the hospitals who had been hit by the careless firing into the air.

We made our way to the downtown area, and Captain Guidry quickly located the power substation, where we were met by the power station operator. He explained that all instructions for starting the electricity would come from the primary plant located at al-Dhora, southeast of the city. He would have the engineers from that plant come to see us the next day at 9 a.m.

We had just started to depart when a man walked out of a building from across the road carrying three AK-47s. Security told him to stop and drop the weapons. He did so willingly, but warned us that there was a Fedayeen squad operating several blocks away.

We left the area in our vehicles and took an immediate right turn, opposite the direction from where we came. There was a tall divider in the road, and I thought veering left and driving against traffic might be the smartest move. But the lead vehicle had already committed to the right and we followed. For about three blocks, people along the road cheered and gave us thumbs up.

Suddenly, there were no more people, just a street and storefronts. At that second I heard a burst of fire. "What the—?" I yelled.

Specialist Graham Porter yelled back that Captain Guidry was shooting, and that I should look to my right. When I did, I saw several men running from a bunker shooting at us. Everything seemed to move in slow motion. I instinctively lifted my 9mm Beretta from my hip and pulled the trigger. On the second shot, a tall, lanky man in a white shirt and dark pants ran out of the bunker while grabbing his stomach. He fell to the pavement.

My translator Salih was sitting behind me and grabbed my shoulder and started shaking me, yelling, "You got him, you got him."

"Damn it, Salih," I yelled back, "shoot, just shoot!" While we were in the midst of the kill zone for only seconds, the slow-motion surrealism of everything made it feel like we were in the fight for several minutes. Both Salih and I continued to fire. Then our vehicle made a U-turn. "What in the hell are you doing?" I yelled at Porter. "Going back through the ambush?" Then I realized the road was blocked, forcing us to turn back into the kill zone and line of fire.

A lot went through my mind at that moment, the clearest thought being, "Oh shit, it is my oldest son's birthday." I did not want this to be the day they knocked on my family's door to tell them I wasn't coming home.

We passed back in front of the ambush site, and there was a loud explosion. I looked into my rearview mirror and could not see the trail vehicle. "Can you see them?" I yelled to Specialist Porter.

He could. At that moment I heard another explosion and looked back to see the other translator hanging out of the vehicle shooting back towards the ambush. We were moving well out of the kill zone and I yelled for him to stop. Specialist Porter, who was driving our vehicle, thought I was talking to him. He hit the brakes and the vehicle went into a skid.

"Not you, Porter," I shouted, telling him to keep driving, and for the translator to stop shooting. He looked at me like I was crazy, and started talking nonsense, trying to rationalize shooting back. I wasn't in the mood to listen.

I radioed back to the vehicles behind us to make sure that we had everyone, but could not get anyone to respond. Because of insufficient equipment, we were forced to communicate with small handheld commercial walkie-talkies that were almost impossible to hear when driving in the humvee. Porter put me somewhat at ease when he said that he could see the trail vehicles. All I could think about was getting to the site and I prayed that there were no injuries.

Cars had stopped about a hundred and fifty yards out. People were abandoning their vehicles, crouching low, and fleeing into buildings. We drove maybe another quarter mile. People lined both sides of the street, cheering and giving us the thumbs up. We drove several miles back to a secluded area and stopped to check on everyone's condition. We determined that in a matter of seconds the team had fired more than two hundred rounds. Several of the vehicles had been hit, but luckily, we had no injuries. I found out that the explosion I heard was a rocket-propelled grenade (RPG) that just missed the back of my vehicle before hitting the sidewalk. The second explosion was another RPG that just missed the rear vehicle.

The adrenaline was still rushing when we reached division headquarters. I reported to Colonel Sterling that we had been ambushed while leaving the power station and that we needed to have some security when we returned there to meet the chief engineers the next morning. Our canvas humvees, flak vests, M16 rifles, and pistols were simply not enough to run through the city of Baghdad. He agreed and would direct one battalion to provide security.

The next morning we went to link up with a Bradley platoon, but one of their Bradley vehicles had broken a track, forcing us to wait for two hours. Making things more difficult, we would not have communication between the Bradleys and our humvees. After waiting for them to set up security, we were ready to move.

We turned onto the dirt road leading to the power generation substation. There were buildings on the left side and a twelve-foot wall on the right, and we noticed that the road was covered in fluid. When the front vehicle hit a pothole, the fluid splashed and covered it. We realized the fluid was fuel. The road was too narrow for the humvees to turn around without becoming easy targets, so we continued along the road.

The first vehicle moved out into an intersection, and suddenly, there was gunfire. I looked to the left and saw a fuel tanker directly in the line of fire. I remember thinking to myself that if a rocket-propelled grenade hits that tanker, this will become Operation Fire Fly. Captain Guidry and his team laid down suppressive fire. He was motioning and yelling for the rest of the vehicles to turn around and get out of the area. We started to take fire from a building on the other side of the road from behind the wall.

Unable to communicate with the Bradley platoon, I ran down the road, waving my arms, trying to get the platoon leader's attention. With every breath, the smell of the fuel filled my nose and mouth; I knew time was not on our side. The lieutenant finally noticed me signaling for him and drove his Bradley toward me.

"There is a shooter behind the wall in that tall building," I yelled pointing to the area from which we were taking fire.

"I'll take care of it, sir," he replied. He then drove forward to the building and the sound of the 25mm guns was comforting.

"Damn," I thought, "I am glad I am not in that building." My next thought was that we had to get out of there. The firing stopped and we withdrew from the area. Ironically, our tardiness that morning probably saved our lives.

When we returned to the division headquarters I went directly to Colonel Sterling and described the attempted link-up, including the fuel covering the road. Maj. Doug Claggett, a Canadian Army officer and the division's chief of operations, looked at me and joked, "Yeah, I can smell you and it stinks."

I curtly smiled at him and discussed with Colonel Sterling the importance of security at the power plant, especially with the Fedayeen lying in wait. The word probably leaked out after the previous day's skirmish that we would be returning to for a meeting with the engineers. Colonel Sterling and Major Claggett agreed that we needed to go back and secure the area, but in force this time. With two near misses in fewer than twenty-four hours and running on less than two hours sleep, I wasn't in the mood to go back, but I knew it needed to be done.

This time, instead of one platoon from the Bradley battalion, we would now have an entire company. We would be going after the power substation with fifteen Bradleys, air support, and fire support. My team and I changed our uniforms and headed back to the battalion area to plan for the mission.

Six hours later, Captain Guidry, Staff Sgt. Kevin Bell, our translator Al-Amir, and I rode off together in a Bradley on a roundabout route to the substation, anticipating a fight. I was looking out of the small porthole as we approached the site. The substation operator from the day stood with a crowd of people. The fuel that had covered the road had by now soaked into the ground with only traces left behind. I told the driver to back up and lower the ramp, and directed Al-Amir to translate what I was about to say word for word.

The ramp lowered and the operator suddenly realized who we were. He had a dumbfounded smile. I walked up and grabbed him by shoulders. "If one more person shoots at me today," I said, "I will blow up everything you can see."

The operator was noticeably scared. "What do you mean?" he asked.

I told him I did not appreciate his attempt at a warm welcome this morning.

Still looking bewildered, he said the engineers had been there waiting for us, but went home when they saw us leave.

I asked him about the fuel and the shooting this morning, and he explained that they had put the fuel down to keep looters from coming up the road. This was unlikely; two other roads leading to the area and had not been covered with fuel. I asked him about the shooters, and he said that the guard at the bus station and the fuel point across the street were shooting into the air to keep looters away.

It did not add up, and I wasn't in the mood for further discussion. "Tell your friends to go and tell the folks not to shoot while we are here, or we will blow up any place from which we hear a shot."

He warned me about a fueling area behind the wall in front of us, to which I responded, "If I hear a shot, you will have a clear view to the road."

He must have understood the implication, because his eyes opened wider and he looked even more frightened. He said, "What about the guard at the bus station?"

I told him to pass the word for the guard not to shoot or there would be no more buses. He motioned to the men standing around him and said something in Arabic. The men hurried off.

The Bradley that had brought me to the substation rolled up and stopped in front of the building where I now stood with the substation operator, who was now very apologetic, and a crowd began to form. Among the crowd were the operator's children, who handed me a rose and offered tea.

Al-Amir told me that the rose was gesture of great respect. I accepted it and thanked them, reiterating our ambition to secure the substation and get the electricity turned back on. Suddenly everyone was eager to help. The children brought out the tea, and for the next hour the substation operator and I talked. Finally, he agreed to take us to the homes of the engineers.

The executive officer from the mechanized infantry battalion arrived shortly thereafter. I overheard him radio a report back to his brigade that infuriated me. He told them that there was nothing to report. He was basically saying it had been a false alarm. But he had not been there that morning and had not had his vehicle saturated with fuel while taking gunfire from behind a wall. I went up to him and told him that his report was incorrect.

He replied that it was not. I told him about the fuel that had been intentionally spread all over the road prior to our arrival. I pointed to the fuel tanker that had been in the line of fire, but now sat against a wall about a hundred yards from us.

He questioned how I could have known that the fuel covering the road had been spread intentionally. I explained that the substation operator had confirmed it, but for some reason, the officer stuck to his assessment. I was about to blow my top, but knew this was no place to pull rank. It was no use arguing, because from a distance, it would be hard to know which of us was being the fool.

After we returned to the battalion area, I drove to brigade headquarters and thanked the commander for his help. I described the events, repeated what the substation operator had told me, and told him our plans to meet with the engineers the next day.

Then I headed to the division headquarters, where I described the events and our plans to meet with the engineers to Colonel Sterling. He told me the team would be getting military police support, that I was to stay in, observe the targeting, and keep tabs on how reconstruction was progressing.

While waiting for Captain Guidry to return with troops from the engineer brigade, I reviewed assessments of the city's infrastructure. While the power and water substations were mostly intact, they were decrepit and in need of major repairs. The sewage treatment plant, on the other hand, had been looted, and hundreds of the approximately thirty thousand kilometers of high power lines were down.

An officer from Corps headquarters came in and interrupted my review of the reconstruction efforts. "I understand that you are trying to turn on the power plant at al-Dhora," he said.

"Yes," I replied.

"Well before you do, I want you to make sure that the power grid is decentralized. Let's look at changing the power from two hundred and twenty to one hundred and ten. Just think of the economic impact it will have."

I knew the officer well and knew it was futile to argue with him. After three days in Baghdad, I had reached the point of exhaustion. All I really cared about was getting the power back on. I had no concern how it operated before or how it would operate in the future. All I wanted was for the engineers to get it running.

I looked at the officer, shook my head and said, "Yes, sir."

He looked at me and asked, "How are you going to do it?"

"Sir," I said, "I have no idea. In fact, I am not going to even try. Some smart guy will have to sort all that out. All I care about is getting electricity back on for the Iraqis. Not tomorrow or the next day while your idea is being sorted out. I want it on today."

Furious, the officer turned and walked away. It was a good thing he could not read my mind at that moment.

Captain Guidry and his team were successful the morning of April 12. At approximately ten o'clock, the team arrived at the division headquarters with a busload of engineers. They were escorted to the engineer brigade headquarters. "These are the right people to turn on the electricity," we were told. Eleven days later, despite complaints that the engineers weren't the most cooperative, it became a reality.

Meanwhile, daily reports came in that some commanders were directing troops to leave the enormous portraits of Saddam that were staring down from public buildings and offices throughout the city intact. I recommended to Colonel Sterling that, barring structural damage to buildings and structures, the images needed to go. The Iraqis hated Saddam, but the average man was scared to death of him. I suggested that to leave the pictures in place would give Iraqis a sense that Saddam would return. By taking them down, we demonstrated that there is no need to fear him; he was not coming back. Colonel Sterling agreed and issued the order to tear down the images.

The momentum we had built up in the restoration of basic services to Baghdad wavered when a group from the Office of Reconstruction and Humanitarian Assistance (ORHA) arrived at the end of April. Iraqis perceived the lack of progress with restoration activities, but media reports were more concerned with the looting of the Museum of Antiquity and the condition of Baghdad's zoo animals.

On April 14, we went to the Palestine Hotel and met with the Marines we would be relieving when they moved to the southern part of Iraq. The Marines had established a civil-military operations center in the hotel and were directly engaged with the Iraqis. They shared the hotel with the international press corps. Demonstrators would walk up and down the street in front of the hotel, stopping in front to perform for the press by repeating anti-American slogans, chanting and waving their arms feverishly, then continue on out of sight. Every thirty minutes, another set of buses would shuttle in new demonstrators, with new signs and new chants. The Iraqis, who had lived under a police state for thirty-five years, were getting a taste of what it meant to have freedom of speech.

The division had directed my battalion to establish a civil-military operations center by April 20. After seeing the mass confusion in front of the Palestine Hotel, I decided not to recommend taking over the Marines' operations center. My recommendation would be the palace area on the west side of the river. On the morning of April 15, we left the airport to conduct a reconnaissance. On the way towards the palace area, we saw families along the road digging up bodies that had been buried during the battle. Burned out and destroyed vehicles were everywhere.

When we arrived at the palace compound, a lieutenant colonel stopped us and came up to the lead vehicle. I stepped out to greet him.

"What are you all doing here?" he asked.

I answered that I was from the civil affairs battalion and we were here to do a recon for a battalion headquarters. The colonel looked my way and said that he had heard we would be coming. He introduced himself as Lt. Col. Philip "Flip" DeCamp.

I introduced myself and told him it was nice to meet him. Flip looked at me and said, "Hey, we are on our way to a bank robbery in progress, do you want to help?" I looked at Captain Guidry and he shrugged his shoulders. I told Flip, "Sure, let's go," and he told me to fall in behind his vehicle. There was a Bradley in the lead along with other elements from Flip's battalion.

We arrived at the bank to find soldiers from Flip's battalion establishing a perimeter. About one thousand or so people had gathered around the bank, some chanting, "Money, money!" A couple of men carrying AK-47 assault rifles ran from the bank and fired a couple of shots.

Flip looked at me. "This a civilian issue," he said. "What do you want to do?"

I told him we should clear the building.

Captain Guidry's security team composed of former Rangers, special forces, FBI agents, and police officers arrived on the scene. Guidry laid out a plan with them to clear different parts of the building. The teams entered the front of the building, and I took my translator and a couple of soldiers around the back. We turned the corner of the bank to find several hundred people gathered at the back gate. They were pushing the gate back and forth, trying to push it down.

Flip told me he had an extra Bradley if we wanted to put it in front of the gate. I said that sounded like a great idea, so Flip turned to a captain and told him to make it happen.

In short order, a Bradley turned the corner to make its way down the very narrow alley. Flip stood a few feet away from me, grinning as people jumped out of the Bradley's way. I started up the stairs in back of the bank and was met by a barefoot man running out of the back door and down the stairs. I reached out to grab him, and he tried to sidestep me. His quick move caused my arm to hook and clothesline him at the neck. He fell on the steps, back first, and began trying to punch and bite me. Trouble was, he had no teeth.

Al-Amir came up to help me subdue the man, and we noticed stacks of U.S. dollars sticking out of his shirt pocket. When we finally had him restrained the man, we removed $100,000 U.S. dollars—ten stacks of $100 bills, in $10,000 bundles—from his pockets.

One of the soldiers handcuffed him and escorted him off. Meanwhile, the teams had caught six other men, and were now escorting them from the building. We discovered a hole they had cut in the top of the vault. The robbers had dropped down a child, who handed the money up to them.

Then Flip received a report about another bank robbery in progress a couple blocks away. Flip's battalion escorted my security team on their way to assess the situation.

Flip and I discussed securing the first bank. We agreed that we should remove the money from the damaged vault. Another vault had been only slightly damaged, and the crooks had not been successful in gaining access. But to secure the bank would further overextend Flip's battalion, who already were responsible for securing some four hundred facilities in his area of responsibility.

We decided to go with our other option, which was to blow open the undamaged vault and secure the contents. Flip's engineers packed about fourteen pounds of C4 explosives on the vault. We cleared the streets, moving the crowd from the area to keep them from being injured by the flying glass.

A couple of Bradleys moved across the street from the bank. Flip and I, along with our soldiers, hunkered down behind the vehicles and prepared for the explosion. At that moment, I felt like I was in a remake of *Butch Cassidy and the Sundance Kid*.

Flip was handed the detonator. He counted to three and hit it. The earth seemed to move under our feet. Smoke billowed from the building, but surprisingly, not a lot of glass. Meanwhile, Captain Guidry and his team returned with a pair of suspected robbers they arrested at the second bank.

Flip and his engineers evaluated the vault we had just tried to blow up. They learned that the explosion did not make it through the rebar. We would have to secure the building, and my team would return to the division headquarters with the money removed from the first vault.

After some questioning, Flip and I agreed that the nine men we had taken into custody were not the actual robbers, but merely opportunists who had not planned the robberies. I told Flip I would take them with me for fear that the crowd would attack them if we released them there, thinking that they had money. My team loaded the nine men into the back of one of our troop carriers. The men shouted at the crowd as we drove off, and the crowd cheered them.

The further we drove along, the more the expressions of the men changed. By the time we stopped about a hundred feet inside the palace gates, they looked terrified. When I told them to get out of the vehicle, they began to cry, begging us not to kill them. I told them to get down and line up. One man urinated on himself, and another younger man cried and begged us not to kill them.

I stood facing toward the line of nine men. "The next time you see a bank robbery," I told them, "you better run away, because if I come and find you there, you will never get out of jail." Then I told them to go on and get out of there.

They looked at each other like it was a trick and then the man that had urinated on himself ran up and started hugging me. The other men followed suit and began hugging both me and members of the team. The men kept looking over their shoulders as they walked away, perhaps fearing we would still shoot them. Once they reached the palace gate, they must have felt that they were no longer in danger and hugged each other in relief.

My team and I took the money (several potato sacks–worth) to the tactical operations center at division headquarters and counted it. It was in excess of $6.3 million. The division's intelligence officer, Lt. Col. Jon Mowers, made a joke that every time we go out we get into something, and judging by the large sum, this time was no different.

The palace complex (later called the Green Zone and then the International Zone) was by now a ghost town. It was eerie to walk through the deserted palace that once housed the former elites of Iraq. Uniforms left behind by Iraqi soldiers, half-full teacups, and a pan of food were the only remaining remnants of the former regime. The next day, April 16, members of the 354th Civil Affairs Brigade would uncover $750 million in the complex.

Our job of locating and installing a police chief had already been done by the Marines the day before. I went to the hotel to meet this officer. Mohammed Mohsen al-Zubaidi would become both a friend and a nemesis before my Iraqi adventure was through. I was sitting with him and his entourage in the coffee lounge of the Palestine Hotel. Suddenly, the side doors flew open and reporters rushed in like a tidal wave hitting a beach. They inundated us with questions from the Arab press. It was obvious that the press had been briefed earlier on Mohammed's personal plans, and had been lying in wait to ambush us.

A reporter asked me if the U.S. Army had any plans to "slow the progress of the Marines." I assured everyone that we would keep up the momentum and capitalize on the Marines' accomplishments. Another asked me about Mohammed's appointment as the "mayor of Baghdad."

"Mayor of Baghdad?" I responded. "No, he is not the mayor of Baghdad, but we intend to work with those concerned citizens who want to move the reconstruction effort forward." I explained that the people vote for mayors; they are not appointed.

Muhammad interjected that he had been elected by the sheiks of the country.

I leaned over and whispered to him so low that my translator could hardly hear to translate: "You are not the mayor, but if you can accomplish what you say, we will work with you in some capacity."

That night, al-Zubaidi announced to CNN that he was the mayor of Baghdad and he laid out his plans to rebuild the city. Over the next ten days, we spent as much time trying to deal with Mohammed's personal agendas as we did trying to reestablish the infrastructure in the city.

The Associated Press reported it this way: "Mr. al-Zubaidi, a recently returned exile, has been busily touring facilities, meeting interest groups, and naming supporters to key positions in the city since he declared himself mayor of Baghdad last week. One of his followers has said he plans to represent Iraq at an Organization of the Petroleum Exporting Countries meeting this week in Vienna." He also announced plans to start his own army, create his own currency, and to start a radio and television station.

Then in July 2003, I learned that al-Zubaidi had taken out a contract on my life. After his arrest, the exploitation of his computer turned up pictures of my wife and me, along with other personal information. I was told that charges would be filed against al-Zubaidi and he would be prosecuted, but he was released on December 4, 2003, and he fled to Jordan.

Maj. Vince Crabb and captains Mike Self and Tim Popek had taken on the responsibility of the police department, doing yeoman's job by the time ORHA arrived. Crabb had played to the international press as the "Sheriff of Baghdad." By the time the bureaucracy arrived, Crabb was already well known in both Washington and London. Crabb and his team had hired more than 5,000 police officers by April 26 and had paid more than 1,200. He had acquired more than 2,300 pistols from confiscated weapons caches from Saddam's palaces, and placed into service more than 3,600 police cruisers.

On April 16, Crabb came to me to report that he, along with Popek and Self, had been involved in the capture of Hikmat Mizban Ibrahim al-Azzawi (number 26 most wanted/eight of diamonds in the deck of cards), the deputy prime minister and finance minister. He explained that a man came to the police station and said that he would take him to the home of al-Azzawi. As the police advisor, Crabb brought along some police officers to the home, where they placed al-Azzawi under arrest. After the capture, the Marines were leaving the police station and agreed to escort al-Azzawi to the prison. On only his first day on the job as police advisor, Crabb was already catching major wanted persons.

Once the Marines left Baghdad to begin moving south, I became the senior civil-military coordinator in the city, and would remain so until the 354th Civil Affairs Brigade could make its way to Baghdad. Maj. Gen. Buford Blount directed that I meet with the appointed interim police chief, Maj. Gen. Zuhair al-Nuammy, and interim deputy police chief, Maj. Gen. Louie al-Khadban, and insure that they understood the position of the Coalition. On April 22 in front of the international press, I laid out the Coalition's demands and expectations for the "new" police department.

I explained that Nuammy and Khadban were the only police department administrators the Coalition would recognize. Their uniforms would now be blue, with a brassard around the arm. Major Crabb coordinated the brassard and was also responsible for a new Iraqi police badge, adopting the crest worn on the Iraqi military's hats prior to the war. The crest would now move to their chest as the new police badge. It would become a symbol of pride, to be worn close to their hearts. When Crabb explained that this is how it is done in the United States, it rated highly in their minds.

The self-proclaimed mayor, Muhammad al-Zubaidi, had appointed a police chief among other city public officials. Nuammy told me that he was being threatened by supporters of al-Zubaidi, and al-Zubaidi's appointed police chief had been coming to police headquarters saying he was the rightful police chief. He had asked Nuammy, "Why are you going into my areas? I'm the chief; I'm responsible there. I have my own men and you need to stay away."

I had told Nuammy that if the man interfered or made any other threats, he would be arrested, as would anyone who attempted to intervene in the reconstruction efforts. I reassured Nuammy that he was the only recognized police administrator in Baghdad—period.

The international press would get the message about the Coalition's resolve on the matter of who was in charge. By April 26, everyone in the coalition was fed up with al-Zubaidi's antics. I invited him to my office, at which time he would be detained. We arrested him and his deputy on April 27. According to an Associated Press report that later appeared in the *Washington Times* and other news outlets:

> U.S. FORCES ACTED FOR THE FIRST TIME AGAINST FOLLOWERS OF A SELF-PROCLAIMED "MAYOR OF BAGHDAD," ARRESTING A MAN WHO SAID HE HAD BEEN NAMED CHIEF OF POLICE BY MOHAMMED MOHSEN AL-ZUBAIDI. U.S. FORCES DETAINED THE MAN WHEN HE TURNED UP AT THE CITY'S MAIN POLICE STATION TO CHALLENGE THE AUTHORITY OF Z[U]HAIR ABDUL RAZAQ [AL-NU(A)MMY], WHOM U.S. OFFICIALS HAD PLACED IN CHARGE OF POLICE.

Before I departed with the self-proclaimed police chief in custody, I told Nuammy that he and his officers would be held accountable for any corruption, torture, or human rights violations committed under their watch. He was to take action against officers who violated this directive, or I would have him arrested. He cautiously nodded his head. Crabb was left with specific instructions on what we needed to accomplish, and there was no doubt in my mind that he was up to the job.

I was getting into my vehicle when I noticed a police cruiser speed up to the police station. What I witnessed next would stick in my mind as an example of how far we had to go. The two officers got out of the vehicle, opened the trunk and pulled two males from inside by the hair of their head. When I told Crabb about the incident, I was pleased to find out that Nuammy had already fired and arrested the officers.

While our efforts continued to focus on the restoration of government services, the Iraqi people were becoming increasingly more agitated with what they perceived as a lack of progress with restoration activities. It was hard to get them to understand that it is not as simple as flipping on a switch. There was only so much we could do given the decrepit infrastructure that was left by the former regime and the limited number of people available to help.

# CHAPTER 4

# Reaching Out

*He who speaks about the future lies,*
*even when he tells the truth.*
*—Arab proverb*

Our battalion settled into our new accommodation in the Presidential Palace with the immediate task to coordinate, monitor, and advise on the reconstruction efforts of Baghdad. Major General Blount and Colonel Sterling from the 3rd Infantry Division (Mechanized) augmented my staff with almost a dozen officers to track every governmental function (utilities, safety, sanitation, etc.).

Flip De Camp was concerned about the location of our offices, which were approximately a kilometer inside the palace gate. He did not want unknown Iraqis walking freely inside the secure area, and I understood his concern. Vince Crabb and Capt. Stacy Simms brought over a bus to shuttle Iraqis between the offices and the gate. This seemed to be a simple answer to the problem, as long as the Iraqis would abide by the procedures. But they did not, and instead chose to walk to and from the gate. So Crabb had newly-commissioned, armed Iraqi police officers brought inside the secure area, and this proved valuable in preventing incidents with other Iraqis.

I considered majors Toney Coleman and Barry McRae and the other staff members heroes in how they managed thousands of people, interviews, and other inquiries. They developed a database that identified Iraqis with specific expertise. This included electricians, translators, and every other imaginable skill. We used the database to hire people for the immediate needs of the Coalition. The database would be transferred and used by the Coalition Provisional Authority (CPA) and other Coalition units when they arrived.

While the international press focused on museum looting and zoo conditions in the first days after the fall of Saddam's regime, which were certainly issues of concern, they were of little or no concern to the average Iraqi. I do not recall a single Iraqi asking about either of issue. Their immediate and overwhelming concerns included health care, medications, safe drinking water, electricity, security, garbage removal, missing family members (including those lost during the Iran/Iraq war), fertilizer and insecticide for their crops, final school exams for their children, anxiety over Saddam's possible return, information about the future government, complaints about the Americans, complaints about the Iraqi military, and so on.

Satellite dishes, which had been banned under the former regime, began to pop up on houses overnight. No longer were they force to watch only government-controlled programming. The window to the rest of the world gave them a clear picture of what they had been missing for thirty years. They wanted everything now, not later, and expected the Coalition to provide it overnight. It was a setup for disappointment. I described it to one reporter as being like the end of *The Wizard of Oz*, when Toto pulls back the curtain, revealing the wizard's "magic" as nothing more than a little old man manipulating levers. There would be no magic solution or quick fix to satisfy the Iraqis.

One success we had was in assisting a young American girl and her mother who had been trapped in Baghdad visiting relatives when the war broke out. At first it seemed insurmountable. Sara and her mother came to my office every day pleading for help. The mother was terribly ill and needed medical attention. I asked Major McRae to assist and he began contacting various agencies. Some offered money to assist them until we could get them a flight home. Finally, McRae found a diplomat from a Middle Eastern nation who agreed to provide medical care and travel. I would later find out that Sara's mother recovered after returning to the United States.

I would soon learn how much Iraqi sheiks value loyalty to their family and tribes. For the most part, legitimate sheiks wield honor and respect in Iraqi society, especially in the rural areas. Their influence was vital in winning their country's approval of the Coalition's intentions. Mass communication was not readily available, so I would communicate what the Coalition wanted through the sheiks who visited my office. These wants included rounding up the former regime elites.

I met dozens of sheiks and clerics in April and May. Most were appreciative of the liberation and wanted little more than reassurance that we were there to give them their country back, not occupy it. I assured them that we were not crusaders determined to undermine Islamic faith, that we wanted nothing more than to eliminate Saddam and build Iraq into a strong nation that would serve as a model for the rest of the Middle East. We also discussed Islam and its similarities to Christianity. For a U.S. military officer to discuss the Qur'an with Iraqi sheiks turned out to be a shocking concept to both Americans and Iraqis.

The reconstruction efforts were slowly but surely becoming perceptible to Iraqis. Our primary obstacle was the decrepit infrastructure and the damage caused by sanctions, war, and looting. The years of UN sanctions had taken their toll on the electric, water, and sewer systems.

Upgrades and repairs to these critical systems had not been made for at least ten years. Saddam's regime had done nothing to improve the systems since about the 1970s. The infrastructure primarily serviced Baghdad, leaving little else for the rest of the country. But with the brutal Iraqi summer approaching, the Iraqis were not interested in whether the UN or Saddam was more responsible for their current state of affairs. The Coalition was now responsible, and they simply wanted their electricity.

On April 20, I was directed to conduct the division's press briefings on our reconstruction efforts. Capt. James "Jim" Brownlee liaised as my public affairs officer. An excellent officer with enormous energy, Captain Brownlee helped me rehearse before the briefings, giving me great confidence before I went in front of cameras. During this period in the operations, most of the members of the press I encountered were professional and simply looking for the current story to report. Only once did I meet a reporter whose apparent personal agenda took precedence over giving an accurate account of events.

At one of the evening press briefings, I was asked why we were not getting all the weapons out of the city. I explained that we were making every effort to remove the enormous cache of weapons; in fact, we were taking dozens of truckloads out of the city every day. I mentioned a news article that reported there were more than seven million AK-47 assault rifles in the city of Baghdad, a number that meant one rifle for every man, woman, child, and baby in the city. It just was not possible to knock on every door.

A reporter asked me to elaborate about the report on the number of rifles. I replied, "As I said, it was in one of the stories that you all reported."

"Well," the reporter quipped, "then that is not credible!"

I smiled and asked, "Can I quote you on that?" The room erupted in laughter.

Saddam had consumed the lives of the Iraqis for three decades. Although he was gone forever as far as the Coalition was concerned, the Iraqi people couldn't shake the belief that he would show up and reassume power. Rumors were running rampant in the city, including one that he was going to return for his birthday on April 28th and lead a revolution.

This was the main topic for many of my press interviews, particularly with the Arab press. I finally said to a couple of the Arab reporters, "He is not coming back, but if Saddam feels like he wants to return, you tell him to stop by my office for tea first." They got a chuckle out of that, and the quote actually made the front page of some of the local newspapers.

Rumors were difficult to manage and even more impossible to stop. There was one particular rumor that involved me. Word quickly spread that I was sent to Baghdad with a fake name (King) to prepare the people for the return of the monarchy. Sheiks and others would come in and ask me for my real name and wanted to know my position on the return of the monarchy. Some even referred to me, tongue in cheek, as "Your Highness" and "Your Majesty." Sharif Ali (the last remaining family member from the former monarchy) and I had a few laughs about it during one meeting.

By April 23, Crabb and his team began developing with Lt. Col. Mark Warman, Military Police battalion commander, a one-week program of training and instruction for the leadership of the newly-formed Iraqi police force. The program would cover human rights training, administration, managing patrols, and a myriad of other specialized topics.

During a briefing, we informed the press that the course would begin on May 4, with Warman's battalion beginning joint patrols by May 11. There was an *esprit de corps* developing among the men and it was getting contagious.

Major Crabb approached me when he returned from the police academy that afternoon. He told me that a civil affairs colonel had come to him asking who authorized the guidance and changes regarding the Iraqi police force. Crabb told him I was the one authorizing these efforts. The colonel became angry and demanded everything stop. After Crabb reported this incident to me, I told him that because the division had approved our actions, the Corps would have to provide any order to stop in writing. Better yet, they could provide an alternative plan. Crabb smiled and in his distinctive southern drawl said, "Roger that, sir."

The day the ORHA team arrived, Crabb introduced himself to its staff and explained what he and his team had accomplished so far. The ORHA staff seemed disinterested and, unknown to us, began implementing its own plan.

Then the April 27 arrest of Mohammed Mohsen al-Zubaidi and his deputy led to a Shi'a cleric threatening to have me killed. My meetings with this cleric were widely known, and my knowledge of the Qur'an's teachings gained me a certain level of admiration among other religious leaders and sheiks throughout the country.

Unbeknownst to me, this Shi'a cleric had been preaching anti-American rhetoric. After meeting me and learning of my respect for Islam, he began instructing his followers to work with the Americans. Kelly O'Donnell and Charlie Ryan from NBC News, who had been following the cleric, heard about his change of heart. Their NBC Nightly News profile of the two of us ran on June 1, 2003. This cleric's path and mine would cross many times during my time in Iraq.

In the days immediately following the fall of Saddam, the battalion was inundated with thousands of people who had seen Saddam, knew where weapons were buried, and had information on various wanted persons. Our battalion's immediate objective was the reconstruction and stability of Baghdad, and we were not prepared, nor were we trained, to sift through this overwhelming amount of information to evaluate its validity.

Thankfully, I had an arrangement with "Daniel," an American whose team was responsible for gathering intelligence, to help sort through such information. I had been introduced to Daniel upon my arrival in Baghdad. He had a colleague, another American by the name of Cyprus.

Cyprus spoke fluent Arabic and had an inherent understanding of the culture. He was aware of the relationships I was cultivating with the sheiks, and he asked me to query them to provide insight about the activities of the former regime. Daniel, Cyprus, and I traveled to the homes of sheiks and were greeted like royalty. On one particular day, sheiks from around the country hosted us with a feast of lamb, goat, rice, and other delicacies.

Looking back on my experiences in Iraq, I see how the fore-sight of Daniel and Cyprus kept my working relationships with the sheiks focused. Developing the contacts with the sheiks on their terms and accepting their culture was a turning point in making these relationships more reciprocal, broadening them by tapping into the sheiks' collective sphere of influence. Daniel's encouragement inspired everything I did with the sheiks from April 2003 until I left in June 2004.

No doubt, the success of the 422nd Civil Affairs Battalion was a direct result of the friendship and working relationship Daniel and I had formed. I became Daniel's medium for Iraqis to pass along information without feeling that they were spies. While my office became known as the "Nest" in many circles, it was because of the access to representatives in the Coalition, not for the information and advice given to me by visiting Iraqis.

The Information Operations Campaign has become more critical than direct action in waging modern war. A successful information campaign involves the synchronization and dissemi-nation or management of information to four essential target audiences: 1) civilians, both U.S. and international; 2) U.S./Coalition military (informing the troops on the status of operations); 3) the indigenous population of the country where the fighting is taking place; and 4) the military we are fighting.

After May 3, 2003, the information campaign's focus seemed imbalanced in favor of news agencies from Coalition countries and, to a lesser degree, the Coalition military. The scarce dissemi-nation of information and incoherent messages, as perceived by the Iraqi people, created anxiety, frustration, and disenfran-chisement, providing the fuel necessary for the insurgency that would soon follow.

Half a million military-trained Iraqi men returned to a society faced with seventy percent unemployment—with one month's severance pay for enlisted soldiers, nothing for senior officers—then were told to become productive members of that society. These trained combatants made ideal recruits for the insurgency. It is a simple matter of economics. Prior to the war, the average annual income for Iraq was less than $2,500. A private in the military made approximately five dollars a month, or $60 a year. Given Iraq's socialist structure, the people were used to surviving on such meager wages. But now, these men literally had nothing to provide for their dependents.

Backed by rich individuals and nations who had an interest in seeing democracy fail in Iraq, the insurgents had bags and bags of money to fund their efforts. According to a number of sheiks I met with, insurgents were offering unemployed Iraqi soldiers $500 a month to fight against the infidels. This was one hundred times more than they had been paid before.

One sheik asked me, "If your family was starving, would you do anything to save them? How can I make someone in my tribe fight for you, when you have taken everything he has away from him?"

The insurgents had a catchall recruiting program—if the men weren't religious, they appealed to their national honor; if their country was second to their religion, then they were asked to do it in the name of God; and if neither of these were important, they appealed to one's greed. Regardless of the reason, the insurgency was happy to have someone who would fight.

Of the thousands of Iraqis I would encounter, the majority were nationalist in their thinking and beliefs. For most, the issues were the occupation of their country, an imperceptible progress on the infrastructure, and the non-existence of security for the average citizen.

In the early days, both sheiks and average Iraqis welcomed the liberation by the Coalition, believing that once Saddam's regime was dislodged, the country would go back to the people. Clarifying our reconstruction and stability operations was an almost impossible message to deliver on a timely basis, especially with the dramatic and continual changes taking place.

If there was a singular turning point, it was Ambassador Bremer's announcement that the Coalition was an occupier in May 2003. He called for the complete de-Ba'athification of the top four levels of government along with the immediate dissolution of the military. The sweeping changes were instantaneous.

It was as if someone flipped a switch, and all the trust we'd built up was lost. The Iraqis felt betrayed, and their support for the Coalition immediately waned, turning instead into hostility. This shift in terminology from guests to occupiers caused a backlash that was, in retrospect, inevitable, given Iraq's history and culture.

Many of the sheiks, former elite, and average citizens with whom I met wanted to know why we had "tricked" them in taking over their country. I tried to explain that declaring ourselves as occupiers was necessary for the international community to understand and accept our security responsibilities. This explanation did not sit well with the sheiks. To them, it was double talk, and we could not have it both ways. They told me that our betrayal left them with no choice but to fight back, for their country and their honor.

Of the several information operations officers I met in Iraq, none seemed to have an understanding or appreciation for the

Middle Eastern culture, religion, and Iraq's unique history as an occupied country. An example was a Coalition-distributed leaflet with a pair of green eyes on it. For the Iraqis, this symbolized the evil eye and enraged even the religious moderates. This was clearly a failure on the part of the action officers to research Iraq's social mores.

Our information operations campaign should have made the former Iraqi military a primary target audience after it was dissolved in May 2003. Iraq's professional officers would have considered a national military the single symbol of sovereignty, and the security it provides makes a country into a nation. A government that cannot provide security cannot lead a nation. The resulting environment of instability renders the government's laws unenforceable.

Before Ambassador Bremer's announcement, the credibility of the United States among the Iraqis had been unwavering, their enthusiasm inspiring. Captain John Smathers, an attorney from Maryland and the battalion Judge Advocate, began to organize former judges and lawyers together. When Reserve Maj. Gen. Donald Campbell, a judge from New York, arrived as the senior advisor to the Ministry of Justice, he was impressed with Smathers' initiative.

Other officers from the battalion had begun to assess schools, trash removal, sewage, postal services, orphanages, and records at City Hall. In late April, a staff officer came to me and reported that two clerics from An Najaf wanted to see me at the checkpoint. He asked if I had called for them; I had not. The clerics said they heard how I had treated the Bedouin who had cut his finger in An Najaf, and thought if I could help a Bedouin, they knew I would help them.

It shocked me how an event I considered insignificant at the time could have made such an impact that these men drove from An Najaf to Baghdad to talk to me. I asked the staff officer to return to the gate and escort the men to see me. Unfortunately, when the officer returned, he said that the men had left, telling the guard that they had to return to An Najaf before nightfall. To the best of my knowledge, I never again encountered the men who came that day, and often wondered about them and their reasons for making the journey.

The morning of May 2 I visited with Nuammy, the chief of police, who had decided to retire. He wanted to spend time with his family and felt that a younger man might be better suited for the position. Deputy Chief Khadban would also be retiring. We would announce his decision in a press conference the next afternoon. On my way back to the palace, it hit me that it was my daughter Kaitlyn's second birthday. My homesickness really hit me hard.

To the gathered press the next day, after announcing his retirement, Chief Nuammy presented me with $380,000 U.S. dollars and a kilo of gold jewelry that had been confiscated during a raid on a gang hideout. Nuammy wanted to make sure that the money and gold was turned over so that there could not be any allegations of improper conduct. Both Nuammy and Khadban worked hard to bring respect and dignity to the police department during their short tenure. Unfortunately, some in the press tried to make the money and gold transfer into scandal, desperate to create controversy. Nuammy and Khadban realized that the near future was going to be a challenge that few would be prepared to accept.

The daily schedule became busier and busier as the month of May progressed. I met people from all walks of Iraqi society. One day, members from the Iraqi Olympic soccer team, whom Saddam's son Uday had tortured for the sin of losing, approached me with the idea to have a game the next day. I thought it was a nice idea to bring some normalcy to the current situation, but could not coordinate security for the event on such short notice. I told them I would do my best to arrange security for a game in one week.

For this, I would turn to ORHA's Don Eberly, senior advisor to the Ministry of Youth and Sports. He was a soft-spoken man, but a visionary who realized the importance a soccer team would have in fostering a national identity for the Iraqis. Eberly was eager to meet with the soccer team. I agreed to arrange a meeting the next day for he and the team to discuss the details of the event. This activity seemed to me a perfect fit for the OHRA.

Soon afterwards, Hussein Saeed, a former Olympic soccer athlete who wanted to have a role with future Olympic committees, approached me. Saeed had worked for Uday as a senior member of the former Olympic committee. He wanted to represent the Iraqi soccer team at the Fédération Internationale de Football Association (FIFA) conference in Saudi Arabia. Saeed had a passion for the sport and had devoted his entire life to it.

I escorted Saeed to the former presidential palace to meet with Eberly. Saeed laid out all of his reasons why he should be allowed to represent Iraq at the soccer conference, Eberly tactfully explained that it was not possible for him to do it. Saeed was heartbroken and tried repeatedly over the following days to make his point. Understandably, his persistence on the matter eventually forced Eberly to cut off future communication with him.

A man came to my office on May 4 and informed me that a sayyid (another term for a cleric who descends from the Shiite martyr Husayn ibn Ali) in Eastern Baghdad declared that I should be killed for my role in the attack on Baghdad. Cyprus checked around with his various contacts and confirmed the story. The sayyid was declaring the American liberation wrong and calling for the people to fight against the United States.

After more thought and discussion, I decided not to arrest the sayyid. Instead, I would make an effort to reason with him. I spoke to DeCamp and asked him to arrange an infantry squad to escort the sayyid to prison should it be necessary. DeCamp agreed.

I directed the squad to back their Bradley outside one of my office's floor-to-ceiling windows and to stand behind it. If I needed to bring the sayyid out, I would walk him straight out the back door to the awaiting vehicle.

When the sayyid arrived, I invited him inside, where Cyprus was ready to translate. I began by telling him I was disturbed by reports that he wanted me killed, and that I was authorized and prepared to arrest him if necessary. He was free to express his opinion, but not to incite violence or call for my assassination. If he threatened or hurt me, my soldiers, people I knew, or anyone else, the soldiers now standing behind the building were coming to call on him.

Then I asked him, as a leader in his community, why he would not encourage his people to work with us to rebuild the city rather than fight against our efforts.

He defiantly declared that I was an infidel—one who did not believe in God—and that he could not possibly ask his people to work with us.

Surprised by his candor, I looked him in straight in the eye and said, "You believe you are better than God?"

He sat back quickly in his chair and prepared to comment.

Before he could answer, I raised my hand to silence him and went on to tell him that the Qur'an refers to Jesus as the Messiah thirteen times, the nineteenth chapter is about the Virgin Mary and the birth of Christ, and the forty-third chapter declares that Jesus will return in the hour of judgment. In fact, the second and fifth chapters declared that Christians were believers, yet here he sat as an audacious judge of God's word. If an infidel such as myself prays to the same God of Abraham that he prays to, then he and his people were infidels too.

He was stunned, caught absolutely off guard, looking even a little frightened. Then I pointed to the Bradley and said, "That is your ride to prison where you will go and pray to God to forgive you of your errors if you ever threaten me again."

He could do nothing but concede that I was a believer.

According to the reports the following Friday, his prayers declared that the people should give the Americans a chance and that they should work with them to rebuild the city. The sayyid became a close consultant for me and before I left, he presented me with a Qur'an as a gift.

Shortly after the 3rd Infantry Division relinquished its responsibilities to ORHA, the direction and information flow ceased to exist. There appeared to be no clear vision for Iraq's reconstruction. For those of us on the ground, we simply had no plan to follow. We weren't the only ones frustrated by the situation. During our daily meetings with Iraqis, we could offer them no clear sense of the intended direction.

Battalion staff officers had worked diligently to implement some structure to the activities. But after meeting the incoming ORHA advisors, they became confused and disillusioned. It seemed that the advisors intended to dismantle everything we had put into place before their arrival. This had a devastating affect on the Iraqi people and the press began to severely criticize U.S. efforts. In one case, an advisor to one of the ministries said he wanted everything we had done to stop, that they were going to take a couple of weeks "to do an assessment."

I tried to explain to him that while they might want to change, revise, or add to our efforts, they should not stop the momentum we had built up. Although the advisors could not articulate an alternative plan, their blasé attitude was disheartening; we would stop what we were doing, as instructed.

The frustration of my staff and I grew as new units and personnel arrived in Baghdad on a daily basis. We had been there since the first day and had witnessed the chaos and seen the recovery efforts along with the return of basic functions to the city. The additional bureaucracy became increasingly difficult to deal with as we listened daily to the Iraqis' complaints and worked tirelessly to rebuild the city with no clear direction.

# CHAPTER 5

# We Wanted You to Win

*While the word is yet unspoken, you are master of it;*
*when once it is spoken, it is master of you.*
—*Arab proverb*

My primary concerns—the restoration of public services, reconstruction, and security—were challenged by the growing bureaucracy in Baghdad. When the ORHA took over responsibility for rebuilding Iraq from the 3rd Infantry Division, what previously took one day to accomplish began to take several days, sometimes weeks. Iraqis continued to ask me when a sense of normalcy would return to their country. We hoped things would be different when the Coalition Provisional Authority (CPA), made up of U.S. officials, was created to replace the ORHA in May 2003.

We were kept busy trying to manage the continuous flow of information, from sightings of Saddam to locations of WMDs. All five-and-a-half million people living in Baghdad seemed to have their own conspiracy theory. Someone had been passing gossip to the tabloids regarding the individuals I had been meeting. One day, a man claimed that one of Saddam's former pilots, with whom he had once been imprisoned, was in the lobby waiting to see me. The man asserted that he witnessed the pilot signing a letter stating that he agreed to fly a plane into an American naval ship.

The pilot and I had an amicable discussion about the malfunctioning sewage system in his neighborhood. I told him I would be sure to have someone assess it. Then I passed him along to another organization to discuss the alleged letter.

We also had a number of inquiries from civil servants, soldiers, railway workers, policemen, and firemen who had not been paid in months. The last paycheck many of them had received was about two months before the Coalition arrived. They couldn't afford to buy even the basic essentials.

Iraq had been a socialist state, "providing what the people needed." Saddam had ordered food baskets to be distributed just before the war, with two-month rations for every family. These rations included staple items such as tea, lentils, flour, rice, and an assortment of other items. But now there were families with nothing left and in dire need of assistance.

I depended on a Palm Pilot to keep track of my growing list of contacts and requests from people who needed our assistance. It was hard to turn people away, but we lacked the manpower and means to help everyone. We were forced to prioritize our work, and this left some Iraqis feeling abandoned.

We began to see a free-for-all as various exiled political groups from Iran, the United Kingdom, and the United States tried to claim government property for their own use. In one instance, a representative from the Iraqi National Congress (INC) came to me wanting to take over some government buildings and property. Major Crabb had sent the representative to obtain my approval after he demanded almost thirty-six hundred vehicles Crabb had secured for police use.

The man strutted into the office wearing a suit, and had his hair slicked back. The beginning of the conversation was pleasant and polite, but when I told him no, he said that he would keep pressuring me, that he would be, in his words, "Very convincing." I did not appreciate the strong-arm tactic and I asked him to leave. He said that he would not leave until I signed off to allow him to take the vehicles. I said I would not, and he made a comment to the effect that I would be sorry. I told him that he could leave the office now, or I could assist him in his departure. He obliged and left on his own.

Where the ORHA was known for inaction, the opposite seemed true of the CPA, at least at first. The senior advisor responsible for the future Iraqi military's design asked if I could provide an escort for him and his team to the former Ministry of Defense building, and I agreed. We approached the defense compound, which was nothing but a shell. Every window, door, and toilet had been removed from every building. Among the documents and manuals scattered about the floor, we found a large map of the invasion of Kuwait. In one basement room, we found smoldering bags of secret and top secret documents. I imagined the chaos of the day when the leadership, realizing defeat was inevitable, must have ordered the building evacuated and everything destroyed by incendiary grenades.

We walked from building to building, and someone came upon an underground bunker. The ministry advisors, my team, and I entered it with caution. The extensive bunker complex had a number of rooms, beds, gas masks, and bottles of antidotes for chemical poisoning. The bunker, beds, furniture, and other items remained surprisingly intact and in place. In one room, a war-gaming sand table with small metal soldiers, tanks, helicopters, and other assorted military symbols lay on the floor where they had been left by soldiers in a hurry to leave before the hardened structure became their tomb.

I wondered why looters did not steal these items; had some of the former ministry workers locked themselves in until the looting outside had stopped? Whatever the reason, the bunker was one of the only government complexes outside the palace area left relatively untouched and undamaged after the collapse of the regime.

Despite being in a war-torn country, people in Baghdad still felt the desire to enjoy themselves. Zumurudeh planned a large party for my fortieth birthday. She had asked earlier in the day how many candles I wanted, but I asked her not to do anything. She persisted, so I told her one candle was enough. I wasn't feeling up to celebrating my birthday with so many more important matters to address.

Later that day, she called my office and asked me to come by the meeting hall. There I found the battalion staff, our newly employed Iraqis, and several reporters gathered around a birthday cake, singing "Happy Birthday." Zumurudeh and her mother exemplified Iraqi hospitality with the delicious meal they prepared: huge platters of chicken, rice, and unleavened bread.

I was grateful for Zumurudeh's thoughtfulness, but I still had those other matters on my mind. It had been exactly one month since our arrival in Baghdad. The enthusiasm of the Iraqis during the first days was uplifting, and it reenergized me in my work each day. I now felt we were losing ground, with the tide of support turning against us.

Ever since the detention of al-Zubaidi, his organization had made daily requests for his release. The al-Zubaidi group claimed to have an extensive network of Iraqis prepared to assist in the reconstruction effort of the country. They claimed to have far-reaching ties into every governmental function, with experts in education administration, national sports, utilities, health, and every other imaginable function. I found these claims to be intriguing, so I asked them to bring in their committee heads to discuss their capabilities.

The group took their seats at the palace's long conference table. Their attire ranged from the informal to the distinguished. For the most part, each member claimed to have extensive experience in his respective field and the credentials to back it up. Additionally, they claimed to have persons of prestige from each field who were actively and openly supporting the group. I asked what we should call their group.

"The Management Group to Rebuild Iraq," one member replied.

I disagreed with this idea, offering instead, "The Volunteer Group to Rebuild Iraq."

An argument over my suggestion ensued among the members, and the financial chairman quickly put a stop to it. I explained that we were responsible for rebuilding Iraq; at this point, we needed their help, not their management.

We went around with each member describing their capabilities, and I asked each one of them pointed questions to verify their claims. To the man who claimed expertise and extensive administrative experience in Iraqi education, I asked how many schools—elementary, middle, high schools, and colleges—were in Baghdad. To the health administrator, I asked how many hospitals needed to be equipped.

From each person the answer was basically the same: "I do not know." I told the group that they needed to find the answers, and then I would reconvene with each one separately.

The first to see me was the committee chairman for sports, who brought with him two other men and a renowned athlete. During our discussion the athlete asked me, "Why am I here?"

I told the athlete that the committee chairman had claimed he supports the chairman's organization. The athlete shook his head and told me otherwise. This surprised the chairmen and the other men who came with him. I realized that this group was even more hollow than I originally thought.

My next meeting was with the chairman for education. Our discussion was over how to finish the school year. Normally there would be end-of-grade testing, but we talked about having everyone repeat the term next year, given the circumstances and the war. The committee chair said he had three hundred volunteers standing by to assist the Coalition in the reconstruction. He then told me how many books were needed, how much furniture, and how many other school supplies would be required.

When I asked him how many schools were in Baghdad, he said he did not know. He explained that what he had asked for was for only two schools. I would not have had a problem with this had he not started off the meeting by saying he was there to represent all of Baghdad and that the supplies were for the entire school system. I needed to know how many schools were in the city, whether they were opened or closed, and I needed a general assessment of the condition of the facilities.

I asked him if he could have his volunteers provide this information to me within two days. He said it would not be possible. I had a rough idea on the number of schools. Given his three hundred volunteers, I estimated he should be able to accomplish this in forty-eight hours, no more than seventy-two. My response angered him, and he told me he did not come to be interrogated. It became obvious to me that his three hundred volunteers did not really exist, and I told him that I did not have time to waste.

When the group's executive committee came by later that afternoon, I explained what had happened during the morning meetings. The group sat silent. I explained that I would continue to meet with their other committee heads, but that they needed to come prepared with the specific information that I had asked for. They all enthusiastically agreed.

Al-Zubaidi's name came up repeatedly during my discussions with the Iraqis and Coalition officials through the end of May. Many believed that with his assets, and if properly directed, he might be able to assist the reconstruction effort. The decision was made to release him, and I would serve as a liaison officer for him.

The condition of al-Zubaidi's release required him to come in every day and inform me about his activities and individuals with whom he had met. Al-Zubaidi brought his deputy and one of his assistants to our first meeting. Each day, his entourage grew larger and the issues and concerns more diverse.

I became close friends with Amir ("prince" in Arabic) Jassim from the al-Zubaidi Confederation. He was an elderly gentleman and lived south of Baghdad, near An Najaf. He was well respected and extremely influential in his area. At Amir Jassim's request, I did my best to assist and support those activities of al-Zubaidi that benefited local citizens. No doubt, al-Zubaidi had the charisma and charm to succeed in his political aspirations, but he did not have the infrastructure that he claimed to have.

Within days of his release, al-Zubaidi began showing, up late for his scheduled meetings. He always provided a ready excuse, but I felt he was testing my tolerance to see how I would react.

On May 12, more than 110 sheiks came to our headquarters for a meeting. A CPA representative canceled at the last second, leaving me holding the bag. Another officer agreed chaired the meeting. The sheiks expressed disinterest in various Coalition positions, and the meeting threatened to unravel. I asked the chair if I could make a few points. He nodded and said, "If you can."

I stood up from my chair and spoke in a normal tone of voice. "Sammy," the translator from the council, spoke loudly and asked the sheiks to listen up. I stated points about their influence and asked that they work together to stop crime in their areas. They agreed, and went on to state their positions about the Coalition, the occupation, electricity, and security in an orderly fashion.

Saddam had a way to maintain contact, control, and monitor the loyalty of the 7,380 individuals his regime officially recognized as Arab sheiks; he had created an office of tribal affairs during his regime. This office distributed a monthly salary to each sheik, and provided the sheiks a means to put forward their "grievances" to the regime. Saddam used the sheiks to help maintain security and to assist with individuals that were conscripted into the army. In fact, the salaries were Saddam's way of buying their loyalty, and he systematically killed those who he felt betrayed him or otherwise fell out of favor with him.

Ra'ad al-Hamundandi was the general secretary of a council for Iraqi sheiks that worked much like a political action committee. They intended to use their collective influence to help guide the Coalition towards its objectives. That changed when we announced we were occupiers. Al-Hamundandi repeatedly asked me to attend functions with the sheiks. It was at al-Hamundandi's home that I had my first Iraqi meal outside the Green Zone. I stood at the table with dozens of sheiks, many whom I had already met during my short time in Iraq, and others whose names I recognized.

It was a nice home, larger than any I had visited to that point. After lunch, we went took our seats on couches and chairs that lined the walls. A member of the security team told me he noticed a pistol under the abbaya (robe) of one of the sheiks. I thanked him and considered my options.

"Gentleman," I said, "if you have side arms with you, will you please keep them concealed?" My words must have been garbled in the translation. Like something out of a *Godfather* movie, every man immediately reached inside his abbaya. By the expressions on the security team's faces, it seemed we were about to have a serious problem.

"La, la [Arabic for 'no, no']," I said, raising my hand to stop them. I then told the translator to please explain that I know they have guns and that I just need them to keep them hidden.

While it was an experience to sit with dozens of elegantly dressed men, my real satisfaction came from meeting them individually, listening to their advice, hearing about their families and their take on the current situation. While the personal relationships I developed were a benefit to the Coalition, I am not sure I would have experienced the same hospitality from the sheiks had we met later on.

Cyprus came to my office late in the afternoon on May 24. He said he had been told that Sa'd Abdul-Majid al-Faisal al-Tikriti (number 55 most wanted/three of spades in the deck of cards) was at a home just blocks away. Cyprus had tried to contact area units responsible for capturing high-value persons of interest, but failed to raise anyone's attention. He asked me if I could help capture al-Tikriti. I knew the entire theater was overwhelmed with the duty of managing the newly liberated Iraq. While this fell out of our area of responsibility, we were soldiers first and foremost, so I agreed to help.

Cyprus was sure that al-Tikriti was unarmed and that there were maybe two other men and two women in the home. I was hesitant, but believed we had a responsibility to act on valid information regarding a former regime official. Cyprus, Daniel, and I discussed the situation. Captain Guidry (a former FBI counterterrorist agent) and Major Crabb (a former Texas Ranger) felt that they and our security team could take down al-Tikriti without incident. The rest of the team included former police officers, special forces, and Rangers. There was no doubt about the credentials of these soldiers, but still, I had concerns about our possibilities for success.

We discussed the plan. Daniel's team would secure the perimeter and my security team would conduct the actual entry. Captains Mike Self and Timothy Popek, who were police officers in their civilian jobs, joined Guidry and Crabb in developing the operations plan and conducting rehearsals.

After Cyprus and his partner Barbados checked out the area in an unmarked vehicle, we decided that we would conduct the operation at 7:30 p.m. We lined up our four humvees and three sport utilities vehicles. A divider in the road forced us to drive down the wrong side of the road to approach the building. We weren't exactly inconspicuous to the neighbors who were standing in front of their homes.

Shortly after we arrived at the building, Cyprus encountered a woman in the downstairs entryway. He pushed her aside and the security team followed him into the house. Captains Self and Popek covered the rear entrance with the help of other team members. Self found an alternate stairway for getting into the house and communicated it back to me.

"Go," I yelled, and Self, Popek, and Sgt. Christopher Cheechov started up the stairs. I saw the security team, soon followed by Cyprus, exiting the back door empty handed. "Look," I said to Cyprus, pointing and directing him to the stairway Self had found.

Cyprus was just beginning to comprehend what I was telling him when we heard Self yelling from inside the house. "Get down!" he shouted. "You—get down!"

I raced up the stairs, noticing a mosque right next door. I knew we had to get out of there before prayers. I reached the top of the stairs and entered the home, which was unbelievably small. Its entrance room was no larger than a large walk-in closet. The kitchen was off to the right. Self and Popek had three men on the ground in a room that wouldn't have held a full-size bed. A woman was sitting on the couch. I checked the bathroom to make sure no one was hiding in it.

Cyprus moved the men to the couch and questioned them in Arabic. Then he turned to me and said, "I do not know if any of these are al-Tikriti." The deck of cards featuring the most wanted regime officials were no help. When there wasn't a reliable photo, the cards listed only their name and position in the regime beneath a generic silhouette; such was the case with al-Tikriti. What we did know was that Cyprus heard from a man familiar with al-Tikriti that he saw him enter this apartment, and he was certain information was accurate.

Cyprus pointed to a slight man with red hair and said, "He claims to be a Red Cross worker." Then he pointed to the others and gave me their stories, too. He suggested that we take all three into custody and let someone else sort it out.

I worried that we might not have found our man, but Cyprus was a bright, savvy operator. I trusted his instincts, and agreed we should take the men into custody. We handcuffed them and led them out of the apartment.

Cyprus walked behind the red-haired man down the stairs. We knew from our reports that al-Tikriti had worked with the Russians in the past and spoke Russian. Cyprus took the opportunity and said, "Comrade Faisal [al-Tikriti's middle name]!"

"*Nam*," meaning "yes," was his reply, and I smiled to myself.

Cyprus told Sa'd Abdul-Majid al-Faisal al-Tikriti it was nice to meet him. The man lowered his head. He knew he had been caught in an age-old trap.

Cyprus led al-Tikriti to our vehicle and I got into the front seat. I noticed Daniel's team in their positions providing security. The neighbors who had turned out to see what was going on did not seem fazed by the sight of armed soldiers. Cyprus and al-Tikriti sat in the back and spoke to one another in Arabic. Barbados called ahead to the unit responsible for the detention of the most wanted regime officials and we headed toward that location.

We finished the processing shortly after 11 p.m. and headed back to the palace complex. It was after curfew, and our white land cruiser looked suspicious to the drivers of two military police humvees. They drove their vehicles over the median to cut us off, then got out and raised their weapons.

I looked over at Cyprus. "Shit," I said, "our own guys are going to kill us." I stepped out of the vehicle so that they could see my uniform and they lowered their weapons. After I explained to the sergeant that we were returning to the palace area, they allowed us to pass.

Our office continued to be inundated with former civil service workers, military officers, tribal councils, and other interest groups throughout the month of May. They sought answers to the Coalition's actions, or in some cases, inaction. Maj. Toney Coleman asked me to meet with a group of thirty former Iraqi general officers.

This group opened the meeting with a list of demands they had of the Coalition. I was stunned. "Look, you all are not in a position to demand anything," I told them, pushing away from the table. "Let's get that straight and end this meeting right now."

I was about to leave when Iraqi Major General Hassan, who I had met a month before, asked if he could speak to me for a moment.

"Sure," I replied.

"Colonel King," he started, "please understand that you did defeat us, but you must also know that most of us secretly wanted you to win. We did not want Saddam and you told us not to fight for him; many of us didn't. Not because we were cowards, but because we wanted you to free us from Saddam. We realized that only your government's strength could free us from Saddam. You and I both know that even if the entire Iraqi military stood against you, you would have defeated us. But if we had all stood and fought, it would have been at a higher cost for both sides. Please listen to these men with an open mind."

I felt like a damn fool. He was right—our psychological operations campaign during the war had told the Iraqis not to fight for Saddam. While there were many who engaged us in battle, there were many more who didn't, including the deserters we had captured in An Najaf. I returned to the table, humbled.

The Iraqi officers at the meeting tended to be well-educated and trained in a system similar to the British military, and were steadfastly patriotic as one would expect of any nation's military leaders. One particularly straightforward general asked me, "Colonel King, if someone invaded your country, would you fight?" Before I could answer, he went on to say, "By disbanding the military, you have taken away our national identity, our dignity, our self-respect, and our ability to defend ourselves against Iran and others. You give the Iraqi people no hope and no money and then you tell the young men to become 'productive members of society.' With the unemployment in the country, where do they go to become productive, Colonel King? Young men will drift to activities that are morally and ethically wrong to provide for their family in the hopes that God will understand and forgive them. There is an Arab proverb that says, 'Sinning is the best part of repentance.' Be careful, Colonel King, not to give them reasons to need to repent."

I thought about how I would have answered his question. If another country invaded the United States, I would fight. But for me, Iraq was different. Saddam was a corrupt and oppressive leader. He held his people prisoner and he proved himself to be a threat to the world. The average Iraqi feared him, and wanted him gone. Most of the Iraqis I met were fiercely patriotic, nationalistic, and loved their country in spite of Saddam. But it was increasingly clear to me that Iraqis did not realize the total cost of freedom, and continued to test the American resolve. It begged the question: what was their freedom worth to *us*?

On one hand, here were Iraqi generals conveying their concerns; on the other hand, sheiks were warning their people about foreign occupation, and clerics were forwarding their own ideological agendas.

One young Shi'a cleric, Ali, came to meet with me about a Fedayeen group operating in his neighborhood. Ali lived near Sadr City, appeared to be in his late twenties, and wore the distinctive Shi'a white turban. He said that he had come up from the south on orders of Hawza (the Shi'a religious seminary). He explained that the Fedayeen group had been terrorizing his neighborhood. He wanted permission to arm a group of his followers to eliminate the threat.

I explained that I was not authorized to grant such permission, but could introduce him to the commander in his area. I knew the commander was unlikely to permit the arming of civilians, but the commander could take the appropriate action once Ali provided him the location of the Fedayeen group.

Ali did not like this answer, but accepted it. He asked if I would come to his home for lunch in three days. Mindful of the security risk to the team, I told him to give the location to one of my officers and I would see him then.

The team and I arrived at Ali's home—a large beautiful dwelling. An Iraqi policeman who accompanied us asked me why we were stopping there. When I explained that this was where we were having lunch, he looked confused. He explained that before the war, the home belonged to a top level Ba'athist who had since fled the city. This information piqued my interest, and I decided I needed to learn more about our host.

Ali served large platters of rice and lamb. The conversation with him was pleasant, but he seemed to be holding something back. After lunch he invited me to his office upstairs. Once we got there, Ali began to whisper so that no one else could hear. He requested a government position from which he could continue his work in an official capacity. I explained that I did not have the power to assign such a position to him. He appeared disappointed, perhaps suspecting I could have done more to fulfill his request.

Late one evening about two weeks later, Ali's assistant came to me agitated and begging for help. He explained that Ali had attacked the building allegedly occupied by Fedayeen. During the attack, an American patrol came by and arrested Ali. I shook my head; he had heard me advise Ali against taking matters into his own hands. I knew what the consequences would be if he did, and there was nothing I could do to help.

In June 2003, I met Ambassador Hume Horan, former ambassador to Saudi Arabia, and now a senior advisor to Ambassador Bremer. Ambassador Horan was fluent in Arabic, a polished diplomat, and he expressed a true appreciation for the work we were doing in the field. He was more than willing to speak with groups at our request when we thought there would be a benefit.

His offer could not have come at a better time. I had been receiving a barrage of requests from the council of sheiks, which included high-level sheiks from throughout the country, eager to discuss Iraq's future with a responsible CPA official. Ambassador Horan seemed the perfect person to address this audience.

I presented the idea to the ambassador. He reviewed the council's membership and credentials and agreed to speak to them. Our next challenge was to find a building large enough to hold that many people and secure enough for someone of Ambassador Horan's prominence. Major Coleman suggested that it take place in the convention center inside the Green Zone. After Coleman succeeded in convincing the commander responsible for

Green Zone security, he was able to coordinate access and use of the convention center.

The sight of about five hundred men dressed in traditional Arab clothing lined up to enter the building was a sight to behold. Once they were seated inside, Ra'ad al-Hamundandi, along with Ambassador Horan and myself, addressed the group from the stage. Al-Hamundandi opened the session by introducing us. I could recognize many of the sheiks' faces from our previous meetings. Upon eye contact with them, we jointly nodded our heads in greeting. For the first time it occurred to me just how many sheiks I had met in my short time in Iraq.

Al-Hamundandi finished introductions, and the ambassador began to deliver his remarks. I noticed looks of disappointment, resentment, and distrust among several sheiks who chose to sit in the back. They were otherwise indifferent to the ambassador's remarks. They were here to offer him the customary respect, but when it was their turn, they would have something to say.

Ambassador Horan completed his remarks. Al-Hamundandi thanked him, then began the question and answer session with the audience. The first two sheiks he called on were orderly in their questions. One asked about the electricity, and the other wanted clarification about the "occupation." Ambassador Horan assured the audience, as diplomatically as possible, that we were, in fact, occupiers. At this, the room began to rumble with angry chatter.

It looked like al-Hamundandi was losing control as sheiks in the back began to stand up and speak. One was from Basra in southern Iraq. He explained that he could not read or write, and did not have prepared comments, but he spoke so fast that Faisal could not keep up with the translation into English. Al-

Hamundandi tried to interrupt, asking the sheik to sit down and wait for his turn.

Then a sheik I recognized from Fallujah stood up and began a campaign speech to be the next president of Iraq. He realized the room was not paying attention, so he turned to the news cameras that were present and continued his speech. Other sheiks wanted him to come down off his soapbox and told him to sit down.

I noticed another sheik with whom I had a trusting bond sitting in the front row looking directly at me. It was as if he was trying to give me extrasensory advice. I then realized that we needed to leave before the group became unruly. I asked Faisal to announce that we needed to return the ambassador for a meeting, then I motioned for the security to come forward to escort the ambassador out through the back of the building. I learned from this episode that it was best to address sheiks in smaller groups organized by their regional influence.

I simply could not keep up with all the requests for meetings with various sheiks. I had to limit one-on-one meetings to the top sheiks in the country. I would meet with mid- and lower-level sheiks in larger groups. On one occasion I was asked to speak to a group of sheiks at the Sheraton Hotel in downtown Baghdad. The Sheraton was across the Tigris River from the Green Zone and next door to the Rasheed Hotel housing the international press.

Meetings at the Sheraton required travel through the city at a specified time, which increased the risk. The security team did an expert job of reconnoitering the area and I felt comfortable that they were prepared for any scenario that might arise. But on this particular occasion, something happened that I could never have anticipated.

I was accompanied by Kent, a British officer, and would be introducing him to a few of the sheiks. There were between 250 and 300 sheiks and other dignitaries present from Baghdad and northern and western Iraq. On my way to the meeting room, I met several attendees and shook their hands. When I entered the room, the sheiks stood up out of customary respect. I took my place at the head table located on a platform at the front of the room.

I began with comments about the current situation, planned improvements, and a recap of where we had been just a couple of months before. For me, it seemed like significant improvement, but for the Iraqis, it was a long way from the relative general security that they had under Saddam. One audience member commented that when Saddam was here, they worried about only him; now they worry about everyone.

After I concluded my remarks, I introduced Kent as someone with whom I worked closely on the reconstruction effort. I handed Kent the microphone and he began: "My grandfather fought your grandfather—" but was cut off mid sentence. The microphone had gone dead, as if someone intentionally pulled the plug.

You could have heard a pin drop. Both Kent and I realized what had happened. The technicians tried frantically to get the problem resolved, with the grumbling among audience members getting louder and louder until it echoed through the room. Then several sheiks in the front rushed forward. At first I was unsure of their intentions.

"Shit," I said to Kent, "I think you just sparked a rebellion."

Then I realized that the sheiks were trying to hand the translator small scraps of paper. One of the notes read, "And our grandfather beat your grandfather."

Finally, the microphone was turned back on. We apologized for the problem and Kent began again: "My grandfather fought your grandfather, but they learned to live in peace. Let us work together for peace as well."

This did little to satisfy the offended sheiks, so we quickly wrapped things up. Kent apologized as we left the meeting area, but there was no way we could have predicted that the microphone would go out at such an inopportune moment.

Back at battalion headquarters, Faisal informed me that a man claiming to be a sayyid was out front, dressed in a business suit, demanding to meet with Ambassador Bremer. He said he had crucial information about issues in An Najaf. I asked Faisal to get his name. The man refused to give it. He would only say that he was sent from Hawza to deliver a personal message to Bremer.

I had Faisal go out and tell the man I was sorry, but I could not arrange such a meeting. Faisal returned with a message that the man was insistent to speak to me. He recommended that I listen to him, so I agreed. When the man entered the room dressed in the traditional Shi'a cleric black turban and black abbaya, I turned to Faisal.

"Didn't you tell me he was in a business suit?" I asked.

Faisal explained that when the man first entered the building, he asked to go to the restroom, where he must have changed his clothes. This seemed strange to both Faisal and me.

When I invited the man to sit, he said there was no time; he had to see Ambassador Bremer immediately. He had a personal message that had to get to him right away. I explained again that was not possible, but if he wanted to give me the message, I would gladly deliver it. I noticed a bag in his hand, and hoped that the guards out front had inspected it. The man was terribly nervous and on edge. He refused again to reveal his name or the subject of his message.

When it became apparent that he was not going to do anything but keep saying that he had to see the ambassador, I thanked him for coming and invited him to leave. A few weeks later, an officer from a unit north of Baghdad approached me and asked if I knew a sayyid who refused to give his name. The officer described him.

I explained that such a man had come by wanting to see Ambassador Bremer, and that when he would not reveal his reason, I asked him to leave.

The officer said this man had been identified as working with the insurgency and was trying to disrupt one of the neighborhood councils. When the man was detained, he stated that he knew me, but would give no further details. The man was subsequently kept in detention, during which the area experienced a week-long reduction in insurgent activities.

But the security situation continued to deteriorate, and the sectarian divide between the Shi'as and Sunnis seemed to grow wider. During my travels throughout the city, Sunni sheiks told me that Hawza was continuing to send clerics into Baghdad to take over the mosques. At the same time, the Shi'as were saying that the Sunnis were trying to keep them away from their own mosques. Everything that was happening outside of the Coalition activities was being blamed on the other side. I investigated some of the allegations and discovered that most of the perceptions were not caused by sectarian issues, but by criminal elements adapting to the concerns of each side.

There were exceptions. In one case, a cleric came to me asking for help in completing the Grand Mosque. Construction on this mosque had been abandoned due to the war. The cleric estimated that the cost would be about $1 billion. I tried to explain that it was up to the future government to make this a priority. For the time being, I could not help him.

He begrudgingly asked me if I could at least have a large cache of explosive that had been stored on the compound removed. At first I thought this was a strange request, but then it made sense. The propagandists would certainly use a raid to secure the weapons. I told him I would send someone to remove the weapons as soon as possible.

Colonel Johnson, the 1st Armored Division, 2nd Brigade commander, agreed to accompany me with a team of his engineers to secure and remove the cache of explosives. When we arrived at the mosque, something seemed out of place. It wasn't until we sat down for tea that I realized what was wrong. The cleric began to explain his concerns about people shooting at him and asked if Colonel Johnson could provide some security at the mosque. The cleric said that Hawza had sent him to take possession of the mosque, which was in a predominantly Sunni neighborhood.

Then it hit me. He was being attacked because to those in the surrounding neighborhood, he did not belong there, whether he was on orders of the Hawza or not.

Colonel Johnson's team finished the removal of mortars and other explosive devices and we excused ourselves to leave. On the way back to the headquarters, I wondered if the respective religious sects were positioning themselves for what they believed was an imminent American withdrawal.

# CHAPTER 6

# This Will Do

*Think of the going out before you enter.*
*—Arab proverb*

The soldiers of the 3rd Infantry Division had transitioned from fierce battles on April 8, to helping the people of Baghdad the next day in their reconstruction effort. This was a difficult transition for any soldier, but from what I witnessed, they did an outstanding job.

The 1st Armored Division assumed responsibility from the 3rd Infantry Division for the security of Baghdad in late May. Almost overnight, the distance between the American soldiers and the Iraqis grew longer than the barrel on a tank. The change in attitude among the Iraqis was largely due to the attitude among the 1st Armored Division soldiers. Unlike the 3rd Infantry Division, they had not fought their way to Baghdad. It seemed many of their commanders were itching for a fight.

"The new soldiers said that they will show us what security means," one Iraqi said about the 1st Armored Division. "Yeah, right!"

It was as if the 1st Armored Division viewed every Iraqi as the enemy. This attitude alienated the Iraqi people. I started receiving requests for assistance from Iraqis who did not like how they were being treated at security checkpoints. By June and early July, most of my meetings with Iraqis began with them expressing animosity over the mistreatment and disrespect being shown to them in their own country.

In early June, Maj. Gen. Ricardo Sanchez directed my battalion to move from our current location inside the Green Zone. In exploring alternative locations, I wanted something that would be both accessible to the Iraqis and secure enough to protect the soldiers. Our battalion was not designed to provide its own security and conduct civil-military operations at the same time, so we had to make sure that we had the support of the area combat commander.

Because we were now responsible for supporting two brigades (due to the arrival of the 354th Civil Affairs Brigade), we contacted both in our search for new facilities. One of the commanders offered us a mausoleum that held one of Saddam's closest friends (and according to the Iraqis, a friend Saddam himself had murdered). I did not think a mausoleum was the proper location to receive sheiks or other dignitaries, let alone the average Iraqi citizen, so we continued our search through the city.

Faisal and Zumurudeh accompanied us and recommended several places. Most had been looted and many would not provide the required security. The day wore on, and my patience grew short. I was prepared to give up when Zumurudeh recommended that we look at the palace of Saddam's youngest daughter, Hala. She said it was near the Green Zone and surrounded by a wall. Faisal also said it might be a suitable location for our purposes.

Lacking better options, I agreed to check it out on our way back to the battalion headquarters.

The palace was an isolated area in a neighborhood, but I needed convincing about our ability to provide security for the compound. A wall surrounded the entire complex consisting of a palace, a bunker, and a smaller building, along with entrances in the front and back. We drove up to the front gate and found a middle-aged man with a two-day beard sitting inside, holding an AK-47 rifle.

"Hey you," I said, walking to the gate. "Come here please."

The man stood to approach us, picking up his rifle.

"Leave the rifle," I directed, "and come here."

The man walked up to me and explained that the building had been occupied by the KDP, one of the Kurdish political parties. In the first days following the fall of the regime, the political parties would paint their names on the sides of governmental buildings all over the city as a way of claiming ownership. I would find out a few days later that it wasn't a political party who tried to take over the palace, but a Kurdish businessman. He had painted "KDP" on it to keep others away.

The man told me he was the security guard. I asked him to open the gate, and he did so with great apprehension. I walked into the building, checking each room and imagining the battalion's operational setup. I then walked out onto the grounds to determine the feasibility of security for our unit. The compound had a huge bunker that was dark inside. According to Zumurudeh, when Hala decided not to move into the palace, the bunker became a disco. Captain Guidry and his team mustered up some flashlights so we could walk through it. It was dusty, but cool and spacious, and nothing but an atomic bomb was going to penetrate it. I envisioned cleaning it up and moving the soldiers into it.

This having been about the twentieth place we had looked at that day, I was absolutely tired of searching. I looked at Guidry and told him that it would have to do. I explained to the guard that he needed to leave because we were taking possession of the building.

The man said that he could not go. "What will my boss say?" he asked.

I told him that he should tell his boss to come and see me in the morning. The man walked down the road, stopping once to look over his shoulder. While my staff and I were apprehensive about moving out of the Green Zone, Hala's palace provided the battalion a headquarters with a great deal of autonomy.

Hala's palace made us part of the neighborhood community. Security was still my primary concern, but 1st Sgt. Hank Jetty did an excellent job of increasing the force protection posture of the complex. We were light on weapons systems to repel a medium attack, but it was a place that we could call our own.

I went to the 2nd Brigade headquarters and met with the commander, Colonel Johnson. He was a good leader and one of the few 1st Armored Division officers I met who appreciated the cultural uniqueness of the Iraqis. I explained the location and our timeline for the move. He agreed to meet me at the site the next day.

Colonel Johnson and the area's company commander agreed we should take possession of the building. Johnson also agreed to provide a platoon at night to enhance our security. This seemed reasonable to me.

Major Crabb coordinated with the police to provide an officer to screen visitors at the front gate before they came onto the complex. Crabb and others from the battalion explained to the neighborhood residents that we were now located in the palace and would like to begin a cleanup effort with them. Our new neighbors welcomed us with food and small gifts. As for security, we received a few threats between June 2003 and August 2003, but were never directly attacked.

Once the sheiks and Muhammad al-Zubaidi discovered where we had moved, the inquiries we received from them quickly reached the levels we'd experienced in the Green Zone. The growth of the Coalition's bureaucracy and frequency in which responsibilities changed hands made acquiring the latest information on the reconstruction and transfer of authority to the Iraqis more and more difficult.

Meanwhile, Daniel's office representatives seamlessly transferred right along with us to Hala's palace. Visiting Iraqis, however, found traveling to our new location to be more difficult due to increased traffic congestion and gridlock. They averaged an additional twenty-five minutes of travel time through the middle of the city.

Once we reached full operating capacity at the new location, the front lobby became so crowded I would have to exit through a side window about ten feet high and walk around the back of the building just to leave my office. We used the same window to escort individuals who wished to surrender to us out of the building. We did this to maintain their dignity and avoid the crowded lobby, where they were likely to be recognized. The crowds congregating at the palace entrances were smaller than those at our Green Zone location, however, making the location more accessible for those who came in to surrender.

In early May, I had been introduced to an Iraqi named Munkethe (pronounced mun-KEE-thee). His number of contacts among the former elites was unmatched, and he would become a close associate of mine. He offered to work for me and help in the battalion's reconstruction efforts. Because of the lack of communications, he became a runner for me, delivering messages to individuals around the country.

I loved Hala's palace. My office was located in one of the bedrooms. It was large and spacious, perfect for receiving appointments. I was still concerned about our ability to secure it, but the staff was making daily security improvements.

Late one afternoon, I was asked to come and speak to a man who had information on the location of artifacts stolen from the Museum of Antiquities. When I entered the room, the man standing in front of Chuck (the replacement for Barbados, who had returned to the United States) was clearly nervous. He explained to me that the individual who possessed the stolen artifacts planned to sell them on the black market, and that the man's son was going to come up from An Najaf in the morning to help his father sell the pieces. Chuck told me that he had worked with this man before, and that he was credible.

Captain Guidry and I discussed the situation. My operations officer Captain Garner and Staff Sgt. Duane Robinson had called the unit that was located near the man's home, but they had been told that the unit was overwhelmed and could not work this time-sensitive mission into their plans. Captain Guidry said he believed his team could get the man and the artifacts without much risk.

Preserving public art, monuments, and archives was on the fringes of our mission focus, but I had taken so much heat from the press about the museum that I felt compelled to conduct the operation. My operations section, Captain Guidry, and I assessed the risk. We determined that the success of the mission outweighed the minimal risk, so I approved the operation.

Captain Guidry and his team departed for the area just before dusk, and returned to battalion headquarters just as night fell with a dozen recovered artifacts, thousands of Iraqi dinars and U.S. dollars, and a few weapons. They had also arrested the man alleged to have stolen the artifacts and the man's son. The man and his son were being held near the bunker in the rear of the compound awaiting transport to the detention facility. Guidry was debriefing me on the operation when one of the soldiers came in and interrupted: "Sir, this guy is becoming belligerent and getting out of control." Guidry and I walked to the rear of the compound.

"I am a Shi'a from An Najaf and you are infidels," the man yelled at me. "You have no right to hold me."

I approached him and whispered, "You are a believer?"

Faisal translated for me. "Of course I am," the man replied. "I am Shi'a from An Najaf. You are infidels!"

"God has directed that you share his message with infidels," I reminded him. "Would you be so kind as to share with me a verse from the Qur'an. The Cow, chapter two, verse sixty-two?"

"I do not remember," he mumbled. "It does not matter anyway."

I stepped closer to him and said, "Well, friend it does matter, because it defines believers and chapter two, verse sixty-two says 'those who believe [in the Qur'an], and those who follow the Jewish [scriptures], and the Christians and the Sabians, any who believe in God, and the Last Day, and work righteousness, shall have their reward with their Lord on them and they shall not know fear, nor shall they grieve.' "

"Yes," the man replied. "You are right."

I continued, "Since you are beginning to remember, will you tell me what chapter forty-three, verse sixty-one says?"

He glared at me with contempt. "I do not remember."

I wanted to make sure I had his attention, so I whispered. My tone was soft enough that Faisal asked me to speak up so he could translate. "What it says is, 'And [Jesus] shall be a sign [for the coming of] the hour [of judgment]: Therefore have no doubt about the [hour of His return], but follow ye Me: this is the straight way.' I believe that and have no fear of it."

The man was agitated now and demanded we release him. "It is religious persecution. I am a Shi'a from An Najaf and I demand you let me go!"

"Excuse me," I replied, "will you tell me what is God's word in chapter twenty-nine, verse sixty-one?"

"I don't remember," he said, growing more and more agitated as I continued.

"What it says is, 'Dispute ye not with the people of the book, except in the best ways [peacefully], unless it be with them that do wrong, but say, We believe in the revelation which has come down to us and in that which came down to you; our God and your God is One; and it is to Him we submit.' You have done wrong and you are not trying to resolve this peacefully as God has instructed."

By now he was furious. "I have done no wrong, and you are the infidels."

I decided to try one last verse: "What does chapter five, verse sixty-nine say?"

He lowered his gaze in anger and replied, "I do not know." He was defeated, and he knew it.

"It is almost the same thing as chapter two, verse sixty-two. This was your last chance to prove your claim." I looked him in the eye and did not blink. "Since you know nothing of the word of God, I know you do not know what chapter nine, verse five says so I will share it with you. What it says is, 'When the forbidden months are past, then fight and slay the pagans wherever ye find them, and seize them, beleaguer them, and lie in wait for them in every stratagem [of war].' Do you know what this means?" I asked.

"*La!*" he shouted, which means "no."

I again looked him squarely in the eyes. "What is means is if one is dealing with a pagan, you can fight the pagans, and right now since I am dealing with you and you know nothing of God's word, I know you are a thief and now I believe you are a pagan, so God has said I can deal with you appropriately. So I suggest you shut up so I do not have to follow God's word."

The man stood in complete silence.

By now a group of soldiers had gathered. I turned to leave, looking around at their faces. They appeared dumbfounded and in disbelief. Chuck stopped me on my way out and said, "That was amazing. Where did you learn that?"

"I read the Qur'an," I said.

We returned to the building with Faisal walking next to me. "Sir," he said, "I never knew you were so scholarly in these matters. I am impressed."

"Faisal, there is no need for you to be impressed. You have impressed me a great deal since I began working with you. I am sure there is much we don't know about each other, but I am sure we will learn together."

The insufferable Iraqi summer was approaching, with tempers beginning to flare and support for the United States starting to decline. In July, temperatures would soar to 140 degrees during the day. Zumurudeh told me that dealing with government employees could be difficult, especially in the summer. Because there was no electricity and people could not run their air conditioners, no one could sleep at night. When temperatures fall to a cool 90 degrees people become even more irritated.

"So for us," she explained, "we are tired and hot, the people we are trying to deal with are tired and hot, and we both are getting angry and want to kill each other." It became more and more difficult to deal with other day-to-day issues when electricity was practically the only thing that mattered. The irritable Iraqis who were not sleeping at night exacerbated the challenges for a Coalition already tested by the many cultural differences.

During late June, I learned that a raid had been conducted on a farm in the Al-Dhora area of Baghdad and a large cache of weapons had been seized. The farm belonged to someone I had come to know quite well: Ra'ad al-Hamundandi. I knew al-Hamundandi was a businessman who lived for making money, and wondered if there was any connection to the weapons cache. When I learned that the unit intended to raid al-Hamundandi's home in the Monsur area of the city, I sent word that he was in Egypt. I would arrange to have him return from Egypt and would notify the unit upon his arrival.

I called Sammy, al-Hamundandi's assistant, and explained the situation. Sammy assured me that al-Hamundandi was not involved with the weapons, and I replied that al-Hamundandi needed to return as soon as possible to help clear things up. If he failed to return, the unit might proceed with the raid, believing that he was still inside, and upset his family. Sammy assured me that he would relay the message.

A few days later, Sammy informed me that al-Hamundandi

planned to return by the middle of July. I asked Sammy to have al-Hamundandi come to my office July 21.

Meanwhile, my network of sheiks continued to expand daily. One day I was approached by a group of men who came to me on the recommendation of Cyprus. They asked if I could help them locate the former chairman of atomic energy. The chairman, Fadil, was among the top 100 most wanted personalities from the former regime.

I told them I wasn't sure, and asked if they planned to detain him if I got him to come in voluntarily.

They told me that was not their intent. If he was willing to come in and cooperate, they saw no reason to arrest him. They assured me that he would return home the same evening.

I asked Munkethe to request for Sheik Adnan from the chairman's tribe to come and see me. Within two days, Sheik Adnan arrived at the palace. He and I sat in my office and sipped tea. I eventually broached the sensitive subject of how we might contact the former chairman. If so, I asked, would he be willing to convince him to meet with some Coalition officers?

"Colonel King," he replied, "I know him very well. Do I have your assurances that he will not be detained?"

"I give you my word."

He paused, then said, "I will have him in your office at eleven on Monday."

I was surprised. This sheik was going to bring in one of the most wanted personalities, a man who might have been responsible for Iraq's WMD program, on just my word. I called the head of the investigating team who originally asked to meet the chairman to verify that he would be in my office at 11 a.m. Monday. He thanked me and said there would be a team of officers there to meet him.

At 10:45 a.m. Monday, the investigating team arrived at my office. The head of the team showed his arrogance, making skeptical comments to his fellow team members. "Why are we here wasting our time?" he asked. "This is a wanted man. He will not show." I did not find these comments to be appropriate and was tempted to have my security team throw him out the door, but I said nothing. My reputation and that of the battalion being at stake, I hoped the sheik showed up on time with Fadil.

With the clock nearing 11:00, the head of the team stood up. "We don't have time to waste," and motioned for his group to leave. I walked with them. Upon exiting the front doorway of the building, one of the team members turned toward me. In an apologetic tone, he thanked me for trying. At that moment, we noticed a pair of men walking through the gate to the palace compound. It was the sheik and the former chairman.

I pointed at them and said, "I believe that is who you came to see," and breathed a sigh of relief. With no comment, the team walked over to introduce themselves to the former chairman. I thanked the sheik for his efforts, excused myself, and returned to my scheduled meeting.

This was not the last time this team would ask for my assistance to locate Fadil.

By August, most of the former team members had rotated back to the States. An individual named "Ann" was now heading the investigation. She came to my office to introduce herself, explaining that she had replaced the former team leader. She had read in her notes that I had previously helped the team locate the former chairman of atomic energy, and asked me if I still had contact with Sheik Adnan.

I assured her that I did.

"Can you ask him to bring the chairman in to meet with us again?" she asked.

Up to this point I had been involved in the capture or surrender of six of the most wanted personalities in Iraq, and had a reached a certain comfort level in making requests of the sheiks. I assured her I could arrange a meeting, but I needed to know if they planned to detain him if I got him to come in voluntarily. "I just need to tell the family what to expect," I said.

Ann told me that if he cooperated as he did last time, the team would not arrest him. "We just want to talk to him."

I told her it would take about two days. She said that was fine and looked forward to hearing from me.

Munkethe went to see Sheik Adnan about bringing Fadil back to see me. The meeting between the team and chairman would last the day, and he could return home late in the evening. Munkethe called later that afternoon, confirming that Sheik Adnan would bring Fadil to my office the next morning.

I contacted Ann and explained the arrangements. She was pleased, and said she would have her time pick up Fadil at my office and transport him to another site to talk.

Munkethe arrived at my office with the chairman on schedule. Ann and her team exchanged pleasantries with Fadil. She thanked me for my help, and said that they would have him back to my office around six o'clock. I would not be back from another mission by then, so I asked Munkethe if he could come back and drive Fadil home. He said that was not a problem.

After Ann's team departed with the chairman, I thanked Munkethe and left to link up with the support unit for my day's mission.

At 6 p.m., my cell phone rang. It was Ann. "Hello, Colonel King, she said. "I am sorry to bother you."

"No bother," I said. "How is the chairman?"

"He is fine, but I am sorry to tell you that we are going to have to detain him."

I was furious. "Ann," I said, "you cannot do this. You said you would not detain him. I gave my word to the sheik. You have to return him tonight."

"I understand, but he has not cooperated and I have no choice. We are going to detain him."

"Ann, I am on a mission right now with another unit. I need someone from your office to come and get me."

She apologized, saying that would not be possible.

"Fine," I told her. "I will be there in a half hour."

"I do not know what you think that will accomplish. We have decided that it is necessary to detain him and that is what we intend to do."

"Ann, I did you a favor," I said. "Now I expect you to wait until I get there."

I had helped this particular group twice using my resources and contacts, and felt double-crossed. I wondered what I was going to tell Sheik Adnan. I had given him my word. I had been working on the surrender of two other wanted persons, but was sure that once word got out about this incident, no one else would trust me.

I called in a favor from Ernie, a friend from another unit in the area, and asked him to give me a ride across town. Ernie said that he was unavailable, but would send someone else from his team.

I grew more and more irritated about the entire episode as I stood waiting for my ride. To me, someone with Ann's youth and inexperience had no appreciation for the operators in the field who were used to working with the Iraqis. All I could think about was the damage Ann was doing to the credibility of my office, and all this after I agreed to help her. She did not understand how her decision put Munkethe at risk for bringing Fadil to me in the first place. In addition, Sheik Adnan would not be happy with me. He would lose the family's respect, or worse. It was possible his life could be in danger. The more I thought about it, the angrier I became.

I tried to thank the guys who were driving me to meet with Ann, but probably came across as rude. It took almost thirty minutes to get to where Fadil was being held. They told me to call them and they would come back to pick me up.

I exited the vehicle, and then turned my attention to Ann, who was approaching me. Nearby, a group of about ten to fifteen people stood around talking. Maybe Ann thought reinforcements would be necessary.

Ann called out my name.

"Who is the translator?" I asked, loud enough for the rest of the group to hear.

A tall, slim, young American man raised his hand.

I walked towards him and asked, "When did you graduate from language school?"

He replied, "About a year ago."

"And do you speak Iraqi dialect, or are you translating in MSA (Modern Standard Arabic)?"

"MSA, but the chairman seems to be fine with it."

I asked him what level of proficiency he was at in Arabic, and he replied that he was at "2/2," or mid-level, non-technical Arabic. I turned to Ann and said, "I am not sure what is going on, but I am confident that the chairman is cooperating with you.

The problem is you all are not communicating with him."

Ann disagreed. She explained that they were talking to him in German and English, two of the many languages Fadil spoke, and he seemed to understand just fine.

"You cannot detain this man," I told Ann. "You will destroy everything I have worked to build in the last four months."

"I am sorry," she said, "but we have to."

"No, you are not going to detain him for your inability to communicate. Look, give me two questions that you know the answers to, and if I cannot get him to give me the answers, then detain him," I said. "Isn't that fair?"

Ann did not see it that way. She was determined she was going to have this man arrested and she did not care what it did to anyone, or any other operation. Her colleagues had circled in and began to resemble a mob. She whispered something to one of them and then replied back to me, "We cannot do it."

"Ann," I said defiantly, "I am taking the chairman with me."

At a loss for words, she uttered, "Well, uh, look, Colonel King, we have asked him questions such as where he lives and you said he had two homes. He only gave us one. He just simply is not cooperating."

"I am going in to talk to him," I told Ann. "When I come out, I am leaving and I am taking him with me."

When I entered the building where Fadil was being held, he stood to greet me. He had a huge smile on his face and reached out to hug and kiss me on my cheek. "Colonel King," he asked in broken English, "what are you doing here?"

"Sir," I said, "they tell me that you are not cooperating, and they want to keep you. They said that you are not answering their questions."

He sat back in his chair and shrugged his shoulders. "I have answered every question they have asked the best I could. There are some answers to their questions I just do not know."

"For instance?" I asked.

"They wanted to know how many trucks we had, but I did not know," he said. "There was someone who was responsible for that and he only came to me when they needed more. I explained this to them and that there were four special trucks, but that is all I remembered." He looked dumbfounded.

His answer seemed reasonable to me. I myself had just left command and could not recall off the top of my head exactly how many operational trucks we had when I left. Next I asked him about his addresses. He confirmed he had two, as he had told me before.

"But sir," I said, "when they asked you this question, you only mentioned your home in Baghdad."

Confused, he sat back in his chair, then leaned forward with an exaggerated hand gesture of frustration. "I told the young man that I had two homes," he explained, "but he only asked for the Baghdad address." He sat back again, shaking his head with a disbelieving look on his face.

I reached over and patted his knee, told him to wait here, then I left to find Ann.

When I walked outside, Ann and her group were waiting for me. "The general is out of town, so I called his deputy, Mel. He wants to see all of us in his office to discuss this."

That was fine with me, I knew "Mel" to be a reasonable man who would understand this situation. When I entered Mel's office, there were a few faces that I did not immediately recognize from the original group. Ann and her colleague, "Mike", explained their position to Mel, saying that Fadil was uncooperative, that it was necessary to detain him for more questioning about his former duties.

Mel listened intently to the comments from Ann and Mike, then asked for my side of the story. I explained that when I coordinated the meeting with Fadil, I had given the sheik my word that the chairman would not be detained.

Mel looked at me and said, "I understand, and that was [Ann and Mike's] original opinion, but since he is not cooperating, things have changed."

I began to lose my temper. I explained about the address and truck issue, then added, "Mel, you know me. You have commented in the past about my successes with the tribes, with all the people I have brought in. If you do this, it will destroy everything that I have worked to develop. Look, let me take the chairman home this evening, I will explain to the family and I will bring him back in the morning. I'll stake my career on it."

Before Mel could respond, Mike said to me, "Look, you are not an expert at these things. You should stay out of it."

I was livid. "You are right, I am not an expert at what you do, but you are not an expert at what I do either. You all came to me. I didn't call you. How many wanted folks have you called to come in and give themselves up?"

My mind raced with other things I wanted to say, but Mel interrupted—"Enough." He turned to another individual in the room (one who was unfamiliar to me) and said, "He is right. It is the damnedest thing I have ever seen. He calls and they willingly come and turn themselves in."

He paused, and I interjected, "Mel, I have two more from the top two hundred ready to turn themselves in. If you do this, I will never be able to help get anyone again."

Mike started to open his mouth, but Mel interrupted him. "I've heard enough, and in the general's absence, I am the only person who can authorize his detention. Alan, you're off the hook, but he will stay here tonight as our guest. We will get a new translator in the morning and decide the next step." He then looked at Mike and Ann and said, "You two will have to do your homework tonight [to prepare] for tomorrow. Alan, you can explain to the family, right?"

I assured him I could. Then, with some hesitation, I requested two more things: permission to bring a translator with a security clearance, and permission to sit in on the interview. One of the men in the room objected, saying it would not be appropriate. I explained that I had met with Fadil on many occasions. If there was something I wanted to know, I could have found out about it long ago.

I was pleased when Mel agreed to my requests. He told me to be back the next morning at nine o'clock. I called Munkethe, explained the situation, and assured him that Fadil would be home the next night.

When I returned the next morning, I brought the translator and met Ann at the house where Fadil spent the night (Mike was not with her). When I entered the house, the chairman was excited to see me, and apologized for his wrinkled appearance. I asked if he had been served breakfast yet. He thanked me and said that he had eaten. I explained that it was very important that he answer every question as completely as possible and that if he did not understand a question, he needed to ask for clarification. He promised he would.

When Fadil went into the kitchen to meet with Ann and the others, I took my place in the living room, listening carefully to the questions in the next room. Despite Mel's direction to Ann and Mike to "do their homework," it occurred to me that they had not. Instead, Ann was shooting from the hip, asking a stream of random, unprepared questions as they came to her. They were phrased in incomplete sentences that I could not even make out, and the translator had to ask for clarification to many of them.

This seemed like a setup to me, so I immediately left to find Mel. When I entered Mel's office, I explained what was going on. Much to my chagrin, Mel directed Mike to sit in on the meeting along with me, then report back to him. Mike's dislike for me became apparent immediately after he took the seat next to me in the living room.

He and I listened for about fifteen minutes before Ann asked Fadil to run down everything they hid before the war.

"Nothing," Fadil replied. "We did not hide anything before the war."

Mike looked at me in disgust. "See," he said, "he is doing what he did last night. We know he hid everything all over the place. There was even an incubator put in the bunker under building three."

I was furious at the lack of understanding. I stood up and moved to where Fadil could see me. "Excuse me, doctor," I interjected, "when you learned that the war was going to begin, did Saddam order you to safeguard everything that was under your responsibility?"

Fadil smiled and said in English, "Colonel King, you know he did. In fact, we brought in containers and spread them all over the yard because we knew you would blow up the buildings. We separated things between the boxes so in case one was hit we would not lose everything. There was one piece though that was so big. He stammered, searching for the right word. "An, uh . . . it keeps things warm, you know?"

"An incubator?" I suggested.

"Yes, I believe that is what you call it. We placed it in the bunker under building three because it was too large for the container."

"Thank you," I said, and returned to my seat. I turned to Mike. "It is the way the question was phrased. Ann had questioned his honor by asking if he *hid* something. He did what he was told to do. But, I am not an expert at these things you know."

Looking furious and embarrassed, Mike stood up and left.

I went back up to see Mel, explained what had happened, and received his assurances that the chairman would be taken home this evening. At about seven o'clock, Munkethe called to confirm that Fadil was safely home, and that the sheik and family send their regards. I breathed a sigh of relief and went on about my mission for the evening.

In November, I was in Basrah and preparing to speak to a group of sheiks when a member of Kent's team told me there was someone on the phone for me. "It's a woman," he said, with mock insinuation. The others on the team laughed, and I wondered who it could be.

"Colonel King," said the familiar voice on the other end. It was Ann, and she wondered if I could help her again. She wanted the chairman to visit a site with her in the morning and explain some of his work in the area.

I told her I would have to see, but without good telephone access I could not promise anything. She explained that if he could not go with her in the morning, she would be forced to cancel the mission. I told her I understood, but it would take at least six hours even if I were in Baghdad. But I was in Basrah, and didn't know if I could contact anyone to find Fadil. She became excited and said she needed an answer immediately.

"Then," I said, "the answer is no."

"What do you mean?" she replied.

"I do not know how long it will take me to find him," I explained. "I need to go to a meeting right now. If you want me to call you back in six hours I will." I repeated that if she needed an answer now, then it would have to be no.

She seemed flustered. "Okay. Please call me back."

I called Munkethe, and amazingly, was able to get ahold of him on the first try. I asked him to find and bring Fadil to me. Since Ann had not specified a time or place, I instructed Munkethe to have him to my office at nine o'clock the next morning. Munkethe agreed and I left for my meeting. I talked to him again at 6:30 p.m. He had found Fadil, who agreed to be at my office at the specified time.

I called and informed Ann about the place and link-up time. She thanked me profusely, then asked, "Can you tell him to be at the checkpoint at eight thirty?"

"No, Ann," I replied. "It will take a minimum of three hours to contact him. He does not have AT&T for me to call him on. He will be at my office at nine. If you are there, he will be there. If you don't want to meet him, don't show up." My frustration level had peaked.

When I returned to Baghdad, a man named Bob asked if I could locate a former scientist. He said he heard I was pretty good at locating Iraqis and wondered if I could help. I told him I would try, and would call him back in a few days. Two days later, I called Bob and said that we had located three scientists with the same name. One was in the north, one was in the west, and one had been killed during the advance of the American forces to Baghdad. He told me that he was looking for the one that had been killed and thanked me for trying. I was proud of my folks' ability to locate people, but I was more amazed at the smallness of the country.

# CHAPTER 7

# Changing Places

*Do not tell a friend anything you would conceal from an enemy.*
*—Arab proverb*

The summer temperatures began to soar, along with the irritation of the Iraqis. The uncontrolled import of cars into the country together with the lack of electricity and police to manage the traffic placed a heavy burden on the city's traffic flow. The added congestion increased the risk for traveling Coalition members. It could take a number of hours just to get gas, with the fuel shortage backing up lines at the pump for miles. Roadsides were lined with black marketers who exploited the crisis for all it was worth.

Everyone remained busy and the battalion was spread thin, with four locations around the city. The headquarters building had become a magnet for top 200 most-wanted regime officials. In June and July alone, former Iraqi ambassadors, Ba'athists, parliament members, and a host of others among Saddam's elite surrendered themselves at our office.

One day Cyprus came to me with information that Munkethe had coordinated plans with the former minister of information and number 168 on the most wanted list, Mohammed Saeed al-Sahaf (a.k.a. "Baghdad Bob"), to turn himself in. Cyprus explained that it was not going to be necessary to detain him, he just needed a quiet place to talk. I told him that he was welcome to use my office. When al-Sahaf arrived, I saw that he had let his hair go gray. He was a slender man that spoke English and wanted to get this ordeal over with as soon as possible.

Of all the former elites I met, sitting with al-Sahaf was the most memorable. This is the man who said on Iraqi television that the Americans were not in Iraq and that the men who I had met with during the first days of the war were not Iraqis. When I asked him about the news broadcast, he did not remember the specific report. He explained that when he and Tariq Aziz went to Saddam and "suggested" they take another approach, Saddam disagreed. "And when Saddam said for you to do something," Al-Sahaf added, "you did it."

Another time I was visited by a man from Fallujah who told me about a staunchly anti-American sheik, Dhari, who was purportedly organizing the resistance in Fallujah. The man also showed me a letter distributed among the sheiks before the war asking them to encourage their tribes to resist the invasion.

Saddam Hussein allegedly sent a note to Dhari in early June congratulating him on his resistance of American forces in Fallujah and offering men and weapons for his efforts. Dhari reportedly had asked for such assistance prior the war, but because Saddam did not assent to his original offer, Dhari lost respect for him. Dhari had sent a reply to Saddam's note that he did not need his men and guns; he now had missiles.

I asked an Iraqi associate if he knew Dhari. He told me no, but he knew the tribe and where he was located and could easily find him. Approximately three hours later, Dhari walked into my office. He held up his arms as if they had handcuffs on them and he said, "If you are going to arrest me, then I am ready." I told him that I had asked him here as a friend, but that our future relationship depended on his cooperation.

Dhari and I sat together and talked for almost an hour. After a while, it became obvious that the translator was holding something back. Dhari kept pointing at the translator asking him to repeat what he had said (I would learn later that the comments were so inflammatory, the translator was too embarrassed to repeat them even after Dhari was gone). At the time, the one thing I was certain of was that Dhari was not offering to rebuild Iraq together.

Finally, it was time for Dhari to leave. "You came here as a friend," I said. "When you cross the threshold, you are not a friend. The next time we meet, it will not be like this." He knew what I had said without the translation, and looked at me in defiance before turning and walked out over the threshold.

The next morning, I drove to Fallujah to give the 3rd Infantry Division commander responsible for the area my assessment of Dhari. I described our meeting, and that I believed him to be a major player in the resistance. The commander thanked me and said he would have his staff look into it.

I learned that Dhari was detained along with a cleric, Jamal, in October 2003. The sheik general from the Albu Issa tribe and a large number of clerics, including one named Abd with whom I had a series of discussions concerning the Qur'an, urged me to help secure their release. In January, I prepared a paper for ambassadors Jones and Schlicher recommending that they consider releasing the two men.

Dhari would be released in April 2004. Afterward, he and I had several meetings about the security situation in Fallujah. Dhari said that the detention increased his stature in the city, with the other tribal leaders referring to him as "the sacrificer." (National Public Radio would feature a story about the two of us on the day I left Iraq in June 2004.)

One afternoon in that middle of July, Cyprus came to me with a message from Munkethe. Mizban Hadi (number 23/nine of hearts in the deck of cards) wanted to surrender, with the condition that I be the one to accept his surrender. The battalion had already been involved in the capture of most wanted numbers 26 and 55 (eight of diamonds and three of spades, respectively, in the deck of cards). Hadi had apparently heard of my office and felt secure surrendering to me.

Cyprus and Barbados coordinated the surrender with all the necessary parties. On the morning of July 8, Munkethe drove north of Baghdad, picked up Hadi and his family, and drove to Hala's palace. By 12:30 p.m., Hadi had arrived. It was surreal having one of the most wanted men in Iraq surrendering at my office. We sat together over tea, talking for almost thirty minutes about various topics, including his career. When I said it was finally time to leave, he told me he understood. He and his family exchanged goodbyes, and I assured them I would check up on their father, and pass messages to them on his status through Munkethe.

The daily inquires from Iraqis became business as usual, keeping us incredibly busy. Then came July 21, a day that would change everything, and one of the two most difficult days of my life. The morning started off well. Zumurudeh brought me a traditional Iraqi breakfast of crepes. Later, she came to tell me that my first appointment had arrived. It was a Shi'a cleric with whom I had met upon arriving in Baghdad.

The meeting was scheduled to last for almost two hours, but at approximately 11 a.m., captains Mike Self and Travis Morehead came into my office. They looked harried and apologized for interrupting, knowing how I liked to give my undivided attention to those with scheduled appointments. I sensed something was wrong, and excused myself from the meeting.

We stepped into the office of Maj. Brent Gerald, my executive officer. "Colonel," Morehead said, "there has been an explosion. Omar [a translator] is dead. [Staff Sgt.] Laverick, [Capt.] Garner, [Staff Sgt. Mark] Killion, and [Spc.] Terry are wounded, and we are not sure about [Cpl. Mark] Bibby."

The public health team had been ambushed on its way to assess a water treatment facility. They believed Bibby had been transported via medevac (medical evacuation), but they did not know his condition. Feeling the tension of the moment, I said, "Well, go get the goddamn information so I know what the hell is going on."

I am usually in control of my anger, but I was furious; not at those who were in the room, but at the people who had killed my men. I did not know what else to say to these men standing before me, looking to me for direction, so I started barking out orders. My mind raced as I tried to remember all the necessary procedures and reports that needed to be submitted. Gerald assured me they had already been started.

I walked from Brent Gerald's office to mine, and noticed al-Hamundandi and his assistant sitting in the waiting area. It was the date we had agreed upon for al-Hamundandi to surrender. They stood as I approached, smiled, and put their hands out to greet me. I shook their hands, but explained that I could not detain al-Hamundandi today. I asked them to come back in one week. They said they understood, and I left to find out the status of my soldiers and Omar.

There is a saying in the army: "Always discount first reports as suspicious." The reporting this day was no exception. The barrage of conflicting reports on the locations of the various soldiers kept coming, making my team's preparations exceedingly difficult. One person had been medevac'd to one place, then another. Majors Gerald and Crabb and Captain Self stayed close by, being careful not to overwhelm me. They knew I needed space to sort the situation out in my mind.

I returned to my office and sat down at my desk. Gerald came with me and sat in a chair in front of me, saying nothing, just trying to give me support. He and I had spoken on several occasions about what we would do if something like this happened. Zumurudeh was sitting on the couch in the office, tears rolling down her cheeks. My inquiries about Bibby were mistakenly interpreted by the Iraqis present to indicate I cared only about the fate of the American soldier. This was not the case. I had been able to verify the status of everyone except Bibby, so that became the focus of my demands for more information from my staff.

Over the next forty-five minutes, four or five more reports came in with conflicting information. I knew the chaotic information flow was not the fault of the staff, but I regretfully took it out on them: "Get the fucking information, and get it now! I want to know the status of Bibby!"

Finally, Maj. Brent Perley called me and confirmed two KIAs (killed in action) and three other medevac WIAs (wounded in action). Corporal Bibby was killed along with Omar, the translator. Staff Sergeants Laverick and Killion and Spc. Shermaine Terry were medevac wounded. Laverick was reported in critical condition. Killion and Terry did not have life threatening injuries, and they had been medevac'd to an area approximately eighty kilometers south of Baghdad. Captain Garner received minor injuries and was located at one of the aide stations in Baghdad.

I prepared to leave, and told Morehead to call the 1st Armored Division. "Tell them I need a helicopter to the area known as Dogwood at 1600 hours," I said. "I need to get down and see Laverick and the others. And get my team together—I need to get over to the support battalion and locate Garner, Bibby, and Omar."

I made it to the 501st Forward Support Battalion at 2 p.m. Within minutes of our arrival, Capt. Mike Slack's team showed up with soldiers from the 1st Armored Division, who accompanied Garner, Bibby, and Omar to the support battalion. I walked with Garner to the aid station. He was in a state of shock, with tears in his eyes. I held him and could not control my own tears. He explained what happened, and apologized for Bibby and Omar. "It is not your fault, you must let it go," I said to him. For both of us, this was easier said than done.

The support battalion staff came in and told me that someone from the chain-of-command needed to identify the remains. Command Sgt. Maj. Mike Chickosky, Major Coleman, and Captain Self accompanied me to the location. I didn't want to believe that it was real. But there they were in front of me, all of their life taken from them. I placed a 3rd Infantry Division patch on Bibby's chest. We had not yet had the official ceremony during which he would have been awarded his combat patch with the rest of the division. "You earned it," I said under my breath. "I only wish that I had given it to you sooner."

When I left the room, I was told a helicopter would be arriving at the palace in the Green Zone at 1600 hours. I was surprised not to have gotten any resistance to my request from the 1st Armored Division.

On the flight down, we flew over my battalion headquarters. I looked down at the building and wondered: why Bibby and Omar? These two truly superb men did not deserve to die like this.

When I arrived at the helipad for the hospital, Perley and his team met the sergeant major and me. Perley explained that Laverick was out of surgery, in critical condition, and still sedated because of his injuries. Killion was in surgery, and Terry was on his way into surgery.

When I went to visit Killion, he was out of surgery and awake. The moment he saw me he began asking about everyone else. Terry had not come out of surgery yet. Laverick was still sedated, but was opening his eyes. I joked with him that I always seemed to be finding him in the hospital. In February I had been looking for him and found him asleep on a gurney in a hospital room.

His nurse took me aside and explained that his injuries were very serious and that the next forty-eight hours would determine his fate. Infection was a major concern because of the depth and size of his injuries. Out of my deep respect for him, I went back to his bedside and said a silent prayer.

I returned to Perley's team area and was surprised at how many people knew about the incident. The division support commander from the 1st Armored Division, whom I had never met before, stopped me in the hall and said he was sorry to hear about our loss. At a loss for anything else to say, I simply thanked him.

I also encountered Brig. Gen. Rhett Hernandez, the deputy commander of the 1st Armored Division. He had been told of the incident and expressed his condolences. He said that he had a helicopter returning to the Baghdad airport in the morning and I was welcome to ride back with him. I was especially grateful for this offer, because until that moment I was not sure how I would be getting back.

The patient administration section had told me that all three soldiers would be flown to Germany at 2:15 a.m. I did not sleep that night because of the many thoughts in my mind. At 3 a.m., I went outside and looked at the stars for a while. I saw the Big Dipper, Orion's Belt (a group of stars that Wesley, my youngest son, had asked me to watch for and remember him by). My thoughts drifted to my family and how much grief Bibby and Omar's families were going to go through.

At dawn the next morning, July 22, I caught the helicopter back to the airport in Baghdad with Brigadier General Hernandez. Chickosky and I were let off at the 3rd Infantry Division headquarters where I had asked Gerald to have the team pick me up. Major General Blount was on his way out just as we were coming in. He had also heard about the incident and expressed his condolences. "That makes forty now," he said, shaking his head.

That afternoon I wrote condolence letters to Bibby and Omar's parents. There were so many emotions and thoughts pulsing through me, I struggled to find just the right words. A few days before, Bibby had asked me to write him a letter of recommendation for college when we got back to the States. I told him absolutely. He was an outstanding soldier, the epitome of what an American soldier should be. Omar was always full of life, with kind words, and never without a smile. These two young men were dedicated to a free Iraq.

Later in the afternoon, Kent, the British officer who had been with me during that disastrous meeting with the group of sheiks at the Sheraton Hotel, paid a visit. He and I had become close friends. He told me that after I had left the previous night, a mutual Iraqi acquaintance had come in stating that he heard about what had happened to the 422nd soldiers. Kent was able to acquire all the necessary names and addresses and would be working on it for us. (Thanks to the information provided by our loyal Iraqi friends, the assailants were captured on August 28.)

Later that day, the news reported that Saddam Hussein's sons had been killed. Then at 11:30 p.m., Spc. Marcus Jones knocked on my door and said we were under attack. From the sounds outside, it seemed like a huge force. I put on my gear and headed out the door. We had practiced our battle drills and everyone had taken appropriate positions. Captain Simms reported that white flares were being sent up and there were at least twenty guns.

What was strange was that all the rounds were going up in the air. It took a few moments to figure out that it was celebratory fire, not an attack. The people of Baghdad were celebrating the deaths of Saddam's sons, the merciless and cruel killers who had terrorized and pillaged the country while living in majestic splendor. I looked into the sky and said a prayer for Mark Bibby and Omar, adding, "This one was for you!"

During the next week, it would be difficult to maintain our focus on the mission while helping almost two hundred soldiers and Iraqis deal with grief and anguish. It was a true test not to let doubt creep in about an important fact: that most Iraqis appreciated our attempts to help them achieve freedom and democracy and were not the enemy.

One afternoon, an Iraqi acquaintance came into my office, pale and stuttering. "Colonel King," he said, "Muhammad al-Zubaidi has contracted with a group to kill you."

"Oh," I replied, lifting my eyebrow.

"Yes," the man continued. "He also has a list of names of individuals who used to serve as agents under Saddam and he is threatening that he will turn them over to the Coalition if they do not pay him money."

I had worked with this man for several months now and usually found his information credible.

"Did you know that Muhammad gets one thousand dollars per person for introducing business and political leaders to you?" the man asked.

"No," I said. "I did not. How interesting." Now I understood why his daily meetings had grown unmanageably larger. I felt myself grow hot under the collar.

"And the men that he works with are intelligence agents from Syria and Jordan."

I abruptly thanked the man, adding that I would be back in touch. Muhammad al-Zubaidi had been pushing the envelope, and my patience had just run out.

I called Guidry to discuss al-Zubaidi, who had not come into his scheduled meetings for days. In light of this new information, I felt it was time to remind him that he was not in a position to test our resolve. We decided to arrest him.

Cyprus supported Guidry's team in the operation. When they returned with al-Zubaidi, they had recovered more than $27,000; a list of former Iraqi intelligence agents that was later described by the National Security Agency as highly sensitive; an expensive satellite phone; his computer; and of special concern to me, a file with pictures of me taken from different angles and a list of meetings I had attended.

Al-Zubaidi sat on the couch in my office slumped over, his face full of defiance and disgust. When I asked him about the allegation, he angrily denied it; it was not a sincere denial, but more of a *you-can-go-to-hell* denial.

An operative named "Lisa" and others who assisted the battalion took turns questioning al-Zubaidi about the list. He pretended not to know what it was, despite several names clearly having been highlighted by him. It was apparent that al-Zubaidi was not going to cooperate, thus violating the conditions of his earlier release. We had no choice but to detain him. He was into more than we could possibly know.

I had reported daily to Brigadier General Kern about al-Zubaidi's activities. Both of us we were fed up with al-Zubaidi's obstinacy. I called and reported to him that we had arrested al-Zubaidi and were taking him to the prison.

Kent later told me that the FBI would be investigating the alleged assassination plot, and al-Zubaidi would not be getting out of prison anytime in the near future. One afternoon in October, before transferring to Basrah, Kent called to tell me that al-Zubaidi was in the Umm Qasar prison in Southern Iraq. He told me he had a hard time locating him because he had registered under his father's name during the transfer.

Kent had met with al-Zubaidi to discuss the basis for his continued detention. Al-Zubaidi fervently denied the charges, but was unable to reasonably explain the photos and. my meeting schedule in his possession. Based on my conversation with Kent, I contacted the office responsible for al-Zubaidi's detention to make sure that his file was clearly marked this time. I did not want to risk his being released over a paperwork mistake. (On December 4, I would receive a report that al-Zubaidi had been released from prison and was believed to be heading for Jordan. In March 2004, I found out that pictures of my family and me, along with other personal and sensitive information, were found on al-Zubaidi's computer, leaving no doubt about his intentions. All I could do was shake my head in disbelief.)

Ra'ad al-Hamundandi returned to my office July 31, as we had rescheduled on the day Bibby and Omar were killed. I explained that the commander of the area wanted to detain him because of the weapons found on his farm. Al-Hamundandi replied that he had not been to his farm since April and did not know who would have placed them there. I assured him that I understood, but to protect his home and the honor of his family, he would need to explain himself to the unit. He agreed, but was concerned about being detained. I told him that while I did not have control of the situation, I could make sure that his family was not affected.

I had Staff Sergeant Robinson call the unit and tell them that al-Hamundandi was in my office. If they wanted to talk to him, they needed to send a team to pick him up.

Robinson came to my office and informed me that there was a team on the way. He added that the officer who took the message was stunned at how all it took was a simple phone call to get al-Hamundandi to come to my office.

When the team arrived, it was headed by a second lieutenant. I explained to him that al-Hamundandi could help them identify potential insurgents in the area if they worked with him. He made it clear that they were going to detain him whether he worked with them or not. I informed him about al-Hamundandi's diabetes, that if they were detaining him they should make sure the detention paperwork identified his medical condition. I asked him to swing by al-Hamundandi's home to pick up his medicine and explain to his family that he was going to have to be away for a while. The lieutenant agreed and al-Hamundandi accompanied them.

Sixty days later, a group of sheiks came to my office, understandably upset and concerned. They had heard that al-Hamundandi was in the Ibn Sina Hospital, and that his leg had been amputated. They explained that they went to visit him, but were refused admittance. One of them, Sheik Mahmood, asked if I would go and visit al-Hamundandi, and I agreed. When I walked into al-Hamundandi's hospital room, tears welled up in his eyes. He said that he knew I would come, and did not hold me responsible for what had happened; he just wanted to go home.

Indeed, al-Hamundandi's leg had been amputated due to complications from his diabetes. I immediately set to work on his release. Meanwhile, I learned he had been transferred to Abu Ghraib prison, and it took me almost thirty-six days to get him out.

During Ramadan, al-Hamundandi invited me for breakfast. He and I sat together in a diwan filled with guests, discussing the security situation and other topics. Then he said to me, "Until you lose a part of your body, you cannot appreciate what it means to have it all." This was the last time I would see him.

On the afternoon of August 2, Kent burst into my office. He explained that a man had just walked in and said that Saddam Hussein's doctor and other associates were just around the corner from us. Kent said that he tried to get the unit responsible for tracking Saddam, but he could not reach them on the radio. The security team Kent normally traveled with had gone on another mission and he did not have the resources to properly search the area. He asked me if I could help.

"Is the person credible?" I asked.

"Trust me," Kent said. He hadn't the time to explain, but we should consider this a legitimate sighting. Kent instructed Lisa to drive by the site and relay back what she saw.

In evaluating the available resources and risks, I realized that I only had one team on site. But I felt that as soldiers we had to do something. I instructed Captain Garner in the operations section to contact the 2nd Brigade and let them know that we needed their quick reaction force (QRF). I remembered the intense fighting when Saddam's sons were cornered, and knew we lacked the firepower to go into something like that. I looked at the map, and identified three ways in and out of the area. I figured the best I could do was cordon off the location and wait for the QRF to show up.

We would use our three humvees to block the roads. Kent, Lisa, and I drove out in SUVs. Communication between our vehicles and Lisa's was difficult at first. Eventually she was able to confirm a vehicle was still present at the site. She added that there were four men in the vicinity, positively identified as the doctor, driver, and two bodyguards. We still had no response from the QRF at this time. Major Crabb coordinated the cordon, which blocked the perimeter positions.

Kent and I stood at the entrance from the main road, wondering what to do next. Kent looked over my uniform and said, in reference to my rank, "It's your call—you're the boss."

I smiled, and one word came to mind: shit.

Before long, Major Crabb drove over to our area and stopped his car. Lisa was with the original informant in her SUV. Crabb and his soldiers helped four men out of his car. The soldiers covered Kent, who lined the four men up like a police lineup beside Lisa's SUV, facing toward the sun. They were unable to see the informant, who sat concealed behind tinted windows.

None of the four men spoke English. Kent frisked them and asked for their identification. He read each name over the radio.

Lisa translated for the informant, who contradicted each name. "They are lying," Kent said, shaking his head in disbelief.

Despite being frightened in the situation, the informant excitedly identified the man standing next to Kent as Saddam's bodyguard. The others were his doctor, driver, and another bodyguard.

Kent then placed his hand on each man's shoulder, and Lisa translated for him the actual identities. The oldest of the four was especially fidgety and was unable to look up at anyone. The younger men had completely blank expressions and said nothing. Kent reviewed the identification documents; one ID photo was clearly of a different person, and could not have fooled anyone. He grew more and more confident that the informant was telling the truth. Moreover, these men had not taken the time to get their stories straight. They all gave different reasons for being at the address. One said he was buying a vehicle, two said they were buying satellite dishes, and the last said he just happened to be walking by.

Crabb's team, Kent, and Lisa searched the vehicle where the men had first been spotted, along with another car in front of the house. In the glove compartment they found the doctor's identification with his picture and real name. They also found satellite phones, a large number of U.S. dollars, Iraqi dinar (currency), a suitcase of new clothes, silk pajamas, and sandals, all in Saddam's reported size.

I asked Crabb to have his team detain the men. We had now been in the area for almost an hour and a half. Kent went back to the detainees in the SUV. A crowd had gathered and members of the international press corps had come up to the soldiers and were asking what was going on. An Iraqi taxi containing an Italian journalist had stopped and began setting up a video camera.

The QRF had still not shown up, so Kent was by now obviously annoyed. "This is crazy," he said. "What do you think we should do?"

"Let's knock on the door and ask if Saddam is in there," I replied.

He looked at me as if he had misheard me, checked his watch, shook his head, then shrugged his shoulders and said, "Okay, we'll follow your lead."

I called for Crabb and Spc. Brandon Ellis, and turned to walk to the entrance of the building where we were told Saddam was located. I walked up and knocked on the door. I looked around and realized that Kent had gone to get Lisa to help translate. I looked back and saw that the man inside had opened the door. Major Crabb was still twenty meters away.

Realizing I was standing there alone, I hurriedly asked, "Is Saddam here?"

The man's eyes opened wide and he said, "No, no!"

"Who is inside there?" I asked.

He said there were three other people, and I told him to ask them to come outside. When they were out and away from the building, I asked the man to escort us through the rooms to allow us to clear the building. Vince took a team in one direction and Lisa came with me.

Afterward, we walked up to Kent, who was containing the detainees at the SUV. "Well?" he asked.

I knew what he meant. "Not this time," I replied. We were all thinking the same thing: if we had been there a little sooner, could we have caught *him*? Had we just missed Saddam? We would find out after he was captured that the answer was no.

Back at the battalion headquarters that evening, we had a chuckle about it. "That was crazy," Lisa said. "I felt like one of Charlie's Angels following you around that house doing room clearances."

"Come to think of it," Kent joked, "Alan does look a little like Bosley."

The next day, Kent and Lisa confirmed the identities and relationships the men had to Saddam. They were indeed Saddam's doctor, driver, and two bodyguards.

My two-year command tenure was approaching and I was scheduled to relinquish command on August 15. This was difficult because I had been with the soldiers from the beginning and had promised to bring them back to their families. Unfortunately, because command is a tenured position in the army and the change-of-command is a necessary event, I would have to leave the care of the soldiers to someone else.

I spent the last days of my command trying to finish tasks and ensuring continuity existed during the transfer from me to my successor. I was not sure where I was going to be assigned next, but I was confident that it would be some staff position at a desk inside the bowels of Coalition Joint Task Force 7 (CJTF-7) or the 352nd Civil Affairs Command.

One night I had dinner with Maj. Gen. Donald Campbell, senior advisor to the Ministry of Justice. He had been my boss and mentor for a long time. I had served under him when he was the commanding general of the Civil Affairs and Psychological

Operations Command. Major General Campbell, as always, had sound advice: the best thing I could do after leaving command was to be as good a staff officer as I had been a commander. To hear it from him meant a lot to me. I braced myself for the change of pace that was to come.

Over the next two weeks I got out and spent time with each of the teams. We traveled throughout the city and they showed me their projects. In the previous four months, these soldiers had really worked hard to bring back basic governmental services to the city. I was so proud of all of them, and was sorry to say goodbye.

In the days just before I relinquished command, Zumurudeh prepared a huge going-away party for me. My Iraqi friends came from all over the country to bid me farewell. They also expressed their concerns about what would happen to them when I left. I tried to assure them that my replacement was a competent officer who would treat them the same way I had. I would still be in Iraq and they could come and talk to me if there was ever a need.

On August 14, I said my goodbyes to my staff members. Zumurudeh helped me obtain small plaques for each of them, and I gave a unit coin to each of the translators. I also gave Faisal and Zumurudeh letters of recommendation to assist them in obtaining future employment.

I did not sleep that night, thinking of leaving the soldiers and Iraqis whom I cared for so much. I got my things together the next morning and the team prepared to escort me to Saddam's Military Parade Grounds for the change of command. I made my departing speech with Ambassador Hume Horan, other dignitaries, former ministers from Saddam's cabinet, and, of course, my Iraqi translators were in attendance.

After the ceremony, Zumurudeh, her brother, and her cousin brought lunch to my apartment. I expected this to be the last time that I would see her. She had decided not to continue this line of employment and was instead going work with her cousin. Zumurudeh and the others presented me with small gifts as tokens of their appreciation for what I had done to help them. It was deeply moving when we said our last goodbyes at the gate. The thought of not continuing to contribute directly to the efforts in Iraq made it especially difficult.

Leaving command is unquestionably the most difficult experience in an officer's military career. Command allows an officer the opportunity to shape an organization and prepare it for its wartime duties. A unit's failure is the result of poor leadership, but its success is based on the soldiers' ability to understand the leader's vision, accept it, and conduct their business with the end objectives in mind. In the case of the 422nd, we had the opportunity to test our preparedness, and the soldiers performed superbly, proving that the success of an organization is the result of its people. After command, the officer is typically sent to a much less exciting staff job, where he or she will apply the experience gained as a commander.

I had been told I was going to be assigned as a liaison officer in the tactical operations center. It was a far cry from the day-to-day contact with Iraqis that I was used to.

I spent the next three days finishing up paperwork and meeting the occasional sheik who showed up at the headquarters looking for me. I appreciated them wanting to talk to me, but I felt like most of the staff at the headquarters did not want the traffic coming in and out.

On August 19, I went to Camp Victory at the airport to receive my duties and an overview of my job description. I listened intently at what my responsibilities would entail, but I kept thinking about what was going on with my Iraqi friends.

The next day I was called to General Kern's office. He told me that he wanted me to split my workdays: half as a liaison officer and the other half working with the sheiks. This would allow me to set appointments with the sheiks and help guarantee they had someone to assist them.

Three days later I was appointed as the Special Assistant for Tribal Affairs to the commanding general of the Civil Affairs Command. It was obvious that I could not be away from the operations center for an extended period of time. I was ecstatic, and called Faisal and Zumurudeh to request that they work with me in the newly created office. Fortunately for me, they both agreed. Major Coleman heard about the assignment and asked me if I wanted Mary to come over. I was pleased to have her back as well. Because of the pace of the meetings, Mary kept notes for future reference.

On August 25, I was officially engaged full-time with the tribes. This gave me my real purpose for being in Iraq and allowed me to continue the work I had started four months earlier. I had a full schedule my first day back. Faisal, Zumurudeh, and Mary showed up early and we discussed the focus of the new office. When we were at the battalion, we were responsible for communicating with everyone in the society, but now we were solely responsible for dealing with the sheiks. While I missed my soldiers, I was happy to be back on the ground trying to make a difference.

# CHAPTER 8

# Bet Your Career

*Ask the experienced rather than the learned.*
*—Arab proverb*

By September 2003, coordinating the advancement of democracy and stability with the Iraqi sheiks was once again my daily routine. The previous efforts of the 422nd Civil Affairs Battalion had garnered considerable trust among many Iraqis, many of whom had grown comfortable enough to help us arrange honorable surrenders of family members who had been active with the former regime.

Every day in October I had meetings scheduled with sheiks and other dignitaries. Keeping up with all the translated conversations, from Arabic to English and back again, was mentally exhausting, especially for the translators who had to do the real work. Early in the month I had a meeting with Sheik Sa'ad, who told me of a family member on the wanted list who wanted an arranged surrender to protect his immediate family from embarrassment. I told Sheik Sa'ad that I would personally be involved with the escort to ensure that his relative was treated honorably.

The family member he referred to was Lt. Gen. Ayad Al-Bayatee, number 85 on the most wanted list. General Ayad was wanted for war crimes. He had been a division commander against the Kurds and later a corps commander during the invasion of Kuwait. Sheik Sa'ad came to me on several occasions to arrange the surrender. We finally agreed to schedule it for October 20, which happened to be my sister's birthday.

On October 18 at approximately 3 p.m., a tall, slender, elderly man who had noticeable back problems entered my office (my office manager, who usually checked people before they entered, was meeting with me nearby).

"Excuse me, is Colonel King here?" he asked in Arabic.

Hasan from my security team stood up, but before he could escort him out, the elderly man added, "I am Lt. Gen. Ayad Al-Bayatee. I believe that I have an appointment."

Hearing this, I got up from my meeting, went over to introduce myself, and asked the general to take a seat. "You were supposed to come in on Monday," I said.

"I know," he said, "but I am ready now. Why wait?"

I excused the staff and said, "General, I am glad that you are here, but I cannot arrest you today."

He looked confused. "But why?" he asked. "I am here."

"I understand, but you are supposed to come in on Monday. I am not prepared to arrest you today. I really need for you to come in at 1 p.m. Monday afternoon as we agreed."

He shrugged his shoulders and said, "Okay, as you like. Would you like me to tell you about my career?" I had no other appointments for the day so I was happy to sit and listen. I offered him something to drink and he began his story.

General Ayad had been a professional military officer. He had risen through the ranks, but had never become a Ba'athist.

According to the general, he had been offered a ministerial position on six occasions, but after refusing to sign the Ba'athist statement, he was summarily fired from his post. He was later renominated for another military position.

I had had conversations with General Ayad's contemporaries, and by all accounts he was a professional officer, a competent and compassionate leader, and someone that was well respected by Saddam. But even if General Ayad had not been personally involved in war crime activities, I suspected that he was probably wanted for the actions of his subordinates.

After retiring, General Ayad went on to become the mayor of a town. He was a pleasant and charming man, but I was sure he was a man few dared to crossed. I thanked the general for coming in and told him that I would see him on October 20 per the original plan. I advised him to spend as much time with his family as he could and to bring a suitcase when he returned because I knew he would be gone for a long time.

When I returned to the headquarters that evening and reported my daily activities to the commanding general, he looked at me with disbelief and said, "Yeah, right, sure. You'll never see him again." Everyone laughed.

It was embarrassing, but I assured the commanding general that General Ayad would show. He stared at me in disbelief. It was clear what he and the others were thinking; they did not expect such naivety from a lieutenant colonel in the U.S. Army. Someone would later dub this the "*Bet Your Career* game show," which was perhaps an accurate reflection of the stakes.

It would all depend on whether General Ayad's honor brought him back. In my head I prayed, "God, please make sure he comes in on Monday!"

I had made arrangements for Munkethe to pick up the general and escort him to me. I called Munkethe Monday morning and asked him if he had made contact with Ayad. To my tentative relief, he assured me that everything was set, that the general would be at the designated point at 1 p.m.

I met the escort at 12:30 and waited. When Munkethe called to say that they were in route, a huge weight had been lifted from my shoulders. They arrived right on time. General Ayad was in a wheelchair because of a back condition that had worsened. We transferred him to my vehicle and drove to the prison.

When we arrived, General Ayad seemed unconcerned with his future fate. Even though he might never see his family again, I assured him that I would check on him and keep his family informed of his status. I explained that after he was processed, he would be transferred in three days. I would return to make sure that he was properly cared for during the move. He was grateful, hugged me, and smiled. He thanked me for helping him during this period and for helping him keep honor among his family. I hugged him back, said goodbye, and told him I would see him in three days.

General Ayad had kept his word to me and surrendered honorably. I reflected back on this and the day's activities, and remembered again that it was my sister's birthday; I needed to contact her and wish her well. The next second, I looked up and saw the lead vehicle of our escort swerve to miss a tractor-trailer that had pulled in front of us.

My driver was unavoidably heading straight for the trailer at a high rate of speed (which he had been doing to avoid improvised explosive devices). I raised my right arm to brace myself for impact. The vehicle hit the truck, and I felt my safety belt pop free. The impact flung me forward across the front passenger seat, my head hitting the front passenger airbag and my back hitting the windshield. My left leg had been caught on the console, keeping me from going through the front windshield. I was then thrown backward, and felt an immediate throbbing on my shin.

A funny thought occurred to me in that instant: my son's birthday had been the date of the substation ambush, and once again, a relative's birthday would have additional significance.

I was taken to the hospital, where my wound was cleaned and x rayed for possible fractures. Fortunately, there were none. That night at the staff meeting, I was able to report that not only were there no serious injuries from the accident, but General Ayad had surrendered as coordinated and was now officially in custody. I was the lucky winner in the first round of *Bet Your Career.*

On October 23, I returned to help transfer General Ayad as I had promised. His back had gotten worse, but he was holding up. I told him that I had contacted his family to let them know he was okay, and that they sent him their best. I asked him if he had any messages for me to pass on to them. He did not. We dropped off General Ayad and returned to the Green Zone, this time without incident.

In return for the assistance of the sheiks and other Iraqis, they requested that I keep them posted on the status of detained family members. One man who approached me was Dr. Ahmed al-Obeity. Dr. Ahmed, who had received his doctorate degree in Ohio, was married to Huda Amash, most wanted number 39/five of hearts in the deck of cards. Dr. Ahmed was upset that his wife was still being detained after turning herself in back in May.

Dr. Ahmed, a patriotic Iraqi nationalist, spoke fluent English. He had once told me he liked the United States very much, but he liked the customs and culture of his country more. He said that he had opportunities to live in the United States, but this was his home and he was proud of it. I could empathize with him. I love my country too and would defend her no matter what.

Dr. Ahmed's requests were simple: to check on his wife and to arrange a visit. Checking on her was no problem, but for him to visit her seemed almost impossible. I told him I would see what I could do, but made no promises. He was grateful and said he would return in a couple days.

I talked to the organization responsible for the detention of high-profile persons about Dr. Ahmed's request. I was familiar with many individuals in the organization, having been involved in the surrenders of several of their detainees. I soon received the organization's response, and was stunned to hear that they approved a visit by Dr. Ahmed and Huda's mother to take place on Huda's birthday. When I passed the news on to Dr. Ahmed, he was ecstatic, but underneath, resentment over her detention still lingered.

Since my arrival in Baghdad in April 2003, personnel rotations forced us to start projects over from the beginning again and again. These rotations occurred every 90 to 180 days. It could take weeks to reestablish projects with the key decision makers. The resulting delays cost us credibility with the Iraqis. The constant personnel changes would be among the most frustrating parts of my sixteen months in Iraq.

By late summer I had become extremely busy, traveling throughout Iraq to discuss our efforts with sheiks, and to the desert to speak to the Bedouin. The Bedouin were beginning their annual migratory move to the south, and it was an opportunity to see how much these nomadic people knew or cared about the efforts to rebuild Iraq.

The ever-increasing opposition to the occupation was evident in the shrinking support of the sheiks in recent months. While I believed the sheiks closest to me would continue to assist in our efforts, they were less willing to accept the exposure that resulted from their assistance. It was a terribly conflicting position for them: if they positioned themselves with the insurgency, they may lose their identity and their heritage; if they allied themselves with the Coalition, they might very well lose their lives.

I visited the Bedouin in the desert on several occasions, many times traveling by Blackhawk helicopter. Our unexpected arrivals would frighten some of these carefree desert people. I asked an Iraqi sheik with whom I had formed a close bond if he would travel with me and introduce me to the Bedouin. He seemed delighted to help out and readily accepted, but I detected some reluctance. I would later learn that he had been in a helicopter crash years before and did not like to fly, to put it mildly.

When I told the sheik that we would drive to his village and pick him up, his eyebrows raised and he quickly declined. "I will be killed if anyone discovers that I am *collaborating* with you." This was disheartening to hear, but I understood.

On the night before I was to visit the Bedouin, the sheik drove into Baghdad and stayed with relatives. He and his son-in-law met me at the Green Zone at sunrise. It was a little chilly, with a morning breeze that was unusual for Baghdad.

We headed down the gauntlet towards the airport. When we arrived, helicopters were ready for us and we loaded up. The crew chief's windows would be open for his machine gun, and I agreed that the doors could stay open as well. In hindsight, it was inconsiderate on my part not to have asked my guest, knowing he was already uneasy about the flight.

We took off, expecting the flight to take little more than an hour. But about thirty minutes out, we had to turn around and head back to the airport. A bird had flown through the windshield of the second chopper. When we landed, we viewed the damage. The bird had smashed the whole window section in front of the pilot. Luckily, no one was injured. The mission for the day was scrubbed. I asked the sheik if he would be willing to come back again. His mouth said, "Yes," but his face said, "Thank goodness I am back on the ground."

The sheik and his son-in-law showed up at the Green Zone on time for the rescheduled mission. Our escort arrived and drove us to the airport. As usual, the sheik was pleasant and warm in his welcome. When the helicopters arrived, the son-in-law asked if we could fly with the doors closed. This time I replied, "Of course."

The vast openness of the desert and the austere way of life for the Bedouin made me value the amenities of the United States that much more. We landed at a Bedouin camp about a kilometer away from the site. I asked the sheik if he would accompany me even though I had no security with me (we did not want to scare the Bedouin people with the sight of armed men). The sheik said he would, that he had no concern. I suspected that the helicopter landing probably spooked them enough already.

I assured our security team that we would be fine with them out of sight. We could always fire a shot to alert them if we needed them. They also gave us a small handheld radio to communicate with, but it lost its effectiveness after we crossed over the first sand dune. Sheik Muthana, his son-in-law, the translator, and I made small talk as we walked towards the Bedouin camp.

Approaching the tents, we saw a small white Toyota pickup truck, with two men working nearby. It was obvious that they knew we were there, but they continued to work, occasionally looking over their shoulder to see if we were still approaching. When we finally came into view of the men, the sheik raised his hand and waived to the Bedouin, and they returned the greeting.

There were two tents tied together at the camp. The one on the right was open with beautiful, thick, and heavy handmade blankets stacked in piles around the walls. There were also blankets and rugs laid out on the desert floor, and a small teapot heating nearby.

Though clearly nervous, the Bedouin managed to be warm and hospitable. They invited us into the open area of the tent. The sheik first declined our hosts' offer of tea, in typical Arab fashion. When they insisted, he accepted.

After the customary exchange of greetings, the Bedouin told us they were from the As Samawah area in Southern Iraq. This was the second year that they had taken this route. Their usual migration took place farther to the east. I asked if they knew the travelers in the other camps, and they said one was an uncle of theirs. They offered to drive us to visit the other camps in their truck. While sitting on the carpets covering the ground of the tent, I could see the faces of small children peeking through the seams of the tent, full of curiosity about the strangers who were talking to their fathers. Radio communication was difficult and erratic, but I radioed the team after we settled in and told them that we were safe.

After a few minutes I looked around and there were a dozen soldiers walking abreast toward us. The security team had been unable to understand the radio transmission and thought that they should come forward to check on us. The sheik assured our hosts that everything was okay, that there was no cause for concern. The Bedouin offered the new guests tea.

When the team arrived, they said that one of the soldiers had become ill from the heat and was several meters away. One of the Bedouin offered to drive their truck out to pick him up. While we were speaking to the other Bedouin, the security team became excited over a newborn lamb. Their innocent gestures and playfulness with the lamb went a long way to help break the ice and make the meeting more relaxed.

I asked one of the soldiers to bring a box filled with stuffed animals and candy that I had brought along. The children were then brought into the tent to receive our gifts. Their youthful excitement and gratefulness was refreshing to us.

The Bedouin drove us to several other camps with similar concerns. Few had given much thought to the new government. As long as they were allowed to continue their way of life, they did not care who was in charge.

We returned to the helicopter and offered one of the Bedouin money for his time and gas, but as expected, he declined by pushing it away. One of the Americans offered him a present of a Leatherman tools, which he laid on the seat of the Bedouin's truck. They expressed appreciation and seemed quite moved by the present.

After a very long day, we loaded up to return home. During the trip I scanned the faces of the team. It had been a long day and everyone was exhausted.

The sheik and his son-in-law said that they felt it was time well spent. The sheik agreed to continue to help us, and would enlist the assistance of some of the other sheiks, too.

I continued to make contact with the sheiks and solicit their support. Munkethe told me he had found some more sheiks that might want to help us. I asked if he could bring them to see me so I could talk to them in person.

The first sheik was Sheik Omar. I realized that I had met him months before. He was a lively fellow and quite talkative. He said that he was committed to the Coalition's efforts and that he would be glad to help.

The routine meetings at the office took up almost all of my time. When I was asked to go visit the Iraqis in their villages, I was happy for the chance to get out of the office. I was asked to attend a meeting with the Bedouin again. Upon my arrival at the airport, I learned that we had information that the Bedouin had packed up their camps and left the area. Those of us going to the meeting agreed that since we already had the helicopter, we should use it to locate the new camps. I had my day entirely blocked off, so it was fine with me.

We loaded into the helicopters and began the hour and fifteen minute flight to the desert. Upon arriving over the area that we believed the Bedouin were located, I heard the pilot's voice on the headset. He had spotted a caravan on the move about ten kilometers away.

"Can you fly toward them?" I asked.

"Roger that," he replied.

We flew over a caravan of five vehicles with what appeared to be Bedouin shepherds, their families, and their sheep. The pilot, who was circling the caravan, asked me what I wanted him to do. I squeezed the microphone: "Fly about two hundred meters in front of them and land, I will get out and speak to them. And do me a favor," I continued. "Make sure you fly circles around us in watch, okay?"

"No problem," the pilot replied.

I was pretty confident that the Bedouin would be warm in their reception, but decided we shouldn't take any chances. I said to the pilot, "If these folks start shooting at us, y'all provide suppressive fire and we'll high-tail it back to where you let us off, okay?" Then I looked across at the translator, pointed down and mouthed the words, "Let's land."

The translator looked over at me like I was crazy. He knew I meant that if I was getting out, he was going to have to go, too. The helicopter circled one last time to land in the path of the caravan, and I prepared to get out quickly. The helicopter hovered and the door slid back. Even from the distance, I could see that the Bedouin were scared. We disembarked from the aircraft and there was a mound of sand blocking our view of the Bedouin. Running from beneath the blades, we knelt on a knee, turned, covered our eyes from the blowing sand, and gave a "thumbs up" that we were okay.

The helicopter lifted off, and the sand settled as we started towards the trucks, uncertain what awaited us. From the crest of a sand dune, I could see that the Bedouin had left their vehicles. The women had formed a circle with their backs to us and the children were inside the circle. The men stood next to the vehicles and three men stood in front of trucks. I waved, but got no response.

"This does not look good," I remarked.

"Yeah," replied the translator.

We continued toward the men, but they remained still.

"Shit, they have to see us," I said. "What is the problem?"

Finally, three Bedouin began to walk towards us, the one in the middle waving. When we got nearer to the group, the Bedouin man spoke. "Do your duty," he said. "We understand, and will not get in your way." They thought we were customs inspectors.

Each of the men wore thick sheepskin coats. One of the men was young, maybe nineteen; the other was missing several teeth, and looked to be in his mid-thirties. It was hard to tell, because the Bedouin are a desert people, and the extreme weather ages their skin prematurely.

The men explained that they had only begun to migrate the particular route they were on two years ago. Before that they traveled fifty kilometers to the east. They explained that they had heard on the radio that the Coalition had toppled Saddam and they wanted to know if it was true. It had been eight months since the invasion, and they were still unsure that the Americans standing in front of them were real.

They cheered when I assured them that the news was true. With the usual Arab hospitality, they offered lodging, and would prepare a sheep for our meal. We did not have time and politely declined. Then we motioned for the chopper to pick us up. We continued to search the ground, hopping from camp to camp, talking to the Bedouin about the Coalition's efforts. Each time they offered us tea and lamb.

On our last stop, I found out from a Bedouin that the sheik for the entire area, Sheik Muhammad, was a man I had met months before. I had assisted in his release after his arrest by the Coalition, and he had subsequently returned to the village. I decided to visit him, uncertain how much resentment he still harbored for the Coalition and whether he would be willing to assist us in advancing a democratic Iraq.

Munkethe made the request to Sheik Muhammad. The next day, Munkethe came to the office and said that Muhammad had remembered me and appreciated what I had done for him during his personal crisis last August. He would be honored to help me any way he could. Munkethe said that the sheik invited me to his village for lunch, an invitation I could not decline.

When we arrived at the village, Sheik Muhammad came out to greet us. He hugged me and gave me the customary three kisses. He was an elderly man, highly revered among the sheiks in the region. We entered the sheik's diwan and took our places around the wall. The building was old but sturdy. Chairs lined the walls and pictures of the sheik's family with British officers in the early 1900s were prominently displayed. It was not long before each of the guests was offered tea. We spoke to the sheik for a while about his family and their history. He was proud of the family's accomplishments as he showed us the aged pictures of his ancestors.

After about an hour, we were told that lunch was ready. There were eight goats on the table along with rice and other assorted delicacies. We stood around a large table and feasted on the food in front of us. It is customary to eat with one's hands. Sheik Muhammad came by and tore meat from the goat and laid it on my plate, a sign of respect for a host toward a guest. Sheik Sa'ad was standing across from me and ate from the gum of the goat. He looked and me, smiled, and offered to put some on my plate. I simply smiled and politely gestured that I was full. After our feast, Sheik Muhammad showed us around parts of his village. The village was in the middle of the desert, with no running water, no electricity, and only a satellite phone for communication.

During the meeting, I learned that the sheik had several items confiscated when he was arrested. He wondered if I could assist him in getting them returned. I promised I would do my best, but was unsure what I could do to help. Because of the sheik's prestige in his area, I decided to ask Ambassador Jones, deputy country administrator, if he would follow up with him.

We walked from the house, and children appeared from what seemed out of nowhere. I had a large bag of candy and offered it to them. They dug into the bag, their faces lighting up, and then played together with some of the soldiers. I thanked Sheik Muhammad for his hospitality and assured him that I would arrange a visit between him and Ambassador Jones to discuss what the Coalition could do in his area to advance our efforts.

Capt. Kevin Guidry searches deserters from the Iraqi Army in An Najaf, March 2003. Captain Guidry would be wounded in action February 21, 2004. *Staff Sgt. Kevin Bell*

Villagers look on as we are served a feast in their village elder's diwan. They seemed to trust and accept us, and I never sensed any fear, only a deep curiosity. *Staff Sgt. Kevin Bell*

The 422nd Civil Affairs Battalion distributed water to more than three thousand villagers during a tactical pause in An Najaf. *Staff Sgt. Kevin Bell*

Someone recognizes me and yells my name during a walk in downtown Baghdad, June 2003. The entire street closed in on me as my security team did its best to remain close and alert to the situation.

We inspect the damage to one of our helicopters after a bird strike smashed out part of the windshield, forcing us to scrub the mission.

Col. Larry Rubini, senior advisor to the Ministry of Justice, sits next to me on our way to meet with the Bedouin people in the desert.

Bookending me at my going-away party are Lt. Col. Rick Welch (my son's godfather and the man who succeeded me) and Sheikh Hussein Ali al-Shaalon.

Masgoof, a traditional Iraqi fish dish, is grilled to perfection during a tribal meeting at Munkethe's farm alongside the Euphrates River.

The entire village chips in to help repair a school. *Staff Sgt. Kevin Bell*

Capt. John Smathers searches a man who had wandered onto the battlefield. Captain Smathers received four Bronze Stars, including one for valor, two Purple Hearts, and an Army Commendation medal. He returned home in March 2004. After enduring difficult physical rehabilitation for his war wounds, he died unexpectedly on February 4, 2006. *Staff Sgt. Kevin Bell*

Maj. Jeff Sliverthorne directs children during the school repair effort. Major Sliverthorne was directly responsible for the battalion's communications, a position for which he was particularly well suited. *Staff Sgt. Kevin Bell*

Several weeks after we provided medical care to this Bedouin man with a severely cut finger, clerics who heard of this "benevolent act" traveled to Baghdad asking for our help. *Staff Sgt. Kevin Bell*

Cpl. Mark Bibby stands guard during a visit to An Najaf, March 2003. He was killed in action July 21, 2003. *Staff Sgt. Kevin Bell*

Mathaan, who is the same age as my son, runs up to greet me during my meeting with a village elder. *Staff Sgt. Kevin Bell*

A procession of more than 250 sheikhs and other dignitaries filled two large tents for a meeting to discuss and assess the progress—and unrest—in southernmost Iraq. *W. Layers*

Sheik Hussein Ali
al-Shaalan and I greet
each other.
*Annia Ciezadlo*

Capt. Damone Garner and Omar pose in the kitchen of Hala's Palace before a mission. Captain Garner was wounded and Omar was killed in ambush on July 21, 2003. *Courtesy of Capt. Damone Garner*

Mohammed Saeed al-Sahaf ("Baghdad Bob"), number 168 on the most wanted list, shakes hands with me in my office, July 2003. (inset photo: *Foreign Broadcast Information Service*)

Maj. Brent Gerald, the de facto fire chief of Baghdad after the fall of the former regime, inspects a newly renovated fire station.
*Maj. Brent Gerald*

Hikmat Mizban Ibrahim Al-Azzawi, number 26/eight of diamonds in the deck of cards featuring the most wanted former regime officials, deputy prime minister and finance minister, was captured by Maj. Vince Crabb (labeled "Sheriff of Baghdad" by the press), Capt. Timothy Popek, and Capt. Mike Self on April 16, 2003.
*Major Vince Crabb*

Sheik Adnan al-Janabi describes the long and illustrious history of his tribe to me.

Maj. Barry McCrea greets children in a village. *Staff Sgt. Kevin Bell*

Staff Sgt. Bob Laverick, 422nd Civil Affairs Battalion medic, with the assistance of translator al-Amir, provides medical support to local villagers outside An Najaf during combat operations, April 1, 2003. Laverick was wounded in action July 21, 2003. *Staff Sgt. Kevin Bell*

This photo was taken the week before Fallah (facing camera) was killed during an ambush that occurred February 21, 2004. *W. Layer*

Capt. Kevin Guidry
greets villagers near
An Najaf. He was
wounded in action
February 21, 2004.
*Staff Sgt. Kevin Bell*

Hala's Palace provided us
with a combination of
autonomy and access
that was necessary to
assist the people of
Baghdad. We would
accept the surrenders of
numerous "most wanted
Iraqis" at this location.
*Capt. Damone Garner*

When we saw this
sign while crossing
"no man's land," we
knew there was no
turning back.

We worked with local businessmen to afford the soldiers one of the first Internet cafes in Baghdad.
*Capt. Damone Garner*

Capt. John Smathers talks to a child in a village during the first days of the war.
*Staff Sgt. Kevin Bell*

A Jubor tribal sheik greets me during a reception of tribal sheiks in Baghdad, June 2004.

An Iraqi journalist snapped this photo in Baghdad after the man in the hat ran to my vehicle and unwisely stuck a "gun" in my face. I rolled from my vehicle with my gun stuck in his stomach. His gun turned out to be plastic, and he insisted he was "just playing a joke."

A villager carries off a bag of
lentils during our food distribution
near An Najaf, March 2003.

Here I stand among
chief of police
candidates, April 16,
2003. A new police
chief was appointed
the next day.
*Staff Sgt. Kevin Bell*

Capt. Stacy Simms
talks to children near
As Samawa. Captain
Simms organized the
first orphanages in
Baghdad after the fall
of the former regime.
*Capt. Damone Garner*

A fuzzy picture, taken in March 2003, captures a moment of special significance to me. From left to right, standing, Spc. Graham Butler, who would receive a Bronze Star for valor; Salah, a translator who was with me during an ambush on April 10, 2003; myself; Major Barry McCrea, Bronze Star; Capt. Kevin Guidry, Bronze Star for valor and a Purple Heart; Capt. John Smathers, Bronze Star for valor and two Purple Hearts; Cpl. Mark Bibby, Bronze Star and a Purple Heart, KIA July 21, 2003; kneeling, Sgt. Carl Meyers, Bronze Star for valor; a child from An Najaf; a translator; Spc. Graham Porter, Bronze Star for valor.

Capt. Timothy Popek, left, and Maj. Vince Crabb help the newly formed Iraqi police lay out a map of Baghdad.

# CHAPTER 9

# Tribal Honor

*Better a thousand enemies outside the house than one inside.*
*—Arab proverb*

## CALL HIM ALAN OF ARABIA

The British Empire had T. E. Lawrence, and the American Army has Alan King, a Koran-toting colonel who woos Iraqi sheiks with verses from the Muslim holy book. . . .

The U.S.-led Coalition Provisional Authority (CPA) has been slow to realize the importance of tribal affiliations in Iraq, earning criticism from political analysts and anger from Iraqis.

But on Dec. 4, the CPA approved Colonel King's pet project—a council of tribal sheiks that will meet regularly and dispense advice to Coalition forces.

As deputy director of the newly created Office of Provincial Outreach, under a State Department official, he will be the liaison to Iraq's major tribes.

*—The Washington Times,*
"From Better to Verse"
January 4, 2004

To fully appreciate Iraqi culture and customs, one must understand the Hammurabi Code, written in 1750 B.C. Tribal laws with origins in this code have weathered numerous past occupations. It has given Iraqis the basis for imposing punishment upon criminals and transgressors, while granting remuneration and reprisal to victims. They see no need for intervention by occupying governments to impose law when their laws have allowed tribal Iraqis to live in relative peace for generations. The Iraqi people spoke often of tribal law, but I only witnessed its application in the most remote and rural areas of the country.

During our preparation for combat in Iraq, many thought that the tribes played a significant role in the country's political structure. Tribal sheiks are indeed crucial to Iraq's social infrastructure, but they span the spectrum when it comes to influence and respect. Only a handful in rural areas exert substantial regional control. The challenge for the Coalition has been to find out who wields the power.

Upon the Coalition's arrival, the balance of control began to shift based on who delivered results and who did not. The real power of the sheiks is their ability to shape opinions. Earning their trust and supporting them is absolutely essential to securing victory in Iraq.

History provides us a window to the importance of trust among tribal sheiks. During Saddam's regime, he lost their trust by manipulating their tribes. He even relocated families to weaken the strength of tribes in specific areas. In the early 1980s, he disallowed the use of family names; individuals could only use their given name, father's, and then grandfather's first names. Saddam only revitalized the tribal system in the 1990s to monitor movement and loyalties and to help with a desertion crisis in his military. Among the 7,300 Arab sheiks identified by Saddam's regime, many were given their title through their former leader's "generosity."

Although this led to a number of "fake" sheik designations, the "real" Iraqi sheiks are a group steeped in honor, history, and tradition. One cannot go to a sheik's home for a simple visit. Tea will be served and the talk will last for several hours. When the subject of the tribe comes up, be prepared to hear about a family tree that dates back thousands of years. In the United States we are lucky to know the name of our great-grandfather. In Iraq, most sheiks know the sons of the sons dating back to the original family patriarch.

Of the more than three thousand sheiks I met with while in Iraq, I found that they all had deep feelings of nationalism. From this arose their seething sense of betrayal and opposition during our meetings after the announcement of the occupation. I tried to explain to them that the occupation was a legal term necessary to describe our responsibility to the Iraqi people, but this fell on deaf ears. For men whose ancestors have lived under some form of occupation for millennia, it was hard to believe that the American occupation would be anything other than permanent.

One sheik explained to me with great candor, "Colonel King, you only need to read the history books to understand the Iraqi people. You may have broken our backs, but you did not break our spirits. If you cut off our arms and our legs, we will use our teeth to crawl to the fight. An Iraqi may commit every sin there is and ask our brothers to forgive us, but we will not forgive a liar. God has to do that. And your government lied to us." Iraqis have a way of exaggerating to make a point, and this one was well understood.

We can only hope that those analysts who overlooked history in predicting an eternal euphoria after Saddam's fall did not (to paraphrase Santayana) condemn us to repeat it. They only needed to look to the past to realize that an occupation longer than a month or two would increasingly try the Iraqis' patience.

The British learned something about Iraq's legacy of resistance in the 1920s. After the defeat of the Ottoman Empire in World War I, the Iraqis prepared for the transition to an independent nation. Instead, their British liberators announced the imposition of direct rule in 1919. Resistance followed the unexpected occupation and a succession of events led to the uprising of the Middle Euphrates tribes in 1920. It only took the arrest of a minor sheik to spark the rebellion. By the end of July in 1920, the insurrection extended almost to Baghdad.

When I first started receiving Iraqis in my office, the numerous daily visits of men dressed in traditional Arab robes claiming to be sheiks and demanding their salaries overwhelmed me. It was difficult determining who was legitimate and who was not. I would receive their grievances and conduct inquiries to determine if there was anything we could do to help them. Majors McRae and Coleman became resident experts in locating and ascertaining the status of these individuals. Their efforts did more to contribute to our reputation and respect among the sheiks than any other single task.

I began actively requesting assistance from tribal sheiks in locating individuals among those featured in the most wanted "deck of cards" who remained to be captured. We would arrange surrenders that maintained the dignity and the honor of their families. Among those left in the deck of cards was number 27 most wanted/eight of hearts, General Sultan Hashim Ahmad al-Jabburi al-Tai, the former minister of defense.

Then, in late June, I was introduced to Sheik Adnan. He was a bright, Western-educated, and the head of one of the larger combined Sunni and Shi'a tribes in Iraq. Sheik Adnan's assistance was a godsend, helping me locate a listing of all the recognized Arab sheiks in the country. Now I could easily look up those claiming stature among the sheiks and identify the imposters. I was also introduced to Ahmad, a tribal scholar who provided a wealth of information to me. He had prepared lists of sheiks, their family members, family histories, and most importantly, the family trees that identified tribal relationships and family loyalties. Sheik Adnan said that he would ask Muhammad, a close associate of General Sultan, to persuade the defense minister to surrender.

I would later receive a phone call from Sheik Adnan. "Colonel King, Muhammad was arrested by the Iraqi police on his way to the north. He is being held at the prison in Baghdad. He stopped to buy a drink and the police raided the shop he was at and they arrested him." I immediately rallied a security team to take me to the police station.

I met great resistance from the police lieutenant in my first attempt to secure Muhammad's release. I was in the middle of arguing my point when another police major (who knew me from a previous meeting) came over to intervene. "Colonel King, what are you doing here?" he asked. When he found out what the problem was, he said that the new chief would have to make the decision.

We entered the office, and I was surprised to recognize the new chief. His name was Kadim. He had been hired when I was responsible for the police department and had been selected after Nuammy retired. I explained the situation, that Muhammad was working with me and I needed to secure his release.

He said that he understood, but Muhammad had allegedly killed an American soldier. I explained how Muhammad had stopped by that store to get a drink just as the police were embarking on their raid. He apologized, but said only Bernard Kerik, former New York City police commissioner and the senior advisor for the police, could make the decision whether or not to release Muhammad.

I phoned Kerik and explained the situation. I told him that I would take custody of Muhammad. This way I could ensure that he was under American control and I would take full responsibility for the man alleged to have killed an American. He approved the release. Throughout August and September, Muhammad and others would try to convince the former minister of defense and his family to surrender to Coalition forces. The family promised that the former minister would surrender soon, but not yet.

In August, Munkethe had approached Zumurudeh and said that one of the tribes wanted to make me an honorary sheik. The request came directly from the sheik general of the tribe. I was humbled by the proposal. It came from one of the larger tribes in the country and was quite an honor. "Yes," I said. "Of course."

On September 8, 2003, I traveled to the tribal diwan in the mid-Euphrates area to meet the tribe's family members and to be accepted into the clan. It was the largest diwan I had yet seen, and was decorated with pictures of the family's ancestors. At the far end of the diwan hung the family's flag. The family had seven branches, six predominantly Sunni and one Shi'a. The symbol for the family was a Turkish coffee pot with seven cups (one for each branch of the family).

The sheiks of the seven branches were in attendance. These esteemed family members included a former supreme court judge and others from around the country. I listened intently to the sheik's explanation of his family's history, structure, and composition, and was introduced to each family member present. Then the sheik declared that I, too, was a member. Afterward, he stated that they now had a blonde-haired, blue-eyed member of the family. Everyone laughed at the comment.

I made my way around to each individual and could see a huge feast being prepared in the next room. The introductions continued as I was led to the table to eat as one of the family. The sheik and Munkethe presented me with a white *kaffiyeh* (cloth worn over the head), a black *abbaya* (traditional robe), and an *equl* (two bands of tightly wound cord that sit atop the Kaffiyeh).

When word spread among the sheiks that I had accepted this honor, many expressed their animosity. One prominent sheik bluntly said to me, "You are like a sheik-of-sheiks in this country. Why would you accept to be identified with one specific tribe over the rest?" I never thought of it this way; I thought of myself as simply a liaison and coordinator for the sheiks. Just the same, I was humbled by the recognition, and should have been more mindful for the consideration of the others. From that day forward though, most of the sheiks that I met dropped the title of colonel and fondly referred to me as "Sheik King."

I spent a great deal of time during my command meeting with sheiks at their homes. After I relinquished command, I had to decline many of the invitations I continued to receive. I did not have a full security team, so getting individuals together to "tag along" was difficult if not impossible. Thanks to the Iraqis and a few others from the Coalition who were interested in my work, I did make my way a number of lunches and dinners.

One day while I was settling into my role as Tribal Affairs liaison, a sheik came in to tell me of a family member who had been approached by the Fedayeen. He was scared and wanted to provide information to the Coalition, but did not want to be arrested. I asked the sheik to bring the family member to me. If he was not working for the Fedayeen, I would not arrest him. The sheik was grateful and said the man would be at my office the next evening.

I called "John," an American who collected information about insurgent activities. I explained that a man was going to be in my office the next day with information about the insurgency. John agreed to come and would be bringing a translator.

When the man arrived, he came with an associate. I could tell that the Iraqi was scared. He explained that the Fedayeen had stolen his car, which had explosives and other materials inside. This of course piqued both John's and my interest. John asked, "Why did you have explosives in your car?" He stumbled around the question and tried to explain that he had been a Badr Corps arms dealer since 1996, but he didn't want to get into it. John demanded a better answer, but the guy refused. John was prepared to arrest him, so I asked John to come into the hall to discuss our next steps.

My concern over detaining the man was twofold. First, the sheik had brought him to me and I needed to explain to the sheik the reason for any detention. Second, and more importantly, I believed we could work with this man if we built up his trust over a few days. He would eventually tell us what we wanted to know, but it meant we could not detain him. John was doubtful about such a plan, but reluctantly agreed.

I told the man that he could go ahead and join the Fedayeen as long as he reported to us what they were doing. "Oh, I cannot do that," he explained. "They will require me to swear on the Qur'an and if I do that, I can never talk to you again."

I told him I understood his concerns, but argued that he could not be asked to swear on a lie. By asking him to do so, the Fedayeen would be asking him to lie and deceive God, which is forbidden. I cited the Qur'an itself to make my point. "So you can still talk to us."

While he pondered, John and I sat quietly waiting for his decision. Several minutes later he looked up and asked, "Can you get an Imam to say this is so?"

"Absolutely," I replied. "I will have three here in the morning."

"I'll do it then."

Having built a trust with this man, he would go on to help us locate several insurgents.

On September 19, I attended a lunch at Munkethe's farm. He had a tent set up alongside the Euphrates River where we feasted and enjoyed the company of some dear friends. Munkethe had a boat and we drove up and down the river. He served an exquisite Iraqi fish dish known as *masgoof,* which had been grilled over an open flame. We sat along the river, eating and enjoying a beautiful day.

The sheiks present at the lunch told me about the detention of Sheik Mit'ab Eneza. Sheik Mit'ab was the sheik general of the Eneza Tribe for the entire Middle East, and that included the royal family from Saudi Arabia. They explained that, of any sheiks the Coalition could arrest, no three put together would be as important as Sheik Mit'ab. I listened and absorbed all they were saying to me.

During the lunch we discussed many of the issues we were working on together. The sheik who was helping me secure the surrender of General Sultan said he believed that the former minister of defense would surrender soon. When I returned to the palace that evening, I received confirmation that General Sultan indeed surrendered himself to the 101st Airborne Division earlier in the day.

On September 21, I was called to Camp Victory at the airport to discuss a sensitive issue. When I arrived, I was ushered into a room filled with people I did not know and had never before seen. I was told that there was a sheik in our custody, and was asked if I knew anything about him. To my surprise, and to the disbelief of those gathered in the room, the sheik to whom they referred was Mit'ab. The sheiks I visited with at Munkethe's farm had provided more information than I could have realized at the time.

The group asked what other information I had received from the sheiks, and why I didn't pass it along earlier. I explained that I prepare a weekly report detailing the issues and concerns of the people I meet with and pass it up the chain. Most of the group appeared interested by my general assessment of the country and the information communicated to me by hundreds of sheiks. Moreover, thanks to the fortuitous lunch a few days earlier, I was able to help coordinate the release of Sheik Mit'ab on September 23.

The lower-level sheiks began to create tribal councils whose purpose was to gain access to the Coalition leadership. Their ultimate goal was to achieve some power in the political process. Most claimed to wield great influence and have far-reaching power, but in reality they had little or no influence at all. I sought to help them organize and focus their legitimate undertakings, knowing they could be a valuable resource to identify the various groups they claimed to represent.

The tribal councils were an alien concept to the historical tribal system. Mid-level and prominent sheiks would laugh about receiving a membership card to an organization they wanted no part of. Not surprisingly, these same tribal councils publicized names of members who had not joined. This was an attempt to leverage their organization's importance with the Coalition and among their peers.

On one occasion, a man came to me claiming to represent one of the top sheiks in the country. I asked him a series of questions, and found him exceedingly rude and demanding. He said that he carried the full authority of the sheik and wanted immediate attention. I knew the sheik he claimed to represent very well. In fact, we had regular lunches and were close friends. While I usually went out of my way to allow those who came to my office to maintain their dignity, in this case, the claims were so outrageous, I let the imposter continue his delusions of grandeur.

When the man was finished making his claims, I asked my translator to call the sheik and ensure I had his permission to deal with the man on his behalf. His face filled with horror, and lost all color. I asked him if it was okay to call.

"Of course," he responded. "As you like."

I wasn't sure if he thought I was bluffing, if he was too embarrassed to get up and leave, or if he was praying that the sheik did not answer the phone. In any case, the sheik did answer. He knew the man sitting with me and was livid that he had attempted to take ludicrous privileges.

By the time the phone call ended, the man in front of me was a white as a ghost. I said, "I have to respect the wishes of the sheik. I am sorry that I will not be able to do business with you." The man stood up, thanked me for my time, and left the office.

My translators were angry and chastised me for doing such an embarrassing thing to the man. "What else was I supposed to do?" I asked. Their reply was vague, but they made me promise that if I were ever in that situation again, that I simply ask the person to leave. I agreed that I would conduct things differently. Later than evening, I still felt a lingering sense of shame over belittling and humiliating the man, which was not my intention.

By November 2004, I had become recognized within the CPA as the go-between person for tribes. On December 4, Ambassador Jones created the Office of Provincial Outreach. It was a de facto political section with a very different focus than that of the Governance section in the CPA. The office included Ron Schlicher, the office's director; Ambassador Ross; and Tom Warrick, a renowned international attorney who was a politically savvy career state department employee. They were all accomplished diplomats and highly educated Arabists with unsurpassed knowledge and understanding of the Middle East.

The rest of the office included Col. Dale Shirasago, Schlicher's military assistant; Capt. Jim Rondeau, a young accomplished special operations officer who was critical to the coordination between our office and the Joint Task Force; and later, Col. Gary Cobe, who was assigned with us for the last couple months of his tour.

I was due to rotate back to the States on February 21, but was asked to extend my duty. For the office to be effective, the leadership considered it imperative to provide input to the sheiks. With the decision to extend my tour, I was selected to serve as Schlicher's deputy.

I was allowed to bring my Iraqi staff for the transfer. I could not have asked for a better group. They had been with me from the beginning and replacing them would have been impossible.

The transfer of responsibility for my work from the 352nd Civil Affairs Command to CPA would be transparent to the sheiks. Now, however, I had access to get their messages to the CPA leadership almost instantaneously. When Schlicher and Ambassador Ross first came to meet with them, the word soon spread among the sheiks that there was now an opportunity for real candor. Because Ross and Schlicher spoke fluent Arabic, the meetings went by so quickly that it was difficult for my translators to keep up. They ended up providing me with a general meeting overview as it unfolded rather than translating word for word.

Having agreed back in November to meet with a group of the local sheiks to discuss their issues and the escalating violence in the southernmost part of the country, arrangements were now being made for my travel. Discussions were underway to create a tribal affairs office in CPA and I had been tapped to fill one of the positions, so this would be a good opportunity to meet some of the regional sheiks.

My good friend Kent had transferred to Basrah and he traveled out to meet me. Kent and his team escorted me back to their office, briefed me about the area's objectives, and explained their work regarding the tribes. Their tribal expert, Martin, had compiled an extensive report. I was impressed by the work he had done and the information he had compiled.

The next day I met the British ambassador and discussed the topic for the day's meeting with the sheiks. The ambassador's obvious concern, as well as the concern of the military leaders in the region, was the increased violence, particularly the roadside bombs. He listed the six sheiks we would be meeting. It turned out that I knew the sheik general of the senior sheik who would be in attendance. The sheik general had told me if I was ever in Basrah I should pass along his greetings. I felt this would be a way to open up the discussion.

When the sheiks arrived, they were polite, but kept an unusually cold demeanor. I was accustomed to very different greetings from Iraqis with whom I had not yet established a relationship.

The sheiks were cordial, but I sensed they were not speaking openly. I said to the senior sheik that Sheik Kassim passed along his greetings. The sheik immediately sat up and became very interested. "You know Sheik Kassim?" he asked.

I said I did, adding, "I told him I was coming and he wanted me to say hello to you."

In an instant, the mood inside the meeting changed. I explained to the sheik that I was there to discuss with them their issues and concerns, which I would take back to Baghdad.

The senior sheik began to speak: "Colonel King, you said you came here to help us. What can you do that we cannot do for ourselves?"

I had not anticipated this question. I thought for a moment, then said, "Maybe nothing, but if I understand your issues, then maybe I can help you help yourselves."

The sheik looked at me intently, almost looking through me. Then he said, "You come here asking how to help. I don't think you can help. You must understand, we feel deceived by you [the Coalition]. I came here once, talked, and had tea, and six days later you arrested me. Do you think I want your help?"

I sat there for a moment, considering a response. I realized he was saying what most others were saying: that the coordination and communication between units and CPA was almost nonexistent.

Then the sheik said, "And you see this man here?" He pointed to a sheik in front of him. "He came here, had tea, and that evening you [the Coalition] raided his house. When you did not find him at home, you arrested his eighty-five-year-old father who has Alzheimer's. You destroyed his home, and then the next day you set his father free. You let his father out of prison the next morning, but he does not know who he is or where he lives. As he walked down the street a member of the tribe recognized him and took him home. What would have happened to him if he had not been picked up?"

He sat there waiting for an answer. I apologized for the misunderstanding and expressed how thankful I was that nothing had happened to the man's father.

The sheik thanked me for my concern. "Colonel King," he continued, "no one has done anything to compensate this sheik for the damage to his home. The soldiers stole his money and they left him dishonored. While I appreciate your apology, I do not control every man in my tribe. There are those who will not accept your apology and will feel driven to attack you for the honor of their family."

A British officer sitting in the meeting disputed the accusations made by the sheik concerning damage to the home and the alleged theft. The sheik assured him it was true and tried to hand him a disk that had pictures of the damage on it. When the officer refused to accept it on the third try, the man returned the disk to his pocket.

The senior sheik said, "You see, you do not want to hear the truth, and we cannot control our young men."

The meeting was effectively over and we made small talk for a few minutes, then everyone stood to leave. While I felt that the meeting was relatively well received by the sheiks, the animosity between the British and the Iraqis was painfully apparent, as it was between the Americans and the Iraqis in the north.

When I was later invited to what I believed was a small indiscreet meeting of sheiks in the Ad Diwaniyah area in the lower center area of Iraq, I was happy to accept. But when I arrived, I found more than 250 sheiks and other dignitaries from the south dressed in the flowing robes of their traditional garb.

There were two large tents like those seen in the movies. I was introduced to what seemed like an endless procession of men. Fallah and Hasan, who were serving as my security, were standing so close to me that I could barely breathe. Sheik Hussein escorted me to a large tent with tables that stretched as far as I could see and were covered with food. I was asked to stand at the head of the table where sheiks walked by filling it up to ensure that it was never empty.

After the lunch, I was escorted into the second tent where I was taken to the front and seated in the center. Along its walls were seated some of the more well-known chief sheiks from the region, who rose when I approached them. They hugged and kissed my cheeks in traditional fashion.

Sheik Hussein asked if I would be kind enough to listen to some of the concerns from the sheiks. That was fine, it is what I was expected to do. The first few sheiks were critical of the occupation, but they were polite and congenial in their remarks. About fifteen minutes after we started, a man in a business suit made his way to a few feet in front of me. Fallah was concerned at the way he approached, and I saw him and Hasan step forward to stop the man. I motioned to him that it was okay. Fallah looked at me with deep concern and then stepped back to his position.

When the man began to speak, though I could not understand Arabic, I could sense the anger and frustration in his voice. The man was speaking so fast that Faisal could not keep up. Faisal continued to ask the man to give him time to translate, but the man had appeared to have rehearsed the speech and was not about to let anyone stop him.

It quickly became apparent that this man intended to belittle me and the United States in front of the sheiks and the other dignitaries. His comments became more rude and direct as he went along, and Faisal became too embarrassed to translate some of the comments. The man started waving his finger at me as if to scold me. Sheik Hussein and a couple of others stood to subdue the man, but he flung his arms and waved his hands to keep them from taking him away.

I motioned to Sheik Hussein that it was okay, he did not need to concern himself with this, but I could see that it was becoming embarrassing for the entire group and they all wanted him to stop.

He seemed to go on for minutes without taking a breath. The other sheiks were getting increasingly frustrated. Finally, the man hesitated and I seized the opportunity. With his permission, I started into a verse from the Qur'an. That proved we were both believers, and as believers we have a duty to resolve our differences peacefully.

The man became speechless.

Out of the corner of my eye, I could see the other sheiks lean to each other and whisper among themselves, then smile, and point at me. Sheik Hussein, still standing behind the man, realized what was about to happen. He smiled at me and stepped back shaking his head in disbelief with what he knew I was about to say. He pointed to the sheiks sitting to my left, smiled, and then motioned for them to listen.

"My friend, you are a believer correct?"

The man stood motionless and speechless.

I continued, "From your comments you are a believer, yes?"

Still no words, he just nodded his head up and down.

"And you know what the message of God is to believers, yes?"

Again, he did not speak, but just shook his head up and down.

I made my way through a number of verses concerning peaceful interaction between, believers, finishing with, ". . . and you know that chapter twenty-nine, verse forty-six says, 'And dispute ye not with the people of the book.' So let us not argue with one another. Let us do as God has instructed and resolve our differences here, peacefully."

The man just kept staring at me.

I stood and shook his hand, hugged him, and then thanked everyone for coming. I turned and shook the hands of the sheiks sitting nearest me and then excused myself to leave.

The sheiks rushed me, hugged me, and grabbed hold of me to lead me out. Three sheiks grabbed Faisal. "He killed us with the words of our religion."

I knew what the sheiks were referring to. They knew that Saddam himself had encouraged the Iraqi people to learn the language of their enemy, English, so that they could think like them and anticipate their actions. In the eyes of the sheiks there that day, I had turned the tables.

I walked out towards my vehicle, with Fallah and Hasan standing on both sides of me. The senior sheik walked forward, smiling at me. "You have earned their admiration and loyalty. Tell us what you want us to do."

Sheik Hussein had arranged a police escort to the provincial border for my group. Police pickup trucks weaved back and forth and the chief of police led the way down the narrow two-lane road toward the Green Zone. I was honored by the gesture, but uncomfortable and concerned with the attention it brought us.

The images of all the sheiks kept going through my mind, as did one particular comment: "Tell us what you want us to do." I wished it was that easy.

When the Abu Ghraib story of detainee abuse broke and the graphic pictures were flashed on television sets around the globe, the Iraqis felt that it was a conspiracy to embarrass and dishonor the entire country. The sheiks and average citizens I met begged me to stop the pictures. One sheik said, "It is disgraceful, but it is done. Punish the people involved, but stop showing the pictures so it does not appear day after day that you condone it."

I was sympathetic to their requests, but tried to explain there simply was nothing I could do. This was what freedom is like. It allows people to say what they want and report the truth, which included terrible events like this.

Soon afterward, a letter came to me from an elderly man by way of his sheik. This letter provides a perspective of the deep sense of honor among the Iraqis:

MR. KING, I AM JASSIM. I AM SIXTY-EIGHT YEARS OLD. I HAVE THREE DAUGHTERS AND HAD ONE SON. I DID MY BEST AS THEY GREW UP TO PROVIDE THEM PARENTAL GUIDANCE, TO TEACH THEM RIGHT FROM WRONG AND GUIDE THEM DOWN THE CORRECT PATH. MY DAUGHTERS GREW UP TO BE FINE WOMEN, GRACIOUS MOTHERS, AND EXCELLENT WIVES, BUT I FAILED WITH MY SON. HE BECAME A THIEF, DRUNKARD, AND MURDERER. HE WOULD DRIVE STOLEN CARS HOME, PARK THEM IN FRONT OF MY HOUSE. HE WOULD COME IN WITH BLOOD ALL OVER HIS CLOTHES AND PASS OUT IN MY LIVING ROOM. THE TRIBES WERE COMING ASKING ME FOR REMUNERATION AND

DEMANDED I PAY FOR MY SON'S CRIMES. FOR THE HONOR
OF MY FAMILY AND TRIBE, I HAVE KILLED HIM. I PRAY THAT
GOD WILL FORGIVE ME AND THAT YOU WILL TOO. I
PROMISE THAT I WILL PROVIDE FOR MY SON'S WIFE AND
HIS THREE DAUGHTERS FOR THE REST OF MY LIFE. I LIVE
AT [LOCATION WITHHELD] AND AM PREPARED TO ACCEPT
WHATEVER FATE YOU DECIDE FOR ME.

I sat at my desk reading this chilling letter. The sheik sat next
to me, searching my face for a reaction.

"What is it he expects me to do?" I thought to myself.

The sheik sat quietly, allowing me to ponder the extraor-
dinary request.

"Sheik Sa'ad," I finally said, lifting my head and smiling, "this
is a civil issue, not one for me. It is one that the police will need to
deal with. As for me, I have no right to condemn this man, as
God will decide his fate on the Day of Judgment. I leave it up to
you to decide what to do for now."

He smiled back at me, let out a huge laugh, and then began
to tell me about his family. I have never taken a civilian or military
course that prepared me for this. For the moment, I could only
hope I did the right thing.

# CHAPTER 10

# No Time for Tears

*Do not stand in a place of danger trusting in miracles.*
*—Arab proverb*

The overcast sky made it an unusually gloomy day in Baghdad. It was February 21, which also happened to be my youngest son Wesley's birthday. Among other things, we were going to travel to villages outside of An Najaf to spend the day with some of the children we had met earlier in the war. My Iraqi staff and I had purchased some gifts and candy to share with the children. Since I could not be with my son today, we were planning on celebrating the day with others and make it a pleasant outing.

There was an uneasy feeling about the upcoming mission, one I had not felt before. Fallah and Hasan, my Iraqi bodyguards, were not sure where we were going, but they were trying to convince me that we should not do it today.

It was supposed to be a standard civil affairs mission to reach out to the people. We had been in the country eleven months, and I wanted to make an assessment of how the people we met early in the war now felt about the Coalition's mission.

It had been a year to the day since I had left my family. The unit I commanded during the war was returning home that day and I should have been with them but had extended my tour to continue my work with the tribes. My boss, Ron Schlicher, was returning home today as well for a visit to the States, and I would be very busy during his absence. This would be my last chance to go on a mission for a while.

Captain Guidry, who was the head of my security team during the war, was now Brig. Gen. David Blackledge's aide-de-camp. He and the general, along with a security detail, would be traveling with my security and translators today. As I prepared to give the movement and security brief, Kevin came to me and asked if I knew the sergeant major from one of the units. I said I did not. Kevin explained that he had just bumped into the sergeant major, a person he had not seen in ten years. Kevin smiled and jested that this was a bad omen. He did not say why, and I did not want to know. I am not superstitious, but I already had an uneasy feeling about the day so I told him he needed to "stop that omen shit."

Faisal was going to be my primary translator for the mission, and he too was very uneasy about the trip. We had been on countless missions and he had never asked to carry a weapon before, but today he asked if I minded him taking one along. I usually trusted my intuition, and today it told me we should postpone this mission.

The general was coming, and I did not know how to explain it to him: "Ah, general . . . sir, I have this bad feeling, so . . . well, I know you want to go on this mission, but . . . well, I don't think we should go because, well . . . I have this feeling . . . " I did not see that rationale going over well with the general.

I had taken the same route the week before and made it with no problems. I usually skimmed through the movement briefing since we had done it hundreds of times, but today for some reason, I took extra time covering all the points, including actions during ambushes, what we would do if we lost a vehicle, actions under fire, etc. We were traveling in three soft-skin (meaning without armor plating) SUVs. I would be in the lead vehicle, the general would be in the middle, and the remaining portion of his security detail would be in the trail vehicle. Fallah and Hasan always traveled in my vehicle, but since they both were familiar with the route, I asked Fallah to ride in General Blackledge's vehicle in case we were split up, "or something."

Fallah looked particularly uneasy about this arrangement. He and Hasan were very close, and Fallah took his job very seriously. Both Fallah and Hasan had been special forces soldiers in the Iraqi Army and they were highly concerned about my safety. I could tell that Fallah wanted to stay in my vehicle, but I needed him in the vehicle with the general just the same.

Hasan drove a white Toyota Land Cruiser and he kept it immaculate, inside and out. He was an expert driver who could move quickly on a road that was six feet one inch wide with a vehicle that was six feet wide. He was an amazing driver, and one I knew would give his life to protect me.

Zumurudeh had been needling me for months to go on one of the missions and I finally gave in to her wishes. But I told her that if we were fired upon, she had better do as I say and not question me. I told her firmly, "I will throw you into the floorboard or on the ground and you had better stay there, because I will be busy and will not have time to argue with you."

She smiled gently and agreed.

I looked at her and sternly reiterated, "I am serious now. If something happens, you better do as I tell you!"

She shrugged her shoulders, smiled at me again, and replied in her usual way, "Yeah, sure, sure . . . okay." Then she left to prepare.

When Zumurudeh returned, she had on a pair of pants and a ladies jacket over a blouse. I had asked her to wear an *abbayah* (traditional Arab dress for ladies) and a *hijab* (traditional Arab scarf worn on over the head) for the visit to the villages. I asked her again to put them on.

"But why?" she asked. "I will put it on before we get there."

I still had a nagging feeling about the day and said, "Just put it on, please."

She finally complied. She sat where I normally sat on missions, the backseat on the passenger's side. Today, for some reason, I sat on the driver's side in the backseat. Faisal was in the passenger's seat, a position usually reserved for Fallah. Everything seemed a little off today.

We started movement thirty minutes later than I had planned, which added to my irritation. We did not usually have communications except for some commercial handheld walkie-talkies, but today the general's security had given me a headset and radio. Finally, we started making our way through the laborious maze of barriers inside the Green Zone palace area. We reached the outer security checkpoint and were on our way.

On our way out of Baghdad, cars jammed like an overflowing sardine can. Somehow, Hasan maneuvered through the city with ease. When we reached the marketplace in the town of Mumadiyah, traffic came to a complete stop. I felt like a fish looking out at the curious onlookers. We continued to inch our way through the city.

I think that we were all a little uneasy in the marketplace, but the traffic finally broke up and we were on a four-lane road driving south toward the town of Al Iskandariyah.

Then it happened. Approximately five kilometers from the city, I heard the burst of gunfire. Out of the corner of my right eye, I could see the tracer rounds whizzing past our vehicle. I knew immediately that we had triggered an ambush. I grabbed Zumurudeh's head and yelled, "Get down!" I threw her into the floorboard as a tracer came so close to my eye that for a split second I could feel the heat against my face.

A tracer round ignited Zumurudeh's clothes and then hit something that caused it to ricochet. I patted out the fire while a cacophony of gunfire continued all around us. When I looked over, I noticed a tracer had landed in the backseat. It had set some papers on fire and was burning through the material. "Damn," I thought, "my hand is going to be burned to a crisp!" But I scooped at the tracer and brushed it away. I looked down at Zumurudeh, "Are you okay?"

"Yes, yes," she replied, in a calm but direct voice. "Stay down."

Faisal and Hasan were focused straight ahead, neither looked injured. I asked them how they were doing. Without turning around, Faisal answered that he was okay. Hassan said nothing, so I assumed he was fine. We were still moving.

By now we were traveling at about 85 to 90 miles an hour, but we were not outrunning the bullets. I jumped up into the back seat and looked out of the back window. The tracers were flying by and they just kept coming. The rear passenger window had bullet holes in it at head level.

I could not believe that Zumurudeh or Faisal had not been hit. The tracers zooming looked like lasers out of *Star Wars*. Since there is usually one tracer for every four or five regular rounds, there must have been multiple shooters, or the guy was burning the barrel of his rifle. The way the bullets kept coming, the shooters must have been in a vehicle behind us, but I could not see them. The trail vehicle was engulfed in flames and my view was blocked by the flames and the billowing black smoke.

I radioed to Captain Edwards, driver of the third vehicle, "You are on fire, get out, get out!"

The rear wheels of the general's vehicle were shot out causing it to fishtail, hit the median, and then cartwheel, front over back, across the road.

"Stop," I yelled to Hasan, "turn around!" I wondered how many were dead. Hasan crossed over the median and stopped about one hundred yards from the crashed vehicle.

I got out and told Hasan and Faisal, who both carried weapons, to watch to the south and not let anyone come up on us. I told Zumurudeh to get out and get behind a small berm that was alongside the road. I ran back to the crash site. Hearing shots but not seeing any tracers, I passed the trail vehicle, which had come to rest halfway between my vehicle and the general's. In straining to see through the flames, I could not see any silhouettes or signs of life. I hoped that everyone got out.

Making my way to the general's vehicle, I crossed paths with Maj. Bill Layer. "Did everyone get out of the third vehicle," I asked?

"Yes," he replied. "Thank God."

I had insisted that half of my battalion become trained combat lifesavers before the war and had myself received training for treating combat wounds back in the United States. You hope you never have to use such training, but you have to be prepared.

I finally came upon the general's vehicle. A few cars stopped about three hundred yards to our north. A crowd seemed to be creeping toward us, so I fired two shots off to let them know not to come closer. I took hold of one of the general's security team and told him to do the same. One fired into a vacant field to the west.

It did not look good. Captain Smathers was sitting in the back seat with Fallah lying face down on his lap. I realized I had left my medical bag in the back of the vehicle. Then Smathers said to me, "Sir, I think he's dead."

I could see the bullet wound in the back of his head. I took Fallah's pulse. Nothing. I could hear the decompression of his lungs, and felt again for his pulse. No use; he was dead. I asked John how he was doing and he replied, "Fallah fell on my arm and I think it is broken. I am not sure about my legs."

I performed triage on the others with various injuries, evaluating which ones needed immediate attention. Faisal came up and asked me if there was anything he could do to help. "Go get . . . " I was having a hard time thinking, my mind racing a million miles a minute. "Uh, Faisal, go get my medical bag in the back of the vehicle." Faisal ran off towards Hasan.

I saw General Blackledge and asked him how he was doing. He said that his back was hurt (compressed vertebrates, as he would later find out) but he could walk. Guidry came to me and said that one soldier had some burns on his face. He had some glass in his arm and face, but he said that no one else had immediate life-threatening injuries; that is, except for Fallah, who could not be helped.

We had lost two of our three vehicles and so my priority turned to getting the team out of there safely. There was still sporadic fire, but I was not sure at this point if it was our team or the insurgents doing the shooting. I looked around and noticed a house with cars in front just a short distance from the crash site. It appeared to be a used car lot. In my movement briefing that morning I had told everyone, "If we lose a vehicle, we commandeer one and get the hell out of the area." It was now time to act.

I walked up to the lot and was met by a man in tattered clothes wearing a very thick tan coat that looked like those of the Bedouin I had seen in the desert. He was surrounded by a group of men that spread out to my right. A few, including a very large man, stayed behind him. I said to the man in the Bedouin coat, "I need this car," and pointed to a white sedan. Though I do not remember anyone speaking, someone must have translated, because there was a pause and then he replied, "*Lesh?*" I knew this as the Arabic word for "why."

"What do you mean, why? Look at those two vehicles. I need to get out of here, and I need this vehicle, now!"

A man at the lot translated. "He said he does not have the keys."

I was furious. I did not have time for nonsense and was literally on the verge of killing someone. Just then I noticed three men running in the field behind the house. One appeared to have a rifle. I fired my pistol twice and yelled over for one of the other soldiers with a rifle to shoot them. I felt that the man in front of me was stalling so the others could have time to set up another ambush.

Suddenly, everything seemed to close in on me. My senses became overwhelmingly strong and focused. It seemed as if I could feel and hear everything around me, and I felt as if the people standing near were starting to close in. Every sound was almost deafening, it was as if I could hear the heartbeat and breath of every person there.

My instinct was to break the window out of the car to startle them, but the hammer was back on my pistol and I was certain it would fire off a round. I could see the contempt in the man's eyes, the absolute defiance. At that moment, defiance was about to meet determination, and I was determined to leave even if I had to kill him. It became obvious he was not going to give in.

Not having time to negotiate, I began to speak in a very low voice that progressively got louder. "You have one more chance, and then your friend gets a turn. Find the damn keys!"

I counted in my mind the number of bullets I had left in my pistol. I had started with fourteen, had fired off four shots—ten. I had ten rounds. I could get a couple of them before they took me down. If they rushed me, I would shoot the big guy. He and I stared straight at each other, reading each other's thoughts. I lifted my pistol to place it against the man's head. In the heat of the moment, I was prepared to make a hasty decision that I could not turn back. My finger was on the trigger, and I tensed up in preparation for the recoil.

Before I could shoot, a voice from behind me shrieked, "I will take you!"

I looked over my shoulder and said, "Get in the car, let's go."

Someone asked me as we walked away, "Were you really going to kill him?"

"You're damn right I was," I admitted. At the time I could not believe the man would have rather died than help me.

I walked back to the crash site and Hasan had already brought my vehicle back. The man from the car lot had driven his car around and everyone was loading up. Guidry was helping Smathers to the rear vehicle and I saw Smathers's legs collapse. Another soldier ran to assist. I went to the general and asked him if he could walk. He said yes. I asked him to get into the passenger seat of my vehicle.

Then I looked and saw Fallah, still lying in the back seat of the general's vehicle. His rifle dangled from his body. I ran over and leaned to grab it while still in stride, but my body jerked back and I felt my right shoulder pop.

Fallah had put the sling of the rifle through a d-ring on the front of his vest. Faisal came over to help me loosen the sling and pull Fallah from the vehicle.

"Sir, what is one more AK in this country?" Guidry yelled. "Come on, we need to go."

I snapped, "Not this one!" I kept pulling, but it was futile.

Someone yelled, "Come on, we've got to go!"

"We need to get Fallah," I replied.

"We can't," came the response. "There isn't room."

I looked back and sure enough, we had crammed thirteen people into two vehicles. I attempted to sterilize the general's vehicle, grabbing his bag and everything I could see.

I looked at Faisal and told him to go back over to the car lot and deliver a message for me. "Tell [the man in the Bedouin coat] I am coming back for my friend. If he is not here when I return, I will personally come back for *him*!"

I bent down, touched Fallah's shoulder, and said a short prayer for him. I thought, "We should take you with us. I am sorry, please forgive me."

I could hear the secondary explosions coming from the burning trail vehicle from the ammunition that had been inside. There was no time for tears now. I knew that we had to get the general and the rest of the team out of there.

Faisal returned from the car lot and informed me that the man appeared extremely frightened by the message. I wasn't sure if Faisal was simply trying to placate me, but I thanked him anyway and said, "Come on, let's go."

We ran back to the vehicles, and I got in the back seat on the passenger side. I directed Hasan to head south. In his grief he did not seem to comprehend what I was saying. Fallah's death had really shaken him; the two were like brothers.

"Hasan," I yelled, but could not get him to compose himself.

Zumurudeh spoke sternly to Hasan in Arabic. Hasan turned and looked at her, then me, then back around. Having regained his composure, he started to drive.

I asked Zumurudeh what she had said. "I told him this is not the time for crying," she replied. "When we get back, we will all cry together. He is the only one that knows where we need to go, if he does not do it now, we will all die."

We drove about five kilometers and saw a police station. There had been a Polish checkpoint here the last time we came through. I told Hasan to pull into the police station. He and Zumurudeh were talking to the police officers and making no headway. The police wanted us to leave immediately. I had opened my door to get the attention of one of the officers.

Zumurudeh said, "They cannot help us. They said that the nearest base is twenty-five kilometers southwest of where we are." That meant that we had to drive through Al Musayyib, a small town known to be a safe haven for the insurgents from Mahdi's Army.

No choice. "Let's go, Hasan," I directed.

Hasan made his way towards Al Musayyib. The image of Fallah was stuck in my mind. We should have taken him with us. I should have put him in the trunk or something, but we should not have left him. I would not have left anyone else.

I tried to reach my office on my satellite phone, but kept losing the connection. When we reached Al Musayyib, the traffic became congested. General Blackledge asked me, "Alan, how much longer?"

"Not too much further," I replied. "On the other side of this town." We inched through the market area when what sounded like a loud shot startled everyone in the vehicle. I turned around to see the car in the opposite lane had backfired. It took a lot of discipline for our soldiers to not open fire right away. I kept trying to reach the office on the satellite phone, still to no avail.

We finally made it out of the town and came up to a Polish checkpoint. Guidry rolled down his window and tried to explain that we needed an immediate medevac. The guards did not understand English. A Polish colonel came up and he too could not speak English. Guidry rattled off some Russian. The colonel gave a look of recognition and the two began conversing. I had no idea Guidry could speak Russian. This showed the advantage of learning to speak a second language. The colonel walked to his vehicle, and I directed Hasan to an area off the road.

Smathers had the most serious injuries, so I told the general, who was in relatively good condition, that I was going to take care of Smathers first. From my combat life-saver bag I grabbed what I needed to begin to splint Smathers's arm. Before I could finish the job I ran out of splints. I noticed some two-by-fours in the back of one of the Polish soldiers' trucks, so I asked them if they could spare a few. They obliged. We moved Smathers into the back of one of the Polish vehicles so he could lie down.

Meanwhile, I tried again to reach the office by satellite phone. First I tried Colonel Sharisago, but the number was busy. I tried a couple others, and kept getting the same message: "User is unavailable." It was no use. Finally, I tried Ben Hatch, who was supposed to be providing movement security for our boss that day.

I heard through the earpiece, "Hello?"

"Ben, it is me . . . "

"Hello?" he said again, drowning out my words. The confusion was a result of the typical delay you get with satellite phones.

"Ben, it's me, Colonel King!"

"Hey sir, what's up?"

"Ben, I am on a [satellite] phone, so there is a delay. We have been ambushed and—"

"Are you okay?" He had cut me off again.

"Damn it! Yes, just listen to me. I have been trying to contact Colonel Sharisago and cannot get through."

"He is just around the corner, I will get him."

"No," I blurted out. "Listen to me I don't want to lose the signal." I tried to calm my voice, "Ben . . . just listen. I will call you all when I get to our next location. I need you to report that my team was ambushed, we have one Iraqi KIA and two Americans WIA—"

The general heard the conversation and corrected me: "Four WIA."

"Ben, four WIA, and one is a VIP. Do you copy?" I asked.

After Ben correctly repeated what I had said, I told him I needed to go, and that I would call Colonel Sharisago when I got to our next location.

Returning to my work, I found an individual by the name of Master Sergeant Blosser with burns covering his face. He had been sitting in the rear of the burning vehicle. One of the medics had gone through my bag a few weeks before to restock it, and they must have taken out the burn pads. I told Sergeant Blosser I was sorry, I did not have anything for his burns, and what I did have in my bag would do little else than worsen the pain.

Guidry came over to me and said that there was a medevac on its way for us. He said he was doing fine, despite small glass fragments in his arm and face. I decided it was better not to touch them and push them in farther.

I went back and checked up on the general. He said that his back was hurting, but he would be okay for now. I had just begun to look around for orange air panels to lay out for the helicopter to find us when the telltale *whoop-whoop* sound from overhead indicated they wouldn't be necessary.

Hasan wanted to return by himself to check on Fallah. I was hesitant, but gave him permission. Then I went over to the Iraqi man who had driven us, handed him a hundred dollars and said, "*Shukran gezeelen,*" which means "thank you" in Arabic.

He pushed my hand back and said, "*La, la* [no, no]."

I insisted, pushed the money into his hand, then reached into his car and cleaned up the wrapping from the bandages. I shook his hand, thanked him again, and then headed off to the waiting helicopter.

There were plenty of onlookers as we arrived at the Polish hospital and it was apparent that the post knew what was going on. I told Faisal and Zumurudeh to wait for me at the hospital and went to look for the American liaison.

I found a helpful lieutenant and explained to her that I needed to send a classified message immediately. I asked her if her unit had any classified communications. She said they had a computer that was classified and led me to her unit's office. She introduced me to a staff sergeant, who logged onto the computer for me. The air-conditioned room felt wonderful after what had transpired.

I could feel the adrenaline leaving me after many hours of intense focus. My thoughts drifted back to when I was a cadet at my officer summer camp. I had been the platoon leader for that day's training and was exhausted by the end of it. When we loaded up into the truck to return to the barracks, I laid my head back and fell asleep. During my after-action critique, the training officer told me that as long as you are the leader, it is never over. You don't sleep until your troops do.

And this day was certainly not over yet. By the time the computer's desktop finally came up, I had caught my second wind. I drafted and sent the message, then returned to check on the others.

Everyone was sitting outside the medical tent except for the general and Smathers. Guidry explained to me that Smathers was being prepped for surgery and the general was going to be medevac'd. I asked if everyone had made it to the mess hall and then went in to see the general. The general and I spoke for a while and I returned to see if Guidry knew where Smathers was. He pointed towards a building and said that he would go with me.

Smathers was lying in a bed being prepped for surgery. The Polish nurse was very polite and joked with us. Smathers smiled. We talked for a while about Fallah, the accident, and the others. Then Guidry and I left to let him get some rest.

I contacted Colonel Shirasago on the satellite phone and updated him on the status. He said that ambassadors Jerry Bremer, Richard Jones, Ron Schlicher, and the Joint Operations Center in task force headquarters had been notified. I said that I was going to try to catch the medevac back with the general and that I needed to locate Fallah.

A Blackhawk had just arrived to transport the general. Guidry ran out to ask its crew chief if I could fly with the two Iraqis, while Faisal, Zumurudeh, and I waited for the response. He explained that we needed to get back to help locate Fallah. The crew chief said they could accommodate us, and Guidry motioned for Faisal, Zumurudeh, and me to get on board.

During the flight, I played the events over and over in my head, furious at the cowards who were responsible and wanting to find out who they were. I was hopeful that the tribes would come through like they had when they helped us locate those who murdered Mark Bibby and Omar. After landing at the Ibn Sina Hospital inside the Green Zone, I handed the crew chief four of my unit's coins to thank his pilots and team, and we disembarked.

There was an entourage to meet the general at the hospital. Colonel Shirasago and Captain Rondeau were at the door to meet me. For the first time that day, I felt a sense of comfort seeing Colonel Shirasago. He is one of the finest officers with whom I have had the opportunity to work during my career, a professional with a strong sense of duty. Fearless, yet compassionate, this night he would exhibit both those traits in spades.

We were told that Hasan had made it back and was up at the headquarters building. I wanted to see him, but I checked on the general first. He seemed to be comfortable and dealing with the pain. He thanked me for everything, after which I excused myself so that I could go see Hasan and look for Fallah.

When I arrived at the headquarters building, Hasan was standing next to his vehicle. I walked up to him and we hugged. He started to cry, and I could barely contain my own tears. He explained that an American army unit had come to the scene minutes after we left. The unit had taken Fallah.

Before I could say anything, Colonel Shirasago was on the phone to the emergency operations center (EOC), trying to locate the unit that had Fallah. I walked alone to the water fountain in front of the headquarters building, where I lost my composure. Hours before, Fallah and I had stood in front of the same building, and now he was gone. What was worse was that I had broken a cardinal rule of war and had left a friend behind. Tears flowed uncontrollably down my face.

Colonel Shirasago came up to me after finishing his call to the EOC, put his arm on my shoulder, and said that the 82nd Airborne Division had picked up Fallah. He was on his way to the Combat Army Surgical Hospital. He could tell that I was hurting deep inside and he found the words to reassure me: I had done all I could do.

Still, I could not help feeling guilty for leaving Fallah. I regained some of my composure and went back up to tell Hasan what Colonel Shirasago had told me. Guidry had just come up with the rest of the group.

Guidry and I went next to the vehicle. "Kevin," I said, "we should not have left Fallah."

"I know sir, but there was nothing we could do," he replied. "There just wasn't any room."

"I know, but if it had been you, John [Smathers], or me, we would have found room. Fallah gave his life for us. We should have found room for him, too."

Guidry looked at me and said, "You're right, point taken."

Colonel Sharisago was back on the phone trying to find out Fallah's time of arrival. He hung up and said that the captain in the EOC said that Fallah was at Ibn Sina Hospital.

I told Zumurudeh to go on home and she asked if she could talk to me for a second. "Will you tell me something?" she asked, staring at me intently.

"Sure, what do you want to know?"

"Did you know this was going to happen today?" she said. I looked at her dumbfounded. "What do you mean?"

"Well, I have seen you get ready for hundreds of missions, but you were different today, allowing Faisal to carry a weapon, asking me to wear the abbayah. I don't know, it was just different. It is as if you knew something bad was going to happen today."

"I don't know, yeah, I guess I had a feeling, it was weird," I stammered. "No, no . . . you are right. Yes, I felt it was going to happen. Now you need to go on home and rest," I told her. "If you don't want to come in tomorrow, I understand."

"No," she said. "I will be here tomorrow. You be careful tonight." She smiled and pointed her finger at me in a scolding manner. Then she stopped and stepped forward, remembering something. "Oh, yeah—and thank you for saving my life today." She smiled again, turned, and walked out the door.

Hasan and Faisal stayed to escort Fallah's body to his family. In Islam, the body must be buried within twenty-four hours, and I was determined to make sure this happened.

When we arrived at the hospital, I explained to them the religious significance of returning Fallah's body to his family right away. They had no idea what we were talking about. I was beginning to boil, feeling jerked around by someone else's ignorance.

Thank God for Colonel Shirasago, who made some calls. He found out that Fallah had been taken to the morgue out at the airport. We both knew that to run the gauntlet in SUVs to the airport at night was tantamount to suicide. The colonel looked at me and said, "I will go with you." Captain Rondeau said he would go too.

I thanked them both and said, "Let me get Hasan and Faisal."

Colonel Shirasago said that he would ask the security team if we could borrow one of their vehicles. While he was on the phone to his security team, I explained the situation to Hasan and Faisal. They looked at me in disbelief; they did not want to drive the gauntlet, either.

This outpouring of support was overwhelming. Colonel Shirasago found out that Ben and his team—Kurt Playle, Craig Hotaling, and Chris Garon—would ride along and provide security, along with himself and Jim Rondeau. I began to get choked up. Ben and his team were due to rotate out of country within days and this was not exactly a drive through the Green Zone.

I didn't want them to get hurt, but their concern for Fallah and for me was a great comfort. They were boldly breaking a tenet of war that says bad things tend to happen on your last days in the combat zone. Most men would never chance it. Hell, I was supposed to be going home that day, and was still asking myself why I extended.

I hadn't eaten anything all day. Just as the hunger pangs were at there worst, Colonel Shirasago came up with enough dinner plates for everyone. One of the members of the security team described the scene of the colonel trying to battle the dining facility staff to get the food. "The colonel was running down the hall [of the palace] with all his gear and was yelling at the dining facility staff that he needed the food and didn't have time to work through the administrative crap to get approval."

The group that was gathered at the vehicles began to laugh—the first time I remember smiling all day. We could see Colonel Shirasago right up in their faces. The colonel was a make-it-happen type of officer, rare in today's military. He didn't put up with bureaucratic bullshit when it came to caring for the soldiers. This is what I loved so much about him.

There was no small talk; in fact, there was no sound at all other than the sound of us shoveling food from the dinner plates into our mouths. Colonel Shirasago later compared it to the Last Supper, a good summation of the general mood that night. After finishing our plates, we loaded up and headed to the airport.

The road was almost deserted on the way to the airport, with only an occasional car. Our convoy of bright SUVs stood out like one huge neon sign in the blacked-out city. Thankfully, we made it to the airport, and then maneuvered through the checkpoint. We asked a number of officers for directions to the morgue. Colonel Shirasago eventually found an officer who escorted us through the maze of barriers, turn after grueling turn, until we finally made to the morgue. Not wanting to break down in front of everyone, I took a deep breath, and entered the morgue to go identify my friend.

Inside, two soldiers passed the time playing cards. It all felt disconnected from reality. This would not be the first time I had to identify a friend's body during this tour, but it was always a dreadful task, perhaps more so this time.

"Hey guys," I said to the soldiers. "We are here to pickup the Iraqi that was brought in by the eighty-second."

"Sure," one replied, "we have been waiting for you." The other one said that he would take me in to identify Fallah, but then we would have to wait around until a medical officer arrived to sign the death certificate. The soldier took me into the room where Fallah's body lay double bagged. He had told me to expect this; there had been a lot of blood.

I put on a pair of latex gloves, and the soldier pulled back the zipper. There he was, my fallen friend, lifeless in a pool of blood. I identified him, and the soldier handed me a small bag with Fallah's belongings. I thanked him, and then he excused himself, leaving me alone with my friend for a few quiet minutes.

When I came out, Colonel Shirasago, Ben Hatch, Hasan, and Faisal were standing there. Hasan went in to see Fallah. The rest of us tried to make small talk while we were waiting for the doctor. About thirty minutes later, a doctor finally arrived to sign the death certificate, officially declaring what we knew hours before—Fallah was dead.

Hasan had laid the seat down in his Land Cruiser and we loaded Fallah into it for his final ride home. The rest of the crew loaded up into the other vehicle. We agreed that Hasan would stay with us until we reached the cutoff for the Green Zone, then they would peel off and take Fallah home.

I was exhausted by the time I arrived at my apartment that night. I moved slowly, almost unsure of myself. I took a long hot shower, washing Fallah's blood from my arm and recalling the events of the day. My shoulder was stiff and becoming difficult to move. I looked at my hand, remembering the flames and the heat against my skin, but there were no burns. Did I put that fire out, or had I only imagined it? I wrote it off as divine intervention, and to this day haven't come up with a better explanation.

I crawled into bed, thanking God for sparing my life, and that my son did not have to experience his father's death on his birthday. I asked Him to watch over Fallah and protect his soul. I thanked Him for the friends that I had made here, Colonel Shirasago, Ben, Hasan, Faisal, and the others who had been willing to risk their lives for friendship. These selfless and dedicated men put the experience of war into perspective that night. It was something that cannot be understood by those who have never had to depend on another for their life. I would always feel grateful and indebted to them.

The hardest part was not over though; I still had to face Fallah's three sons, the youngest only 10, and explain how brave their father was, and why he died. Tears welled in my eyes, and I drifted into a deep sleep with that thought weighing heavily on my mind. Thank God, I thought. Tomorrow is another day.

I awoke the next morning, still sore, still thankful to be alive. I found it difficult to lift my arm, but managed to get dressed and went into the office. My entire Iraqi staff came into work, and my office was inundated with both American and Iraqi visitors paying their respects. I set to work planning Fallah's memorial service.

Just before lunch, Zumurudeh came to me with some surprising news. A sheik had called from the area where we had been ambushed and provided the name of the gunmen's tribe. I immediately called the tribe's sheik, who assured me that he would look into it. The following day, I received the names of two of the suspected gunmen from the tribe. I never learned what happened to them, but was grateful for the information just the same.

# CHAPTER 11

# The Intifada

*Put a turban on a scorpion and he is still a scorpion.*
*—Iraqi proverb*

Toward the end of the summer 2003, I began to sense an under-current of resentment and defiance that started to percolate like coffee over an open flame. In my conversations with the sheiks, they warned that the tempers of the Iraqis were about to explode. By the end of March 2004, the resentment and defiance had reached its boiling point and the entire country seemed to come apart and erupt into total mayhem.

Through the months of February and March, complaints from moderate Iraqis turned into direct threats of unrest; and Iraqis who had defied the Coalition from the beginning began to be more violent and deadly. Muktada Al-Sadr in the south and the Sunnis in the west were secretly making alliances for an advancing confrontation.

March 31, 2004, was the flash point with the brutal murders of four American contractors in Fallujah. The crowd dragged their bodies through the streets and then hanged two corpses off of a bridge. That same day, thousands of Sadr's followers demonstrated in front of the entrance to the Green Zone. The gathered crowd chanted, "Just give the word Muktada, and we'll continue the 1920 revolution."

On April 3, Mustafa Yacoubi, Sadr's deputy, was arrested on a warrant for his involvement in the murder of a moderate Shiite cleric, Abdul Majid al-Khoei, outside the Imam Ali shrine in An Najaf on April 10, 2003. Sadr's followers immediately rebelled and reports began to come in from all over the south that CPA and Coalition offices were being stormed.

Sadr City in eastern Baghdad ignited. The 1st Armored Division surrounded the Baghdad neighborhood and marines cordoned off the city of Fallujah. The Office of Provincial Outreach (OPO) was staffed with some of the most knowledgeable and professional Arabists in the State Department. They were charged to look for political solutions to this extremely volatile situation.

OPO divided responsibility between Ambassador Ross (assisted by Jim Rondeau), who focused on the south and the issues concerning Muktada Al-Sadr. Schlicher assumed responsibility for Fallujah. Tom Warrick and I were tasked to work our contacts throughout the country and identify individuals who could assist or advise on possible solutions.

Everyone in Iraq was focused on the immediate situation. Reconstruction became a distant secondary concern as security and stability became the only topic for briefings. A friend from a local unit approached me and asked that I meet with some sheiks concerning the violence. Apparently the senior sheik had asked to meet with me and the unit believed these sheiks were influential and had information that would help provide insight. I agreed, although it required us to travel inconspicuously through the city at night with no security. By the sheik's insistence, the meeting had to be covert so that he and his family were not exposed as collaborators.

The uprising in eastern Baghdad and western and southern Iraq continued to rage. A translator, driver, and I loaded into an armored sedan and left the Green Zone to meet with a sheik for the first of several meetings. I had driven this route many times, but usually with a significant security force.

The streets were so much different at night than during the day. There was no hustling and bustling of the daily grind. It was more like a ghost town than a sprawling metropolitan city. The only signs of life were an occasional car or men sitting in front of their homes to avoid the heat due to the lack of electricity. We drove along our route, wondering if people realized we were Americans, and if they would be hostile towards us if they knew.

When we drove up to the ten-foot gate, we flashed our lights and the large metal door slid back. With the curtains drawn in the back of my vehicle, I could not see out the sides as we drove into the driveway. Before my door opened, I heard the squeak of the gate rolling shut. I wondered what was waiting for me. When my door was opened by one of the sheiks, I stepped out onto an immaculately landscaped yard. It was one of the most amazing yards I had seen. The sheik greeted me with the traditional hug and a kiss on both cheeks. He and I walked through the yard with his other guests into his large and spacious home.

I was invited to sit on the couch in his diwan and we made small talk about the weather and other meaningless issues. I mentioned to him the name of a prominent sheik who had asked me to meet with him a month before. My host knew the sheik well and it appeared to give me instant credibility. As the conversation lingered on, it slowly drifted toward a discussion on Fallujah. The sheik explained that the Shi'as in the south had sent fighters to Fallujah to train for their battle and support their cousins.

I said that this seemed strange to me because of the ideological differences between the two. My assessment was that Sadr wanted to establish an independent Islamic government, which would anger the Sunnis. I believed that if the Coalition left Iraq, a civil war was inevitable between the two religious sects.

He smiled at me, sat motionlessly in his chair smoking a cigarette, then spoke softly and slowly, "My dear friend, you of all people should know the Arab proverb, 'My brother and me against my cousin, my cousin and me against a stranger.' The Sunnis will fight the Shi'a later. For now the enemy of my enemy is my friend, and for both of them, you are the enemy."

I shook my head in disbelief. I had heard that members of Sadr's inner circle had traveled to Fallujah just before the murders of the American contractors, but I did not realize that it was to form an alliance for an intifada.

As the first anniversary of the fall of Saddam's regime on April 9 approached, rumors were widespread about impending attacks against the Coalition. On that day, Ambassador Jones had planned to travel by helicopter to southern Iraq to meet with Sayyid Farqad al-Qizwini, a prominent cleric in Hilla, and a group of sheiks from An Najaf to discuss deteriorating security conditions. Since the meeting was supposed to include the sheiks from the south, Schlicher asked me to travel with the ambassador.

I readied myself that morning, and could not help but think what the city had been like a year before. The chaos created by the fall of the regime was mixed with the exhilaration of the people as they celebrated the arrival of the American forces into Baghdad. So much had changed since then; I was frustrated by the likes of Sadr and his erratic and unlawful actions. Sadr had set up an illegal Sharia court in An Najaf and his militia was actively detaining individuals who were forced to appear in front of the court and then were unlawfully held captive by Sadr.

Mahdi's Army, formed by Sadr, wore a distinctive black outfit. When they descended on Baghdad, they immediately began setting up unlawful checkpoints, turning women away from the university for not wearing the hijab over their head, and there were reports that they had killed several professors.

The militia was comprised of predominantly unemployed, easily influenced young men. Most were uneducated and Sadr gave them a purpose for existence. Several sheiks from the south had reported that Sadr's militia was openly training in areas west of An Najaf and there was evidence that they were receiving support and financing from Iranian agents. They explained that Sadr had established weapons distribution points in the areas of Sheik Sa'ad near Kut and Al-Hai Town near Nasiriyah over a month ago. For the sheiks, there was no doubt that Sadr was preparing for a showdown with the Coalition.

I arrived at the CPA headquarters to accompany Ambassador Jones to Hilla for our meeting with the sheiks. We were then to fly over to An Najaf to meet with the provincial governor. After we arrived at the helipad, Ambassador Jones smiled and asked, "Alan, do you have any relatives who have a birthday today?"

I looked at him, smiled and said, "No."

Laughing, he said, "Are you sure? I mean, down to third cousins?"

I assured him I did not as the helicopters made their approach. After my last ambush, it had become the joke in the office not to allow me out on any of my relatives' birthdays.

Until then, I had not thought about the incidents from the past, but as we loaded up on the helicopters, a thought came to me: on the anniversary of Saddam's fall, the country was in utter disarray.

I looked out the window, observing hundreds of pilgrims making their way towards the An Najaf. We arrived about thirty minutes before the sheiks. Ambassador Jones received an overview about the expected discussion points, who would be in attendance, and what expectations we should anticipate from the attendees.

When the men filed into the room, I realized I had met several of them. I immediately recognized al-Qizwini's deputy, who entered with one of the sheiks. Al-Qizwini's deputy came over and hugged me and then introduced me to the sayyid. The meeting was informational, but we left without any specific plan of action.

From Hilla, we flew to An Najaf, where we met with the governor. Our discussion was focused on how to resolve the Sadr issue. An Najaf is divided into quarters between three primary tribes, one having two divisions in the city. The sheiks wanted a solution, but they did not want to act without the Coalition's approval for fear that they would be considered hostile too. We discussed several possible alternatives and then departed for Baghdad.

When I returned from An Najaf, we were told that Ambassador Bremer had ordered a unilateral ceasefire in Fallujah to explore political options, allow for medical supplies and food to be delivered, and to give the people of the city a chance to bury their dead. Two days later, the insurgents agreed to the ceasefire, but skirmishes between the marines and insurgents continued in several parts of the city.

That same evening, I was called by an Iraqi friend who informed me that Harith al-Dari, the head of the Association of Muslim Scholars, had called for everyone to fight the Americans, and that the occupiers were now legitimate targets. He instructed the Iraqis during the day's prayers to kill Americans at every opportunity. I had met with Harith in February and found him to be a shrewd and learned man who was well informed about current affairs and international events, but he had his own rigid view of the events in Iraq.

The next day, an Iraqi told me I should meet with Harith as soon as possible because he was promoting a course of action that would lead hundreds of Iraqis to their death. I explained the time for talk was over; if the upcoming Friday's prayers were as inflammatory as the previous week's, there would be no future opportunities for talk with Harith or anyone else from his association.

On April 13, Ron Schlicher informed me that members of the governing council had assembled a group of Iraqis from Fallujah to discuss options for resolving the standoff in the city. Apparently, Sheik Gozi al-Shammeri, in partnership with other Sunni leaders from the governing council, had coordinated for the Fallujans to travel to the palace in the Green Zone to speak to representatives from the Coalition.

By now, some members of the governing council were publicly criticizing the Coalition and several threatened to resign. Ambassador Bremer had directed Ambassador Jones to put together a delegation to open a dialogue with the group. Ambassador Jones headed the delegation, and the others included Ambassador Ron Neumann, Ron

Schlicher, Tom Warrick, and Maj. Gen. Joseph Webber—a marine and the deputy commander of the joint task force—were designated to represent the CJTF-7. To my surprise, Schlicher asked that I sit as a member of the delegation, too.

When the group from Fallujah arrived, of the eight who showed up, I realized I had met four of them at the end of 2003. The team included a doctor from the hospital and a former commander of one of the Iraqi Civil Defense Corps (ICDC) battalions. Because they arrived late, we all took our seats without comment and introduced ourselves from the table.

After Ambassador Jones introduced me, the four men I had met looked at me, raised their eyebrows in unison, and nodded as if to say, "We told you so!" They had warned me that Fallujah was a powder keg about to explode, and during their opening comments, they made sure that they let the delegation know they had told me.

The talks were direct, but respectful. The Coalition had its issues and the Iraqis were delicate in presenting theirs. The exchange of comments had gone on for what seemed like hours, and then someone suggested that we take a break. I went to get something to drink.

During the break, one of the Fallujah negotiators made his way to me. He was a tall, well-groomed man. "Colonel King?" he inquired.

"Yes?" I replied.

"How do you do? I am Abdulla, the brother of Abd. Do you remember Abd?"

"Of course I do. How is he?"

"Abd was shot two months ago for working with [U.S. forces]," he said, his voice trailing off. "He has been in bed ever since."

I was at a loss for words to express my condolences. "I am sorry. I hope he will be okay."

"Colonel King," Abdulla continued, "Abd told me to look for you when I came here. He said you are a believer and that if you were here, everything was going to be okay. He asked me to give you this from him." Much to my surprise, he hugged me, then stepped back. "Abd has told me so much about you, I feel like I know you too. I am glad that you are here." I started back toward my chair, and found that Ambassador Jones had been standing right behind me and had heard the exchange between Abdulla and me.

Abd was the Sunni cleric who had met with me months before to petition for the release of Barakat Albu Issa and Jamal Nazzal. Abd was a good-natured man who was deeply religious and committed to his beliefs. He had shared his concerns about the attempts by extreme religious groups to infiltrate mosques in Fallujah, about anti-American sentiments in the city, and about the fear that the extremists would misdirect the followers. Abd had asked me to assist him in driving the extremists out of the city. I suspected that he might just get what he was asking for, and sooner rather than later.

Earlier I had received a message that a man by the name of Safaa from Sadr City was trying to reach me. I had met Safaa in April 2003, and he was now working in Maktada Al-Sadr's office in Sadr City. The 1st Armored Division was fighting a tough battle against Sadr's Mahdi's Army. Safaa asked if I would meet with Maktada's representative in an attempt to look for a peaceful solution to the situation.

Because it was late and all my translators had gone home for the evening, what normally took twenty minutes now took a few hours. I could not reach Faisal on his phone. I finally contacted

Zumurudeh, gave her a message, and asked her to call Safaa. For the next two hours I went in and out of the meeting with the Fallujans while I exchanged messages with Safaa through Zumurudeh. I finally asked Safaa to come into my office in the morning to discuss the matter in person.

The meeting with the Fallujans went on for seven-and-a-half hours. It was grueling as the two groups attempted to get each other to see their own point of view. In the end, General Webber contacted the marines in Fallujah and they agreed to open the hospital and remove the barricades from the bridge leading to the hospital. The assembled group did not realize the enormity of these concessions or how difficult it was for us to allow, because we knew the insurgents were using ambulances as a means to transport weapons.

We agreed to meet in Fallujah in three days. This would give both sides the opportunity to evaluate the others' actions. There was little change inside the city during the ceasefire. Insurgents continued fighting and it seemed more like an opportunity for the insurgents to reconstitute their resources than a legitimate attempt at a peaceful solution.

The next morning, Safaa was in my office. He explained that there was a misunderstanding between the residents of Sadr City and the Coalition. He believed if we opened up a dialogue between the "legitimate" representatives of Sadr and the Coalition, we could find a reasonable solution to the situation. I called Schlicher, who in turn coordinated with ambassadors Bremer and Jones concerning the requested meeting.

My instructions were to simply conduct the meeting—to listen but not offer any solutions. I told Safaa that I would provide safe passage to Sadr's representative, but he should come just before the convention center closed so that we would not bring unnecessary attention to the group.

While preparing to receive the group from Sadr's office, I received a call from a prominent Sunni cleric. He said that he was concerned about the issues in Fallujah and wanted to talk immediately. He was a leading figure and I was not in a position to say no. I called Schlicher and told him about the call. The cleric was to arrive about an hour after Sadr's group and I felt that I would need some assistance. Ambassadors Ross, Ron Neumann, and Marc Seivers would represent the Coalition.

When the Sadr representatives arrived, they wanted the Coalition to stop the attacks against the "innocent people of Sadr City." The spokesperson was an Iraqi-Canadian citizen.

When I told him there was little I could offer because Mahdi's Army was conducting unlawful searches, checkpoints, and assaults against Coalition forces, he tried persuading me otherwise. He explained that he was a member of Mahdi's Army and he too wore the distinctive shirt, but that should not make him an enemy of the Coalition. I assured him that it did and that, at that point, there was little I could do until I spoke to my leadership.

The meeting with the Sadr representatives had progressed a while before I was informed that the Sunni cleric had arrived. I excused myself for a moment so I could introduce the others who had been sent to handle the meeting. I introduced the esteemed representatives from CPA.

Upon finding out that my current meeting was not finished, the cleric became upset. "But we came to see you," he said. The security a personal relationship provided was important to the Iraqis. I assured the Sunni group that the men gathered could do much more than I could and that I would return as soon as possible.

I returned and finished my meeting with the group from Sadr and then returned to the Sunni group. As I entered, Ambassador Ross explained that the cleric wanted to take some medical supplies, water, and food to the city in the morning and asked if I thought I could arrange his entrance into the city. I said I would look into it, and Rondeau volunteered to coordinate with the CJTF-7. Apart from a short standoff with a platoon of American tanks on his way, the cleric was able to enter the city and deliver his relief supplies.

On the evening of April 15, we flew to Fallujah and prepared for the next day's negotiations. On the way, we were scheduled to pick up the governing council representatives. As we made our way toward the city, we learned that the landing zone scheduled for the pickup was being mortared. Because we did not have contact with the Iraqi representatives, it was decided that we would have to attempt the pickup on that LZ anyway. We sat down, and I looked over at Col. Steve Bucci, Ambassador Jones' military assistant. We sat there for over five minutes, waiting for the group, Colonel Bucci and I continuing to look at one another shaking our heads in disbelief. The delegation finally arrived and we flew on to the marine compound without incident.

When we arrived, Lt. Gen. James Conway received us. He was straight-thinking, sociable, and a gracious host. I remembered reading newspaper reports about General Conway when he was on his way to Iraq. The reports stated that he wanted to have a partnership with the Iraqis in Fallujah to rebuild their city. Unfortunately, events beyond his control forced his marines to fight rather than facilitate the city's reconstruction. He made it clear to Ambassador Jones that he wanted an alternative solution for Fallujah, but his marines were in place and had the city cordoned off. It seemed almost certain that there was going to be an urban battle.

The afternoon of April 16, the U.S. delegation met with the representatives from the Iraqi Governing Council and discussed at length the issues that had been raised during the meeting on April 13. We discussed the overall assessment of the immediate situation and most agreed that the Coalition had fulfilled its commitments, but the Fallujans continued their resistance. These would be the points of discussion when the Fallujah delegation arrived later that afternoon.

When the Fallujans did arrive, Abdullah was not present. Several additional members who had not attended the previous meeting were among the representatives. I recognized a representative from the Association of Muslim Scholars, Harith al-Dari's group. I called back to Baghdad earlier in the afternoon and learned that Harith did not give the prayers that day, but the assistant who did had delivered a much more moderate message. I wondered what role Harith was playing in all of this. The meeting included more of the same requests from the Iraqis, but they claimed that they needed an agreement to each point to convince the insurgents that they were making progress.

We were belaboring our points when mortars began to fall extremely close to the building in which we were meeting. I leaned over to Schlicher and whispered in his ear, "I wonder if that is celebratory fire coming down, or a sign of disapproval at our progress." He glared over his glasses at me, raised his eyebrows, and said nothing.

The Coalition's demands were few, but specific. One included turning in weapons. With Schlicher and Ambassador Jones' approval, I called Faisal on a satellite phone and asked him to pass along a message to the cleric that we wanted peace, but the talks were not progressing well and they might collapse unless we saw some cooperation from the people inside the city. We needed to see weapons tomorrow, a couple hundred, or the talks were over.

Faisal was supportive as always and said I should call him back in a couple of hours. When I reached him, he said that the conversation went well. The cleric also wanted peace and we would see the weapons we asked for in the morning. The news the next day reported several hundred weapons being turned in, but all were rusted or inoperative.

I knew al-Dari was shrewd, but this was ridiculous, and I felt deceived. I called Faisal and asked him to once again call on the cleric. I said that today was not amusing. If there were not serviceable weapons turned in tomorrow, the talks would cease, and the marines would enter Fallujah.

The next day, weapons were turned in. Rockets, mortars, machine guns, but only a fraction of what we believed were in the city. The Iraqis were stalling, not realizing that the patience of the Coalition was wearing thin.

Major General Webber notified Ambassador Jones that Barakat Albu Issa was scheduled for release and he expected him to be processed out within the day. I asked about Jamal Nazzal, and we were told that he was not on the list. Ambassador Jones asked me that evening to discuss Nazzal's position in the city. Nazzal was the Imam for the largest mosque in Fallujah and appeared to be very influential. I believed that if he was willing to cooperate, he could help advance our efforts.

Ambassador Jones scheduled a flight to Abu Ghraib and asked me to accompany him so we could speak to Nazzal in person. He wanted to determine Nazzal's position on the Fallujah issue. Nazzal was a slim man, around sixty years of age. He was jovial and seemed unconcerned about being held at the prison.

Ambassador Jones spoke to Nazzal for almost forty-five minutes. At the end of their discussion, Nazzal agreed that if he was released, he would give the city a message at prayers that they should work to build the city together rather than let the Coalition tear it down.

On Thursday, Nazzal was delivered to my office and I arranged for an intermediary to return him to the city. During our conversation, he agreed to send a message of tolerance and for the Fallujans to work with the Coalition. He would incorporate this message into his Friday prayers.

Over the course of a few weeks, Nazzal asked for the release of hostages, for patience from the Fallujans, and—the most encouraging of requests—"For our foreign guests to leave." By asking the foreigners to leave voluntarily, Nazzal was telling them that the Fallujans wanted the siege to end.

The dialogue between the Fallujans and the Coalition continued on numerous occasions throughout the month of April. We traveled to Fallujah and many traveled to meet us in Baghdad. Each time the Fallujans would ask for one more thing and we continued to demonstrate good faith. One of the members of our delegation made the observation that the Iraqis have never won a war "and they have never lost a negotiation." They were persistent if nothing else.

When I returned to Baghdad from Fallujah on April 25, Zumurudeh told me that Sheik Hassan from Sadr City had come to the office asking for a meeting. I asked her to contact him and explain that I could not meet with his group right away, but that I would contact them as soon as possible.

On April 29, General Conway announced the creation of the Fallujah Brigade to provide security for the city. The brigade was to be comprised of former military officers and soldiers. The thousand-man Fallujah Brigade was to take over security of the city and the marines would pull back from the city.

With implementation of a plan for Fallujah, Tom Warrick and I turned our complete attention to dealing with Sadr in An Najaf. I asked Zumurudeh to call Hassan and ask him if he still wanted to meet. If he did, I would meet with him on May 3.

Sheik Hassan's group arrived as scheduled, but they were strangely cold and aloof. I thought it might have been because I could not meet with them when they asked, but whatever their reason, they were not themselves.

Hassan skipped the customary greetings entirely and went straight to his prepared speech: "Colonel King, before we start, you must understand why we are here, because we are willing to die for Muktada al-Sadr."

I held up my hand and interrupted, looking Hassan in the eye: "And Hassan, you need to understand right now that I am willing to kill you for him, so let's look for more common ground." I was in no mood for threats.

Hassan understood English and his expression of disbelief was immediate. During the translation into Arabic, I could see the smugness slide from the faces of the others. This group of low-level sheiks from Sadr City had asked for this meeting hoping that I would intervene on their behalf and that it would somehow stop the Coalition's fight against the uprising. According to my Iraqi advisors, my reputation among them was well known. It was apparent that they knew I was serious.

The meeting was frank and deliberate. The sheiks explained their resentment toward the Coalition and the occupation. They made the usual comments about disrespecting the women and children and the harshness towards the detention of men. They were aware that I had prepared a paper in June 2004 that outlined suggested procedures for conducting raids, checkpoints, and detentions that would maintain force protection but preserve the cultural customs. In fact, a few of the men in the room had provided input to the paper.

While I appreciated the sheiks' position, I could no longer agree with the procedures we had discussed almost a year before, because their recommendations had come before the total collapse of security in the country.

Since my arrival a year prior, I had met many of the tribal leaders and clerics and had tried in every case to help them when I could. Now they wanted me to help stop the fighting, but the time for talk and intervention was over. What they failed to realize was that the fight had been brought to us, and the Coalition was no longer in the mood to talk.

I briefed Schlicher that evening concerning the discussions and events for the day. When I told him about the conversation with the group from Sadr City, he looked at me and said, "That's one approach at diplomacy. You can get away with saying that in the military. I could not have gotten way with it." Schlicher told me that Ambassador Bremer wanted me to prepare a talking paper based on my discussion that day that outlined ways to bring the situation in Sadr City to a peaceful conclusion.

By the end of April, CPA was focused on bringing a political solution to the situation. They wanted to keep moving the country forward, and the issues in the west and south were serious distractions to the effort. The military commanders wanted to end the fight, not to give the insurgents time to reconstitute or have the ability to fight again in the future. This disparity of philosophical approaches caused a division between commanders and staff in the CJTF-7 and the staff at CPA.

On May 5, the U.S. Army attacked an area of Karbala where Sadr's Mahdi's Army had stored weapons. The fight continued against Sadr's militia around the south over the following days and weeks. The news reported the fights taking place in the graveyards and around other sensitive sites. It is my understanding from the sheiks that Sadr had ordered the fighters into those areas in a deliberate attempt to force the Americans to cause damage to the sacred sites.

Sadr continued to reject requests from leading Shiite clerics to withdraw his troops, so I was asked to seek counsel from some of the leading sheiks in the south. On May 18, I asked a group of Shiite sheiks from the mid-Euphrates to come to Baghdad to discuss the ongoing Sadr issue.

When we met, I thanked them all for coming and reminded them, "Each of you has asked me what your role will be in the future government, and each time I have told you the Iraqi people will decide. Today will determine if you should have a role, or if the age-old role of the sheik has passed. Sadr has challenged both the establishment of a free and democratic Iraq and any future role you might intend to have. If you want to continue to wield influence within the society, you must decide what role you will allow Sadr to have."

Finally, I reiterated, "You have a decision to make," thanked them again for coming and left the room.

About an hour later, one of the senior sheiks present explained that they had decided to go and speak to Sadr: "If we cannot reason with him, we will raise an army and fight him."

I hoped it did not come to that, considering the ramifications for a longer war.

On the May 19, I accompanied Ambassador Ross to An Najaf to meet with the CPA officials and the military commanders engaged with Sadr's militia. When we arrived, we were met with a platoon of military police. We traveled from our location into the city past a number of homes. I could occasionally see a man lift his head over the wall and then quickly duck back down.

When we arrived, Ambassador Ross and the area commander addressed the ongoing concerns with Sadr's tactics. Of particular concern was the issue of Sadr's militia fighting from the mosques in an attempt to draw us in so they could stage a propaganda campaign against the Americans for desecrating their holy sites.

Ambassador Ross explained the sheiks' proposal to the general, about raising a tribal army to fight Sadr if their attempts to reason with him failed. The ambassador went on to explain the advantages of having the Iraqis face Sadr rather than the Coalition. It is an Iraqi phenomenon for the tribes to rise up against a threat, and when the threat is eliminated, the men return to their homes.

The general became angry and began to tell the ambassador how much he disapproved of the idea. I thought he stepped over the line when he stated, "You all will make this mess, go home, and leave us to deal with it."

Ambassador Ross was visibly angry and replied, "It is not your problem, it is our problem." With that, he walked from the room.

Part of the problem was the military's desire to rid the country of Mahdi's Army without considering allowing the Iraqis to solve their own problems with our sideline support. To the credit of the Iraqis, some sheiks did indeed take it upon themselves to solve problems in the areas near Kut and Diwaniya. Sadr finally acknowledged the interim government in June and many of his fighters returned to their homes.

While waiting for my flight back to the States on July 2, I received a call from a member of the former CPA. He asked if I had heard the message during prayers that day. I told him I was at the airport waiting to go home and did not have access. He told me that Nazzal had said, "The Americans are loons. They are chasing al-Zarqawi like they did WMDs. Neither one of them exists."

I wondered if Barakat had told Nazzal I was leaving and he felt free to do as he liked. I was certain that before Iraq found any sense of security, Fallujah would fall, and it would be Nazzal and Barakat among those who would lead it to its doom.

# CHAPTER 12

# Facing a Stateless Enemy

*Seek counsel of him who makes you weep,*
*never of him who makes you laugh.*
—*Arab proverb*

Having arrived with the first American forces entering Baghdad in April 2003, I had the opportunity to experience the war from the beginning of Iraq's liberation, to its occupation, and finally to the beginning attempts of the transfer of sovereignty to the Iraqi people. From this experience, my life and my perspective of world events were forever changed—changed in ways that I cannot begin to explain. I will provide a summary of my personal observations about what brought America to this historic point, what went wrong after the liberation, why the United States and its allies cannot leave now, and, most importantly, what the United States must do to regain the trust of the Iraqi people

On the day after the fall of Saddam, Iraqis were challenged by the fact that freedom has limitations and must be organized. We have experienced similar situations in the United States, most recently during the looting in New Orleans in the aftermath of Hurricane Katrina, or, earlier, during the 1992 Los Angeles riots.

Humans are just human. The Coalition was chastised for not stopping 5.5 million people from looting the city of Baghdad. As a soldier on the street during those days, I may have been able to shoot at the looters, but it would have more than likely caused a riot and endangered my soldiers, illustrating what happens when human consciousness of right and wrong is unexpectedly unchained. It was obvious in the early days after the fall of the regime that many Iraqis did not understand, or did not care, that their freedom ended when it impeded or infringed on the liberty of others.

The majority of Iraqis want freedom and democracy, but we in the West may not fully understand or necessarily agree with the Iraqi definitions of these terms. For Iraqis, the true meaning of freedom is that they can choose what democracy means for them. The concern, of course, is that those in power might create a government that will be as repressive as its predecessor, and the people will be *forced* into something worse than they had before.

The Iraqi military could have been maintained and unwanted soldiers culled out through attrition and forced retirements. This would have kept the trained soldiers capable of conducting security operations and allowed the government a method to closely monitor their activities. Iraqi units could have been dispatched to the borders of Syria, Jordan, Turkey, Saudi Arabia, and Iran to reduce and control the crossing of foreign insurgents.

The disruption to governmental services could have been lessened had we conducted the de-Ba'athification process in a more prudent manner than by discharging the entire military leadership and personnel all at once. By directing the civil servants back to work in the first days following the fall of the regime, we appreciated, as did the Iraqis, the progress made to return basic functions to Baghdad. This could not have been accomplished had we not called for the return of everyone back to work in early April.

While it may have been difficult, we should have forced the dismantling of the Shiite and Kurdish militias. The Associated Press reported the actions of these militias, but I personally read the assassination lists by the Badr Corps and witnessed the destruction caused by these militias. These armed groups operate independently and with total disregard for the government seated in Baghdad. They carried out the agendas of their respective parties, not to mention individual objectives. The attempt to have them operate as part of the Iraqi government security forces was a good plan, but we should have insisted that they be fully integrated into an Iraqi national force. We should have not allowed them to stay as intact operating units with full autonomy. These militias have conducted assassinations, kidnappings, and committed numerous acts of intimidation on the government and the public. Even today, they continue their attempt at consolidating their control over northern and southern Iraq.

For those who have never served in the military, it is impossible to understand that a true soldier prays for peace daily. For a soldier is well aware that in war, he may be forced to kill another human being, or die himself. For most soldiers, this is in direct conflict with their moral and religious values, as well as the lessons they are taught all of their lives. To rationalize the killing of another human being, to make sense of it all, many throughout history have found it useful to dehumanize their enemy; using such derisive names as "Huns," "krauts," "nips," "gooks," "commies," or "hajis." The fact is, in spite of surviving ambushes, experiencing the death of my friends, being forced to kill men who are trying to kill me, and enduring threats against my life, I have never dehumanized the people I was sent to liberate. It would have been very easy to allow myself to feel this way; in fact I witnessed it everyday, by both Americans and Iraqis. But most of the Iraqi people I met, especially the ones I worked with, had the same goal—the freedom and democratization of their country. To categorize all Iraqis as bad is as ignorant and simple-minded as racism and stereotyping is in the United States.

As we engaged our stateless enemy in what we refer to as the "Global War on Terrorism," our many misconceptions between the East and West became painfully obvious. Western media reports the Islamic Jihad to be everywhere and then group a billion Muslims into a single terrorist movement. And, as for the Middle Eastern press, Al-Jazeera's brand of television news defines the term "tabloid journalism."

The likes of Osama bin Laden and Abu Musab al-Zarqawi thrive on validation from the world media. These and other international criminals have successfully exploited Islam in the same twisted way the Ku Klux Klan uses Christianity—all in an attempt to justify their prejudices and criminal acts. We need to stop labeling these criminals *Islamic* terrorists and simply call them the terrorists or criminals that they are. Attaching religious labels alienates millions of God-loving people and gives these criminals a level of prominence among their followers. The majority of Muslims in the world are peaceful people.

I have spoken to many westerners since returning to America and have tried to enlighten those who misunderstand the Iraqi people. But I have encountered many people who have made up their minds and don't want to be "confused with facts." To debate them or to debate religion is not my purpose. I only wish to convey how my successes in Iraq were due to the understanding and the respect that I have for the world's religions, including Islam.

On the other hand, religion is part of the context of understanding our future challenges and gaining perspective on the real enemy. On several occasions during my tour of duty in Iraq, I had the opportunity to discuss the idea of *jihad* with young Muslims and Islamic clerics. I explained that I had studied the Qur'an and failed to find where the average Muslim, like Osama, had the God-given right to declare a jihad.

I asked one cleric if he would be kind enough to prepare a report for me to dispel the authority of criminals like Osama bin Laden to call for a religious war. The cleric's paper was revealing and showed that he, too, understood what I suggested to him about the misuse of jihad by al Qaeda. Unfortunately, the man was so immersed in the current trends and novelties that he had failed to recognize the message of the Qur'an, which calls for believers to work their differences out peacefully.

In fact, according to the teachings of Islamic religion, not only are the likes of bin Laden neither qualified nor authorized to call for a religious war, but no one else on this earth is, either. Only the Prophet Mohammed was specifically and explicitly given the authority by the Qur'an to call on all Muslims to wage war. When he died, the authority to do so died with him.

Men claiming the right to call all Muslims to war violate the teachings of Islam. This is only an empty promise for their followers to achieve salvation and an attempt at fame for themselves. They have done nothing more than condemn themselves to the terrorism and misery that such "religious warfare" engenders.

Let us remember the havoc that the Crusades inflicted upon the Christian societies of Medieval Europe and those of the Islamic Middle East. It is here we see the precedence for all these unjustified calls to arms "in the name of God." Just as Jesus did not sanction such violence upon other children of God, neither did the Qur'an or the Prophet Muhammad. But just as no one could ever convince the European Crusaders of the fallacy of their self-righteousness, so it is today that no one can convince the terrorists of the evil of their acts and the fallacy of crediting them to God's orders.

In chapter 39, the Qur'an states that individuals have the right to fight their enemy, but it does not give them the right to kill innocent bystanders by claiming that it is collateral damage. Those Muslims around the world who have been fooled by these dema-gogue killers—which by no means constitutes anything like a majority of Muslims—will sooner or later realize that these crim-inals who feign being devout followers of Islam are, in fact, violating the letter and the intent of the Qur'an.

Peace-loving people of all religions, including Muslims, must call for an end to the violence and convince their young radicals that the ways of al Qaeda are in violation of God's message. Ironically, these "followers of God" have managed to kill more Muslims than Christians or Jews. In fact, chapter 2, verse 62 of the Qur'an maintains that Christians are believers as are the Muslims and Jews. Therefore, killing a Christian or Jew is as wrong as killing a Muslim.

The God of Islam is the same God as that of Abraham to whom Jews and Christians pray. Jesus did not cry out for God from the cross in English; he spoke Aramaic: "El'i, El'i, La'ma Sabakhthan'i?" which means, "My God, my God, why have you forsaken me?" Isn't it fascinating that the Aramaic term "El'i," means the same as the Arabic term "Allah" (which is derived from the Arabic words "al" and "ilah," meaning "the God")?

I told the villagers who invited me to pray in the mosque that we all pray to the same God and we both ask for victory. The difference is that I pray on my knees and you pray on your hands and knees. Our God, however, hears both of our prayers. I often wonder what God thinks of all of us all asking for the same thing but from opposite standpoints.

In 1979, in the wake of the Islamic revolution in Iran, the American Academy of Religion held a conference in New York. It was a joint sponsorship by the Inter-Religious Peace Colloquium: "The Muslim-Jewish-Christian Conference of the Trialogue of the Abrahamic Faiths." Clerics and scholars from all three religions attended this conference. These men set aside their differences to meet with one another and share their thoughts on religion.

Upon closer inspection, one learns that we are much more alike than we are different. A few men were determined to change the world for the better by attempting peacemaking through profound understanding of our commonalities. This, of course, was disrupted by the September 11 terrorist attacks on America.

Individuals such as al-Zarqawi and bin Laden use our lack of understanding about the Islamic culture and religion against Westerners. They are masterful propagandists and they use our cherished freedom of speech and press to their advantage. They violate the teaching of the Qur'an when they force us to be disrespectful towards the Islamic customs and social mores as a matter of force protection.

While I was somewhat casual about my security in Iraq when I was there, if I returned today, I would not be so nonchalant. The environment has changed too much. Unfortunately, the esteem that I earned through respecting Iraqi customs in the beginning would be lost today because of the precautions I would be forced to take due to the criminal elements in Iraq.

To put to rest some of the ridiculous comments being made today about this war and the military, I have this observation: Every soldier, sailor, airman, and marine who has gone to Iraq has been a volunteer. They were not conscripts forced to join the military against their will. These men and women defend the freedoms that every American cherishes, particularly the freedom of speech. Yet, some individuals in our country use freedom of speech to violate the honor and dignity of the men and women who have paid the ultimate sacrifice to defend the freedom of others.

Nothing upsets me more than demonstrators who use the names or images of fallen servicemen in their political protests. These demonstrators should have to obtain written permission for such usage from the families of the service members killed in action. Freedom of speech is a privilege, and we must protect the individual honor of our fallen heroes who fought to protect this and other freedoms.

Future success in this war is dependent on proper identification of the real enemy. Islam is not to blame for this war, no more than Christianity is to blame for the despicable acts of the Ku Klux Klan, for the mother who hears a god tell her to drown her children, or for religious cult leaders who exploit Christianity for their own selfish ambitions. The enemy is not the God-fearing religious people in these cases, but the fanatical fringe that hijacks and twists the message of sacred texts. Both Christianity and Islam sentence such criminals to Hell.

The terrorists today are using religion to justify their flawed ideological ideas; flawed in the same way that Timothy McVeigh's ideological reasons were flawed when he blew up the Murrah Federal Building in Oklahoma City.

If one thinks that Islam is a religion that oppresses women, just take a look at predominantly Muslim countries that have been led by women. Until the end of 2004, the largest Muslim country on earth—Indonesia—had a woman as its president. Bangladesh and Pakistan have had women heads of government in recent ears. Turkey has had a woman prime minister and Iran had a woman vice president as recently as July 2005.

On the other hand, the U.S. Congress is made up of approximately 15 percent women. Compare that to the 25 percent women in Iraq's parliament. Pakistan's parliament also has a larger percentage of women members than the U.S. Congress. Iran has more women parliamentarians than France, and Muslim Malaysia has more female government officials than Russia. Meanwhile, the highest position that a female has held in the U.S. government is Secretary of State.

It is an astonishing fact that in the past fifteen years, more than half of the Muslims in the world have elected women to lead their countries. The same cannot be said for predominantly Christian countries. That does mean, of course, that Christianity is more restrictive of women's rights and upward mobility. Although Islam does not oppress women, the cultural norms in the Arab countries use Islam to promulgate the oppression of women in their societies.

Outside of the Arab world, Muslim women enjoy a great deal of autonomy and positions of influence. The male-centric Arab world does what its male-dominated history tells it to do. Other Muslim countries, as listed above, do what their less male-centric history tells them to do. Islam's role in all of this is minimal. Societies do what their traditions dictate: in the non-Arab Islamic world, which constitutes 83 percent of all Muslims, women have traditionally reached positions at the highest levels of government.

But before jumping to conclusions and crediting Islam for this, please note how the non-Muslim neighboring countries compare. The governments of the Christian-populated Philippines, the Buddhist-populated Sri Lanka and the Hindu-populated India have had women as heads of state. One can easily see that, regardless of the type of religion practiced, those societies—from Turkey and Iran to Indonesia and the Philippines—have more enlightened views toward a woman's rank in their respective societies.

Arabs, on the other hand, just like the Latin Americans, have traditionally disallowed women high political positions. The Arabs are predominately Muslims, and the Latin Americans are predominately Catholic Christians.

Islam, like Christianity, can neither be credited nor blamed for what the societies that practice those religions do. Societies follow their own traditions and interpret their scriptures in a way that is supportive of their inclinations—whether good or bad. Religions are as good (or bad) as the people who practice them. If the people are enlightened and educated, their interpretations of their scriptures are enlightened and liberal. If they are uneducated and prejudiced, their interpretation will likewise be uneducated and prejudiced. If we are to accurately identify our enemy's objectives and ideological standpoint, we must not allow ourselves to be confused by the differences between social mores and religious teaching.

There will always be the "armchair generals" who believe it is time to call the team from the field. I suggest they stop for a moment and recognize that the threat to freedom in the world is real. There is definitely a movement by extremists to create a world of anarchy and fear. Under the cloak of religious duty, these men deliver anti-American messages to stir the emotions of the weak-minded and cold-hearted to attack an enemy who is not their enemy at all.

As we define what we expect the outcome of this war to be, we must reevaluate who, or what, it is we are fighting. To say we are fighting terror is like defining World War II as a war against the Japanese suicide pilots—the Kamikazes. Terror is only a method, like criminals who use gang tactics to control the streets. Like a gang, "terror" tactics are just one weapon in the arsenal of these thugs. If we allow ourselves to believe that it is terrorism alone we are fighting, we will find ourselves fighting like a soldier in battle, killing the foot soldier and ignoring the tanks behind them. If we are not careful, the larger threat will kill us as we focus on the smaller and easier targets.

We must understand that the terrorists have a more overarching strategy. We continue to diagnose the symptoms but not the disease. We believe that the terrorists' aims are to take away the freedom that we all hold so dear. We have diagnosed this threat as terrorism, not what it is—a truly worldwide insurgency. In order to win this war, we must approach it in such a fashion, *as a war*. Bin Laden uses terror as a means to take our attention away from the real threat, which is to force us to willingly give up our rights for the sake of security and turn the innocent against the innocent.

In order to defeat the international insurgency, we must not only acknowledge, but we must understand, the ideology and motives of the enemy. We must consider the social and even demographic trends that lead to religious/ideological radicalism and consequential terrorism.

History proves that we cannot fight and win an insurgency with conventional tactics. All we have to do is look at the insurgencies in Central America, Southeast Asia, or Asia to know we cannot win with brute force alone. We must earn the trust, confidence, and respect of the people that the insurgency is targeting. We must understand that fighting an insurgency, requires a long-term commitment and desire to win. We must let the politicians that use the war in Iraq as a political football know that they need to realize the insurgents have committed themselves and their lives to their endeavor, and so must we.

To leave Iraq immediately would be to accept that we will give up our own freedom and our grandchildren will live in a police state. This insurgency is absolutely committed to destroying our way of life, and we must fight it on all fronts if we expect to win.

The criminals laugh and declare victory each time we give up one of our civil liberties to fight their "terror" tactics." If these criminals want to use religion to justify their acts, we must understand the religion enough to know that these suicide bombers will not go to "Paradise." We must embrace the principles upon which America was founded and truly accept the right to religious freedom. We must not condemn the whole for the wrong of a part. The true followers of Islam must stand shoulder to shoulder with the Christians, Jews, and other peaceful religions to denounce the criminals that defile the message from God.

If we allow our own radicals to group all of Islam into a stereotyped package of terror and evil, our grandchildren will be apologizing to the world the way we apologize to the Japanese and African Americans in the United States today. If all Muslims were terrorists—over a billion of them—you would not be reading this book. You would not be here.

On September 22, 2005, I was watching CNN and the ticker at the bottom read: "Jewish activist sentenced to 20 years in prison for his part in an attempted bomb plot." If this man was going to set off a bomb and kill innocent people, then he was a Jewish terrorist, or better yet, just a terrorist. We have allowed ourselves to categorize the world into an "us and them" scenario while ignoring one of our nation's founding principles—that of religious freedom. In the words of former President Ronald Reagan, "One man's terrorist is another man's freedom fighter." As a nation that espouses religious freedom, we need to keep the categories equal. Whether a Jew, Christian, or Muslim, a person who tries to kill another human being is a terrorist or a criminal, none are merely activists. All are acting under the cloak of religious fervor while all the time acting against the will of God.

It is necessary for us to recognize that the terrorists of today are very different from the terrorist of the 1970s. Terror tactics in the 1970s were geared toward some political gain or ideological recognition. Today, the suicide bombers are more than terrorists; they are martyrs for their cause. We cannot approach and fight them the same way as before. What is our deterrent against someone that has decided his cause is so just that he is going to give his life for it? We cannot say, "We will kill you if you don't stop." He has already decided to die.

I want to share with you a few misconceptions about Islam and the misuse of Islam on the part of our enemy, al Qaeda. My dear friend and colleague in Middle Eastern studies, Dr. Mike Izady, has dissected the term "jihad," and how it has come to be misused. He and I have had talked at length on the issue, and I will share with you just a few of the thoughts from these discussions.

When al Qaeda calls for jihad, one must realize that "jihad," like the word "crusade," is a vague term. In Arabic, a jihad is a struggle or endeavor. It is not used in a military context in the

Qur'an, and it did not have a military context in the Arabic language until 1828 when a group of ayatollahs from Persia used it during the war in the Caucasus with the Russians.

Since the words of God are timeless and never changing, the meaning of the Qur'an cannot change to fit the human purpose. While "jihad" now has military as well as nonmilitary connotations in the Qur'an, the term does not refer to a violent or military endeavor in its proper use. Instead, the clearer and more straightforward term "qattal" (fighting/violence/ killing) is used to mean a violent act on the part of the believers, whether they be Muslim, Jew, Christian, or Sabian.

In the Qur'an, the cause for "qattal" is permitted and/or prescribed in two cases, though it is not easy to clearly distinguish the two reasons from one another. Most often, however, when "qattal" is prescribed or required in the Qur'an, it is reserved for Muhammad himself. In chapter 2, verse 216, "Qattal is ordained for thee [Muhammad] although it is hateful unto thee. But it may happen that thou may hate a thing, which is good for thee, and it may happen that thou lovest a thing, which is bad for thee. God knoweth; thou knowest not."

On fewer instances, qattal is allowed, prescribed, or required from the believers themselves with or without the leadership of the Prophet Muhammad. Chapter 22, verses 39 and 40, for example, belong to this category. These verses are most often quoted as sanction for violence in the cause of justice (particularly in regards to the ongoing Palestinian dilemma) and by the believers (chapter 2, verse 62 defines believers as Muslims, Christians, Jews, and Sabians). In verse 39, one finds: "Sanction is given unto those who fight because they have been wronged; and God is indeed able to give them victory. Those who have been driven from their homes unjustly only because they said: 'Our Lord is God'—for had it not been for God's repelling some men by means of others, temples and churches and oratories and mosques, wherein the name of God is oft mentioned, would assuredly have been pulled down. Verily God helps one who helps Him. Behold! God is strong and almighty."

It is in these examples that al Qaeda violates the intent and the message from God. As written in the Qur'an chapter 22, verses 39 and 40, the sanction to fight is given *only* to those who have been wronged and not to those who have not been affected. The above example is among the extremely rare occasions where a qattal is permitted to the believers without the clear need for Muhammad to lead the campaign. In all other cases, it is Muhammad who is addressed to do so, and therefore, it had been presumed for the first one thousand years or so of Islamic history (and to many well-educated Islamic jurists today), that qattal is only required from all Muslims during the life of Muhammad, not thereafter. Even in the verses above, permission is given to those who are wronged to engage in violence, and not made a duty for all other Muslims to participate if they were not the direct subjects of that wrongdoing.

What is important here to understand is that there are no instances in the absence of Muhammad that qattal is required for *all* believers. On other occasions, in fact, clarity is missing altogether, and one is left to interpret whether the vague statements pertain to people, or Muhammad, or both. Here is a good example of the latter: (chapter 4, verse 74) "Let those fight in the cause of God who sell the life of this world for the hereafter. Whoso fights in the way of God, be he slain or be he victorious, on him we shall bestow a vast reward." (75) "And why should ye [all] not fight for the cause of God and for the feeble ones among men, women, and children who are crying: Our Lord, deliver us from this place where the inhabitants are oppressors! Give us from Thy presence some protective deputy/chosen one. Give us from Thy presence some defender!" (76) "Those who are believers will battle for the cause of God, and those who are unbelievers will battle for the cause of Satan. But Satan's strategy/tricks are ever so weak." (77) "Hast thou [Muhammad] not seen those . . . who would say: Our Lord, why hast Thou ordained fighting for us? If only Thou would give us respite yet a while" Then say (unto them, oh Muhammad): "the comfort of this world is scant; the hereafter will be better for him who wards off [evil]."

These words are interpreted to connote that warring is prescribed only while Muhammad himself is alive and can answer the questions put to him about the requirements of violence in the cause of justice and equity for the oppressed. But, due to the inconclusive nature of these verses, there are those criminal elements that interpret the same to sanction a call to arms.

Now, as to the usage of "jihad" (an endeavor and/or to strive), unquestionably at the time the Qur'an was written, and until 1828, the word in Arabic denoted peaceful undertakings. Since there are so few references found in the Qur'an, the following constitute *all* the applicable verses: (chapter 9, verse 20) "Those who believe and have left their homes and endeavored [jihad] with their wealth and their lives in God's way are of much greater worth in God's sight. These are they who are triumphant." This verse is a clear example of a jihad [struggle] for true faith in God. In chapter 22 verse 78, "And strive for God with the endeavor [jihad] which is His right. He has chosen you [all] and has not laid upon you [all] in religion any hardship; the faith of your father Abraham is yours. He has named you Muslims of old time and in here [the Qur'an], that the Messenger may be a witness [shahid] against you and that you [all] may be witnesses [shahid] against mankind [if they fail]. So establish worship, pay the taxes, and hold fast to God. He is your protecting Friend; a blessed Patron and a blessed Helper." Here the word jihad is used in a general sense and applies to all true and unselfish endeavors for spiritual good.

It is worth noting that in this last verse, the term "shahid" (witness), is the same used by Muslims for "martyr." And yet, neither "jihad" nor "shahid" are used here in the violent context, but endeavor toward self-improvement and dispensation of simple duties of worship, prayers, fasting, and tax payments.

The following verse has been wrongly used to justify the term jihad having also violent connotations: (chapter 25, verse 52) "So obey not the unbelievers, but strive [jihad] against them herewith with a great endeavor [jihad]." Realizing the Qur'an always uses the term "qattal" to denote violent endeavor, it is ludicrous to interpret this verse as equating jihad with violence. It does not. This is a directive for a peaceful endeavor (jihad), not a violent one (qattal).

I could continue, but I think that the point is made. The enemy, al Qaeda, has attempted to propagandize the Western world. They have endeavored to show this is not a nation that observes individual religious freedom as promoted. And to this, al Qaeda uses prejudices to turn Americans against all followers of Islam.

If we do not uphold and observe one of the fundamental principles that our nation was founded on, that being religious freedom for all religions, then we allow al Qaeda to use the public intolerance they have created against us. This is one of their primary objectives, to attempt to show our hypocrisy, and we contribute to their strategy through our actions . We will supply their recruiting base with angry young men who feel slighted by the inference that their belief is wrong and because they perceive that we are a nation filled with hypocrites.

Whether one agrees or disagrees with the religious beliefs of Islam, we must remain ever mindful that the United States was founded on the idea of religious freedom. In fact, Islam clearly recognizes Christians and Jews as believers in the God of Abraham. The basic inference from God for the followers of Islam is not to war with other believers. Al Qaeda—not Islam—is guilty of stating Christians are not believers. Yet it is the members of al Qaeda who prove that they are not believers.

There are few Americans who believe that the average citizen is willing to risk his or her life to turn in a criminal. We see everyday people who turn a blind eye to crime. In Iraq, those who expose the insurgents risk their lives for their belief that freedom is invaluable. Yet, they are labeled as collaborators and are killed by the insurgents or subjected to false charges and then arrested by the Coalition or Iraqi security forces.

I unfortunately witnessed this in Iraq too many times. The man who risked his life to help me locate former Ba'athists became a target for his adversaries, and they used the Coalition to arrest him on several occasions to warn others that we (the Coalition) have no loyalty to our friends.

Islamic nations that refuse to accept United Nations resolutions to denounce terrorism must do more than simply declare bin Laden a criminal. Their fear of reprisal by a criminal organization only weakens their credibility among their constituents and gives stature to bin Laden and a perceived influence among his followers.

While writing this chapter, I flew into Las Vegas for business at 11 p.m. As always, the neon lights and the flash of the city makes it a remarkable sight. It occurred to me as I was looking out of the window on our approach that the forbidden jihad that al Qaeda has declared, is a hoax. As a nation, we must realize that the attacks on our country or the countries of our allies have not been part of a jihad, under the guise of a Holy War. If al Qaeda's actual motive were religious purity, would Las Vegas not have been the primary target instead of office buildings in New York and Washington, or public transportation in London and Madrid? Since al Qaeda believes we are an immoral nation of infidels, wouldn't it have made more sense to look at targets that were of religious or moral significance? Again, we must remain cognizant of the fact that this is not a religious war. Osama bin Laden has recruited young men to carry out his criminal activities by convincing them they will go to heaven. The fact is, the God I understand of Christianity, Islam, and Judaism would not accept such acts. It is a sin in these religions, and men who are committing sin in the name of God do nothing but ensure their eternal damnation according to the beliefs of their own religions.

Instead, look at what al Qaeda has targeted—our mass transportation (airlines on September 11, 2001), political symbols (embassies), tourist spots (resort in Egypt), subways and buses (Spain and Britain). We must clearly identify the intent of al Qaeda, which is not representative of even religious bigotry, but worse. The targets of terror have not been an assault in the name of God as part of a greater "religious war," but have been more of an attempt to spread chaos and take away the freedom that we hold so dear while they turn man against man.

Since my return from Iraq, I have listened to the comments of the sanctimonious individuals who have never had to pay a price for their freedom. It is these same individuals that espouse their right to free speech in such a zealous fashion. I have heard them refer to the military and our leaders as murderers. They exercise their right of free speech because the United States military puts the lives of it service members on the line to defend it everyday. And, if the American service members were not prepared to die defending your rights, we would all lose those rights together.

As a nation, we should fear those individuals who place greater value on their lives than on freedom. I have never taken a man's life who was not trying to take mine, and if I were placed in the position to do it again, I would change nothing. The people I went to liberate from oppression and tyranny did not have any of the freedoms that we enjoy.

I shared with you some of the countless stories from Iraqis who had family members murdered by Saddam Hussein's regime for disagreeing with his policies. The cemeteries and mass graves of Iraq are filled with Iraqis who attempted to exercise free speech.

The Iraqi insurgency today, although largely Sunni, is not solely made up of them; it is multifaceted and compromising—not just those with their ideological differences (Sunni, Shi'as, and Kurds), but with religious fanatics, foreign insurgents, independent militias, and a significant criminal element that contributes to the insecurity and instability throughout the country.

Iraq cannot create a single strategic insurgency plan without taking into account the criminal elements that create such volatility within the society—and Iraq cannot ignore the influence of its neighbors.

Bordered by six countries, it is in the interest of several of those neighbors to see Iraq fail as a democracy in order to protect their oppressive, tyrannical, and corrupt regimes.

Though Iraq has successfully held an election, today Iraq is a country with a government that cannot yet provide security to its people. As the last act of malice and contempt to the people of Iraq, Saddam freed common criminals from the prisons into neighborhoods causing fear and anxiety among the people. How can one expect the citizens to respect the government—any government—and support it after having witnessed such callousness? And, if the current government condones or is unable to stop similar acts, the people will be forced to turn to the local gangs and insurgents for security.

As our memories of September 11, 2001, begin to fade, our nation has begun to feel we are safe once again. In this complacent atmosphere, there are those who believe we should leave Iraq. For them, the United States has no responsibility to that country and the people there. They judge our victory or failure by the news headlines that report how many soldiers have been killed or how many bombs have exploded in Baghdad that day.

Then there are still those who declare the Iraqi government inept for failing to reach a consensus on a constitution. They obviously did not attend American History 101, or they have forgotten that it took the United States thirteen years (1776–1789) to reach agreement and ratify our Constitution. We cannot expect, nor should we expect, that the people of Iraq would adopt every principle of America's way of life. As one U.S.-educated former Iraqi elite explained to me, "If I had liked everything about your country, I would have stayed when I was there. We have our own customs and we are different, not better or worse, just different."

In September 2005, there was a story by the Associated Press on the MSNBC website talking about Cindy Sheehan, whose son Casey's death in Iraq prompted a vigil outside President Bush's Texas ranch. "I love my country," she said. "But how many more of our loved ones need to die in this senseless war? I know you can't bring Casey back. But it's time to admit mistakes and bring our troops home now." I cannot begin to imagine the grief from her loss. I know when I had to identify the remains of my fallen comrades, I always thought about the grief that their families would endure in the future. But Ms. Sheehan, if we left now, we would not only do a disservice to the credibility of our country and the people of Iraq, we would disrespect the memories of Mark Bibby, Fallah, Omar, and your son Casey, along with the thousands of other Americans and Iraqis who have given their lives in the name of freedom and democracy in Iraq. Because the fact is, our work there is not done.

The Coalition went to Iraq, regardless of whether one agrees or disagrees with the reasons. We toppled an oppressive regime and, as a nation, now have a moral responsibility to finish what we started. If we left today, the country of Iraq would fall into civil war. The western deserts of Iraq would become a safe haven for training areas for insurgents and terrorists. The sanctuary of their new home would allow them to train new fighters who would find their way to the heartland of America and other cities in the Western world. These new fighters would do their best to surpass their predecessors in the awe of September 11, 2001.

The fact is, whether the Iraqis want us in their country or whether the citizens of the United States want us out, for the security of the Middle East and the rest of the world, we have to stay and finish what we started. The failure to understand this on the part of those who want us to leave demonstrates that they do not appreciate the impact America's departure would have on not just Iraq, but on the United States too. Before anyone calls for our withdrawal from Iraq, let him sit with a fanatic who is hell bent on killing him and they will soon realize that we must stay and finish the job we started for the safety of future generations of Americans and Iraqis.

I mentioned earlier that there are things we could have done differently in Iraq, wholesale de-Ba'athification and the dissolution of the military, for instance, or allowing the independent militias to maintain some form of organization. But, we did not. The world and historians can second-guess what we did and how we did it. But that will not make Iraq safer today; nor will it rid the world of terrorism or stop the worldwide insurgency that we are facing.

I believe that those in the Iraqi government who take such a hard-line attitude towards the former Ba'athist could lessen the insurgency and resistance if they allowed all members of the country to participate in its future. The Arabs are proud people, and to disenfranchise so many of the Sunnis from the process is certainly a prescription for disaster.

# CHAPTER 13

# Conclusion

*Sunshine all the time makes a desert.*
*—Arab proverb*

After sitting at the Baghdad International Airport for a week, I was finally on the plane for the United States. Ironically, it was July 4, 2004. As I loaded the C5 Star-lifter and took my seat, it occurred to me that I was at last returning to my children and the American way of life, and, on Independence Day. So much had changed since this journey started seventeen months ago. I could not escape my thoughts about those I was leaving behind.

Sitting on the plane waiting for takeoff, my conversation with Zumurudeh a week before continued to run through my mind. Having gone from liberator to occupier in my translator's mind, I was about to discover another shift in someone's perception of me, and one even more surprising.

"Colonel King," she continued. "Did you know that Faisal and I were standing behind the Land Cruiser when you spoke to Captain Guidry about leaving Fallah behind after the ambush?"

"No, I didn't." I wondered why she would mention it.

"Well, I saw you try to bring Fallah with us and it hurt me that everyone was yelling at you to come on and leave because there was no room. I know that we needed to leave right away, but I was hurt thinking that it could have been Hasan, Faisal, or me that you were leaving behind."

As she spoke, I relived the moment in my mind. A chill came over me with the image of Fallah lying lifeless in front of me. I could feel myself fill with the emotions from that day.

She continued, "When you told Captain Guidry that we should have taken Fallah, you did not accept his response that there was no room. When you told him that we would not have left any of the American team behind and Fallah was part of that team, I was ashamed at how wrong I was about you. I realized that you truly saw the Iraqis who worked for you as your friends, your equals, and your responsibility. Colonel King, I am so sorry, because you truly are a liberator."

After all of this, I was once again "liberator," not "occupier" in the minds of those I was sent to help. I wish it were true in the larger scheme of things. The more we come to be known as occupiers, the more our nation's credibility and our soldiers' ability to accomplish the mission is put in jeopardy.

My feelings of excitement about returning to my children were competing with my emotions about leaving before the work I had started was done. Even today, as I finish writing this book, I still agonize over the fact that I left a job unfinished.

At 4:40 a.m., July 4, my plane finally made its way onto the runway for our flight to the United States. Before having to turn off my cell phone, I sent one last message to my Iraqi friends: "God Bless you. You are in my prayers." By their responses, I was confident I had regained the trust I had from them when I first arrived, but a lot of lives were lost along the way.

The Iraqis, along with Americans, are learning that the price of freedom is not cheap. When the people of a nation begin to value their lives over their freedom, they can expect to lose both. And to expand on the comments of Arthur Goldschmidt Jr., the Middle East might be the Cradle of Civilization, but we must not allow it to become the world's grave.

# Postscript

*A promise is a cloud; fulfillment is rain.*
*-Arab Proverb*

It has been almost a year since I finished writing my original draft of *Twice Armed*. In light of recent events, I would like to read-dress some issues that have gained additional relevance and poignancy over the past year, particularly those addressed in Chapter 12. The debate continues to rage concerning whether we should have gone to Iraq and, now, whether we should stay. This subject remains one of the political talking points heading into the midterm 2006 elections. I hope our lawmakers remember our nation's commitment to the Iraqis before they make any rash political decisions.

In one case, the Coalition made a clear promise to the Iraqis in leaflets dropped over An Najaf, Iraq, in late March 2003 (see Appendix B). The message: "We are here to remove Saddam and his regime from power. We are completely committed to this task, no matter how long it takes, and to restoring peace and prosperity to Iraq." That message conveyed our commitment to the Iraqis to complete the mission we started. But our mission is not complete. It requires intestinal fortitude to stay the course we chose as a unified nation following 9/11.

As a soldier, I pray for peace daily, and while I am prepared to defend our nation with my life, I have no desire to do so unnecessarily. But after my service in Iraq, I believe we were justified in removing Saddam, and we should stay and live up to the promise we made to the Iraqis more than three years ago.

It is unfortunate when success and failure in Iraq is judged by numbers reported in the daily media—success by the number of insurgents killed or detained, failure by the number of American servicemen and women killed. This kind of linear thinking about war is both shortsighted and archaic. We can't approach an unconventional war with a conventional mindset or we are bound for failure, as proven many times in the past.

The modern enemy is a networked organization that is technically and tactically proficient. Killing seven insurgents a day is irrelevant when their organization is not hierarchal and their numbers are unknown. We will not help the Iraqis win this war through brute force or attrition; in fact, we will exacerbate the worsening situation by continuing our heavy-handed use of unrestrained conventional tactics. To effectively engage the non-state enemy, we have to do so through assured security for the Iraqis, proportional force, and a campaign of information that accurately reveals the true motives and nature of those who engage us and challenge the fledgling democracy in Iraq.

In other words, we cannot continue to fight in a reactive mode or disregard the propaganda of the insurgents. We must become proactive in our communication. That means doing more than simply sharing the "good news" of reconstruction; we must also counter the insincere religious overtones of our adversaries with convincing, unified messages.

These counter-messages must circulate to the insurgency's five target audiences, which are 1) the insurgency's supporters; 2) Iraqi non-supporters and/or undecided; 3) U.S. and Coalition policy makers; 4) U.S. citizens, who influence the decisions of policy makers; and 5) neutral countries. This approach leaves little or no room for error, so those who develop the counter-messages must be versant in Islam and Middle Eastern culture.

The effectiveness of this campaign requires action that backs up our messages. Iraqis value security, and realize that the safety of their families depends on their taking a stand against the insurgency. The desire for personal security will be the driving factor that empowers Iraqis to overcome the fear instilled by the insurgents. We must support them by stepping up our security presence, one person, one village, and one town at a time.

Once one area is secured, those in other areas will want to achieve the same level of security. More and more Iraqis will risk their lives to expose the enemy until Iraq becomes a true nation-state, not merely a country with a government. But to maintain itself as a nation, Iraq has to provide security to its people, either on its own or through the proxy of the United States. This is not the case in Iraq today.

Our accomplishments in Iraq are more abstract than the concrete achievements that politicians and members of the media have demanded. The new Iraqi constitution and the successfully held Iraqi elections are momentous events accomplished in a relatively short amount of time. Consider that it took the United States 13 years to ratify our Constitution, 89 years to abolish slavery, 144 years to give women the right to vote, and 185 years to enact civil rights legislation. For a culture that is more than 5,000 years old, the Iraqi people have made significant strides in the last three years in comparison to our own still-evolving democracy.

As the great philosopher George Santayana said, "Those who do not remember the past are condemned to repeat it." In recalling Iraq's past, we need look no further than the following excerpt from T. E. Lawrence's report on Mesopotamia (the lands that now constitute Iraq and parts of northern Syria), written in 1920. The issues he addressed more than eighty-six years ago have resounding implications to the issues of today:

EX.-LIEUT.-COL. T.E. LAWRENCE,
THE *SUNDAY TIMES*, 22 AUGUST 1920

*MR. LAWRENCE, WHOSE ORGANIZATION AND DIRECTION OF THE HEDJAZ AGAINST THE TURKS WAS ONE OF THE OUTSTANDING ROMANCES OF THE WAR, HAS WRITTEN THIS ARTICLE AT OUR REQUEST IN ORDER THAT THE PUBLIC MAY BE FULLY INFORMED OF OUR MESOPOTAMIAN COMMITMENTS.*

THE PEOPLE OF ENGLAND HAVE BEEN LED IN MESOPOTAMIA INTO A TRAP FROM WHICH IT WILL BE HARD TO ESCAPE WITH DIGNITY AND HONOUR. THEY HAVE BEEN TRICKED INTO IT BY A STEADY WITHHOLDING OF INFORMATION. THE BAGHDAD COMMUNIQUÉS ARE BELATED, INSINCERE, [AND] INCOMPLETE. THINGS HAVE BEEN FAR WORSE THAN WE HAVE BEEN TOLD, OUR ADMINISTRATION MORE BLOODY AND INEFFICIENT THAN THE PUBLIC KNOWS. IT IS A DISGRACE TO OUR IMPERIAL RECORD, AND

MAY SOON BE TOO INFLAMED FOR ANY ORDINARY CURE. WE ARE TO-DAY NOT FAR FROM A DISASTER.

THE SINS OF COMMISSION ARE THOSE OF THE BRITISH CIVIL AUTHORITIES IN MESOPOTAMIA (ESPE- CIALLY OF THREE 'COLONELS') WHO WERE GIVEN A FREE HAND BY LONDON. THEY ARE CONTROLLED FROM NO DEPARTMENT OF STATE, BUT FROM THE EMPTY SPACE WHICH DIVIDES THE FOREIGN OFFICE FROM THE INDIA OFFICE. THEY AVAILED THEMSELVES OF THE NECESSARY DISCRETION OF WAR-TIME TO CARRY OVER THEIR DANGEROUS INDEPENDENCE INTO TIMES OF PEACE. THEY CONTEST EVERY SUGGESTION OF REAL SELF-GOVERNMENT SENT THEM FROM HOME. A RECENT PROCLAMATION ABOUT AUTONOMY CIRCULATED WITH UNCTION FROM BAGHDAD WAS DRAFTED AND PUBLISHED OUT THERE IN A HURRY, TO FORESTALL A MORE LIBERAL STATEMENT IN PREPARATION IN LONDON, 'SELF-DETERMINATION PAPERS' FAVOURABLE TO ENGLAND WERE EXTORTED IN MESOPOTAMIA IN 1919 BY OFFICIAL PRESSURE, BY AERO- PLANE DEMONSTRATIONS, BY DEPORTATIONS TO INDIA.

THE CABINET CANNOT DISCLAIM ALL RESPONSI- BILITY. THEY RECEIVE LITTLE MORE NEWS THAN THE PUBLIC: THEY SHOULD HAVE INSISTED ON MORE, AND BETTER THEY HAVE SENT DRAFT AFTER DRAFT OF REIN- FORCEMENTS, WITHOUT ENQUIRY. WHEN CONDITIONS BECAME TOO BAD TO ENDURE LONGER, THEY DECIDED TO SEND OUT AS HIGH COMMISSIONER THE ORIGINAL AUTHOR OF THE PRESENT SYSTEM, WITH A CONCILIATORY MESSAGE TO THE ARABS THAT HIS HEART AND POLICY HAVE COMPLETELY CHANGED.

YET OUR PUBLISHED POLICY HAS NOT CHANGED, AND DOES NOT NEED CHANGING. IT IS THAT THERE HAS BEEN A DEPLORABLE CONTRAST BETWEEN OUR PROFESSION AND OUR PRACTICE. WE SAID WE WENT TO MESOPOTAMIA TO DEFEAT TURKEY. WE SAID WE STAYED TO DELIVER THE ARABS FROM THE OPPRESSION OF THE TURKISH GOVERNMENT, AND TO MAKE AVAILABLE FOR THE WORLD ITS RESOURCES OF CORN AND OIL. WE SPENT NEARLY A MILLION MEN AND NEARLY A THOUSAND MILLION OF MONEY TO THESE ENDS. THIS YEAR WE ARE SPENDING NINETY-TWO THOUSAND MEN AND FIFTY MILLIONS OF MONEY ON THE SAME OBJECTS.

OUR GOVERNMENT IS WORSE THAN THE OLD TURKISH SYSTEM. THEY KEPT FOURTEEN THOUSAND LOCAL CONSCRIPTS EMBODIED, AND KILLED A YEARLY AVERAGE OF TWO HUNDRED ARABS IN MAINTAINING PEACE. WE KEEP NINETY THOUSAND MEN, WITH AEROPLANES, ARMOURED CARS, GUNBOATS, AND ARMOURED TRAINS. WE HAVE KILLED ABOUT TEN THOUSAND ARABS IN THIS RISING THIS SUMMER. WE CANNOT HOPE TO MAINTAIN SUCH AN AVERAGE: IT IS A POOR COUNTRY, SPARSELY PEOPLED; BUT ABD EL HAMID WOULD APPLAUD HIS MASTERS, IF HE SAW US WORKING. WE ARE TOLD THE OBJECT OF THE RISING WAS POLITICAL, WE ARE NOT TOLD WHAT THE LOCAL PEOPLE WANT. IT MAY BE WHAT THE CABINET HAS PROMISED THEM. A MINISTER IN THE HOUSE OF LORDS SAID THAT WE MUST HAVE SO MANY TROOPS BECAUSE THE LOCAL PEOPLE WILL NOT ENLIST. ON FRIDAY THE GOVERNMENT ANNOUNCE THE DEATH OF SOME LOCAL LEVIES DEFENDING THEIR BRITISH OFFICERS,

AND SAY THAT THE SERVICES OF THESE MEN HAVE NOT YET BEEN SUFFICIENTLY RECOGNIZED BECAUSE THEY ARE TOO FEW (ADDING THE CHARACTERISTIC BAGHDAD TOUCH THAT THEY ARE MEN OF BAD CHARACTER). THERE ARE SEVEN THOUSAND OF THEM, JUST HALF THE OLD TURKISH FORCE OF OCCUPATION. PROPERLY OFFICERED AND DISTRIBUTED, THEY WOULD RELIEVE HALF OUR ARMY THERE. CROMER CONTROLLED EGYPT'S SIX MILLION PEOPLE WITH FIVE THOUSAND BRITISH TROOPS; COLONEL WILSON FAILS TO CONTROL MESOPOTAMIA'S THREE MILLION PEOPLE WITH NINETY THOUSAND TROOPS.

WE HAVE NOT REACHED THE LIMIT OF OUR MILITARY COMMITMENTS. FOUR WEEKS AGO THE STAFF IN MESOPOTAMIA DREW UP A MEMORANDUM ASKING FOR FOUR MORE DIVISIONS. I BELIEVE IT WAS FORWARDED TO THE WAR OFFICE, WHICH HAS NOW SENT THREE BRIGADES FROM INDIA. IF THE NORTH-WEST FRONTIER CANNOT BE FURTHER DENUDED, WHERE IS THE BALANCE TO COME FROM? MEANWHILE, OUR UNFORTUNATE TROOPS, INDIAN AND BRITISH, UNDER HARD CONDI-TIONS OF CLIMATE AND SUPPLY, ARE POLICING AN IMMENSE AREA, PAYING DEARLY EVERY DAY IN LIVES FOR THE WILFULLY WRONG POLICY OF THE CIVIL ADMINIS-TRATION IN BAGHDAD. GENERAL DYER WAS RELIEVED OF HIS COMMAND IN INDIA FOR A MUCH SMALLER ERROR, BUT THE RESPONSIBILITY IN THIS CASE IS NOT ON THE ARMY, WHICH HAS ACTED ONLY AT THE REQUEST OF THE CIVIL AUTHORITIES. THE WAR OFFICE HAS MADE EVERY EFFORT TO REDUCE OUR FORCES, BUT THE DECISIONS OF THE CABINET HAVE BEEN AGAINST THEM.

THE GOVERNMENT IN BAGHDAD HAS BEEN HANGING
ARABS IN THAT TOWN FOR POLITICAL OFFENCES, WHICH
THEY CALL REBELLION. THE ARABS ARE NOT AT WAR WITH
US. ARE THESE ILLEGAL EXECUTIONS TO PROVOKE THE
ARABS TO REPRISALS ON THE THREE HUNDRED BRITISH
PRISONERS THEY HOLD? AND, IF SO, IS IT THAT THEIR
PUNISHMENT MAY BE MORE SEVERE, OR IS IT TO PERSUADE
OUR OTHER TROOPS TO FIGHT TO THE LAST?

WE SAY WE ARE IN MESOPOTAMIA TO DEVELOP IT
FOR THE BENEFIT OF THE WORLD. ALL EXPERTS SAY THAT
THE LABOUR SUPPLY IS THE RULING FACTOR IN ITS DEVEL-
OPMENT. HOW FAR WILL THE KILLING OF TEN THOUSAND
VILLAGERS AND TOWNSPEOPLE THIS SUMMER HINDER THE
PRODUCTION OF WHEAT, COTTON, AND OIL? HOW LONG
WILL WE PERMIT MILLIONS OF POUNDS, THOUSANDS OF
IMPERIAL TROOPS, AND TENS OF THOUSANDS OF ARABS
TO BE SACRIFICED ON BEHALF OF COLONIAL ADMINIS-
TRATION WHICH CAN BENEFIT NOBODY BUT ITS
ADMINISTRATORS?

Lawrence's message is relevant to a number of issues we have been facing during the war in Iraq. From the debate about troop strength, to the prisoner controversy, and the reasons for going to war in the first place, these words are highly instructive. The difference today is that Iraqis have self-rule in an infant democracy that teeters everyday from the internal and external influences that challenge its success. If we leave the job unfinished, the countryside would surely erupt into a full civil war. The terrorists of the world would flood the area, establishing training camps and espousing their fundamentalist ideas for the next generation of al-Zarqawi.

As the challenges in Iraq continue, we must understand that the death of al-Zarqawi closed only one chapter and opened another. Numerous friends and reporters queried me the day after his death, all wanting to know what I thought it meant. I told them it was good that he is dead, and that there is one less terrorist in the world, but there would soon be a new leader to fill his place. The press reported almost immediately that a successor had been selected by the name of Abu Ayyub al-Masri.

Time will tell if the new terror leader in Iraq has the charisma necessary to lead the movement forward, or whether his selection will provide an opportunity for us to seize the initiative. While this movement looks to its leaders for inspiration, the ideology of our enemies is not the idea of one man or small group of men. We must recognize that the war in Iraq did not end with the capture of Saddam Hussein. Although I was in Iraq at the time and the event was cause for celebration, the war continued to rage on.

Nor will it end with the death or capture of Osama bin Laden or any other leader of the fanatical movement. Winning this war begins here in the United States with every citizen. In confronting today's terrorist, whose acts more resemble the random violence of the anarchists one hundred years ago, we must understand that the ideological movement of today has more advantages than those of the anarchists a century ago.

Both then and now, terrorism directed its violence as much against innocent civilians as it did against political figures and financial institutions. Whether by dynamite attacks on the police, assassination of world leaders (including President McKinley), blowing up telephone booths with innocent people inside, bombing financial institutions (including JP Morgan Bank, which stood only three short blocks from the future site of World Trade

Center), the tactics of the anarchist movement were eerily prescient of the modern wave of terrorism. One major difference was that anarchists did not cloak their actions in religious fervor, unlike al Qaeda. To them, it was merely an ideology.

The al Qaeda leadership took it a step further, displaying remarkable insight into the psyche of man. Instead of attempting to recruit followers to a new idea, as did the anarchist, they connected it to something that more than a billion people already hold dear: the religion of Islam. As groups such as the Ku Klux Klan have done with Bible verses, al Qaeda reworked selected verses from the Qur'an to suit their own agenda, altering the larger meaning when necessary. By taking items out of context, placing periods where there were commas or continuing text, they have, in a very real sense, created half-truths on which to base their movement.

To better understand the current extremist movement and the comparison to the anarchists in the early twentieth century, today we face the *Takfiris*. These Islamist extremists follow a violent exclusivist ideology. Takfiri ideology demands the murder of any non-Muslim, and any Muslim opposing the Takfiris' goals. These include Muslims who are viewed as being "no longer Muslim," and thus legitimate targets for attack. Muslim opponents of the Takfiris often view them as modern-day analogues of the Khawarij, the seventh-century terrorist movement that waged war against the Caliphate of Ali.

As with the anarchist movement, terrorism against the West has grown steadily since the early 1970s. Much like the anarchists of a century ago, terrorism attracts a fanatical and outspoken group of people. But unlike the anarchists of the past, today's terrorists can circulate their messages worldwide in an instant by way of modern communication technologies.

Western governments scrambled to deal with the post-9/11 terrorist in much the same fashion as the World governments did against the anarchists in the 1900s. After President McKinley's assassination in 1901, the United States moved swiftly to implement radical measures, passing an act prohibiting individuals from entering the country that professed to be anarchists. Around the world, from Asia, to Europe, to America, anarchist groups were destroyed; and the individual followers imprisoned or killed. Though only a small fraction of anarchists advocated violence, all were reviled around the world.

The reaction of the United States in the aftermath of Pearl Harbor followed a similar pattern, when an awestruck country directed its panic-stricken hostility against the Japanese, including Japanese-Americans. The overwhelming backlash led to attacks with eerie similarities to those on Arab-Americans in the days following September 11. Japanese community leaders along the West Coast were labeled and marginalized almost overnight. In December 1941, the FBI began detaining all "suspicious" Japanese and placing them in internment camps. After 9/11, influential religious and political leaders called for a similar response; if some of the policies and laws they demanded were a threat to our civil rights, so be it.

Today we revile the terrorist in the same manner that our ancestors did the anarchists and the Japanese. Yet, the terrorists of today and the anarchists from the movement a century ago have distinct differences. Real-time communications allow them to react and adapt to our tactics within minutes of the first contact. The modern terrorist network is more elaborate and cannot be decapitated. Killing one, ten, or a hundred will not stop the spread of terrorism. Rapid dissemination of information and people is its trademark.

We must not allow ourselves to alienate more than a billion people from the Islamic nations through self-righteous, uninformed conviction. This is exactly what al-Qaeda expects us to do, and if we allow ourselves to stereotype an entire religion, we fall into their trap. Instead, we must ally ourselves with all nations and all *religions* to fight the criminals that threaten freedom and the security of the world.

To reiterate a point I made earlier: this is not a war about religion, as Osama bin Laden and others would want us to believe. Unfortunately, outspoken religious figures and other leaders in this country would certainly like us to believe just that. Imagine how you would feel if someone questioned your religious beliefs. Judging Islam based on the activities of al Qaeda is no different than judging Christianity based on the activities of the Ku Klux Klan. Christians should be outraged by the thought, and feel hatred toward anyone who expressed such a thing, as do I.

Christians do not need to believe or even agree with the teachings of Islam, or vice versa. But when religious figures decree that Islam or Christianity is wrong, they are the ones who are wrong, for their own religions warn against taking it upon themselves to pass God's judgment.

The 9/11 attacks were not directed solely against our economic, political, or military infrastructure, but were designed to demoralize our country, causing instability by turning the innocent against the innocent. The day after September 11, where were you? What were you doing? What were you thinking? I recall comments being made about this or that individual (mostly of Middle Eastern descent) acting suspiciously, and every unattended package was suspected of being a bomb. When we pointed fingers, we caused the innocent to become defensive and to point fingers back at us, the same problem that made the McCarthy era so divisive.

It is natural for humans to fear the unknown. We struggle to understand those things that are foreign to us. That is why some insist on promulgating war through the manifestation of rumors. But by doing so, we become al Qaeda's best recruiting tool.

There are those who believe al Qaeda initially underestimated the American psyche, and speculate that if al Qaeda had studied what happened after the assassination of President McKinley or the bombing of Pearl Harbor, they would have more accurately predicted our reaction to 9/11. Because they have the advantage of today's mass communication, al Qaeda's leaders were quick to discover their miscalculation.

For a nation-state to use a tactic similar to al Qaeda's would have been suicidal. Few countries can compete with the United States in a conventional force-on-force war. An astute unconventional non-state actor might use such a tactic to bait the larger power into using brute force, thus alienating the Islamic masses and driving them to his cause.

Our military and political leaders have been preparing for this kind of enemy for many years. In the words of President John F. Kennedy, speaking about Vietnam to the graduating class at West Point in June 1962: "This is another type of war, new in its intensity, ancient in its origins—war by guerrillas, subversives, insurgents, assassins; war by ambush instead of by combat; by infiltration, instead of aggression, seeking victory by eroding and exhausting the enemy instead of engaging him . . . It requires in those situations where we must counter it . . . a whole new kind of strategy, a wholly different kind of force, and therefore a new and wholly different kind of military training."

As with Vietnam, we cannot apply Western action against Eastern thought and expect the same result as when Western action is applied against Western thought. And thus far, both sides in the current war have had their share of miscalculations.

I will leave you with these final thoughts: For all the effort on the part of al Qaeda, the world's Christians, Muslims, and other religious followers remain predominately peace-loving and rational. But all religions must unite to fight the plague of al Qaeda. We must continue to fight this unconventional war in an unconventional way. Before victory can be declared against al Qaeda, we must stand united as a world against those few extremists who threaten the *security* and *freedom* of us all.

# Acknowledgments

*Dwell not upon thy weariness, thy strength shall*
*be according to the measure of thy desire.*
*-Arab Proverb*

There are many individuals to whom I am grateful and eternally indebted who have made this endeavor possible. Besides those who are mentioned in the book, my family, friends, mentors, and colleagues who shared their past experiences and knowledge prepared me for much of what I was asked to accomplish in Iraq. However, it was their presence in my life that allowed me to accomplish the task of writing this book. To mention everyone by name would take a whole book by itself. But as much as I learned from these individuals, good fortune allowed me to implement what I had learned. As Napoleon Bonaparte once said, "Ability is nothing without opportunity." Iraq was certainly my opportunity.

To each person who has touched my life, I thank you now, but I would be remiss if I did not mention those individuals who were so instrumental in making my tour in Iraq successful and this book possible. To my mom and dad, Bill and Carolyn King, my sister and brother-in-law Pam and Dale Monjar, my grandparents

Walter Beasley, Lee and Louis Gregory, and my extended family Richard Beasley, Gary Beasley, and Judy Grigg, I am thankful for your encouragement over the years and particularly after my return from Iraq. To my family, Barbara, Wesley, and Kaitlyn King, I give my loving thanks and devotion for your understanding, and for your unwavering love and support throughout the preparation, rewrites, and edits, and all the times that I was absorbed in the writing of *Twice Armed*.

I am grateful for Tom and Becca Davenport's encouragement, along with that of my grandmother, Nina King, who compelled me to achieve the education necessary to be prepared for my duties in Iraq. Throughout my career, I have worked for or with people who not only encouraged me, but also pushed me to succeed. I am appreciative for Maj. Gen. Donald Campbell, Brig. Gen. Sandy Davidson, Col. Dave Borresen, and Col. Richard Hayford for believing in me enough to give me a chance to work in the Special Operations community.

To Maj. Gen. William Berkman, Maj. Gen. Tom Matthews, Brig. Gen. Dennis Wilkie, Col. Herman Frankel, Col. Wendell Hodgkins, Col. Jack Basil, Col. Kal Oravetz, Col. Bill McCoy, and the late Col. Eli Nobleman, I am indebted for your mentorship over the years in civil affairs and for your patience in sharing with me your experience and historical perspective of civil-military government. The collective experience of these men became invaluable on April 8, 2003 when I learned that the 422nd Civil Affairs Battalion would be at the spearhead with the 3rd Infantry Division (Mechanized) to initiate the reconstruction effort in Baghdad. To the Civil Affairs Association that works tirelessly to support the soldiers and their families, I am grateful for your service.

Dr. Mike Izady, Dr. Brad McGuinn, Dr. Drew Ziegler, and Dr. John Handley gave me the depth of knowledge necessary to see the international stage and the Middle Eastern culture not for its differences, but for its commonalities. Through your teaching, I was able to experience Iraq through the eyes of the Iraqi people. Not by going "native," but by realizing that I was in their country and should accept their culture before I tried to expose them to mine.

The most significant part of my Iraqi experience is what was documented in the press. I am grateful to many, but specifically Staff Sgt. Kevin Bell and Sgt. James Allen, the combat camera crew who captured on film so much of the 422nd Civil Affairs Battalion success during the early days of the war. To Annia Ciezadlo and Betsy Pisik from the *Washington Times,* Mohamad Bazzi from *Newsday,* Charlie Ryan and Kelly O'Donnell from NBC News, Emily Harris of National Public Radio, and Michael R. Gordon of *The New York Times,* I am appreciative for your reporting of our story.

To my longtime friends who have been by my side through the ups and downs of life, I thank Dr. (Lt. Col.) Pat Cello, Dr. Mike Martin, the Honorable Rick and Mrs. Hoa Welch, Lt. Col. John Somich, Jim House, Gene Keaveney, and Ellis Saums. There are three individuals who actually brought the idea of *Twice Armed* to fruition, Suzanne Rucker, Col. Martin Stanton (author of *A Road to Baghdad*), and Bob Kelley: I appreciate the guidance, phone calls, contacts, and support to make this possible.

Ambassador Ron Schlicher, Ambassador Chris Ross, Ambassador Ron Neumann, and Ambassador Dick Jones, Maj. Gen. Buford Blount, Brig. Gen. John Sterling, Tom Warrick, Bob Kitrinos, Col. Dale Shirasago, Col. Emilio DiGiorgio and Col. Larry Rubini, I am thankful for the opportunity to have served and learned from each of you. Then of course there was my Iraqi staff to which I am grateful for truly making my tour in Iraq an incredible experience and a success.

I am indebted to Maj. Brent Gerald and Lt. Col. Phil Rosso for their dedication and service to our country. It was their commitment and loyalty to soldiers that made my command tenures successful. To Sgt. 1st Class Sylvester "Sly" Harper, my drill sergeant: soldiers in my command benefited from your instruction and I cared for them the way you taught me to.

I cannot forget my publisher Richard Kane, my publicist Callie Oettinger (who is responsible for the title of this book), my editor Steve Gansen, and my agent E. J. McCarthy, the professionals behind the scenes of publishing *Twice Armed*. I appreciate the assistance of Jim Hill, Department of the Army Office of Public Affairs for his assistance in getting the manuscript reviewed and Mary Alice Davidson, who so kindly assisted me in preparing the book proposal.

For their care during my recovery at Fort Bragg, North Carolina, I want to thank Dr. Marjorie Cannon, Dr. Cheryl Ledford, Dr. Michael Sebastia, and my physical therapist Jerry Griffin.

To the soldiers and families of the 422nd Civil Affairs Battalion, whose personal sacrifices and individual safety weighed on me daily: I am proud that I had the opportunity to serve with each of you. You are truly among the best our country has to offer.

Finally, to the fearless operators whom I cannot mention by name: it was your dedication to duty and silent professionalism that made the 422nd Civil Affairs Battalion operation and my personal mission a success. To each of you, I am forever grateful!

—R.A.K.

Edgewater, Maryland

June 2006

# Appendix A

## SADDAM'S MEMO

In May 2003, the Assyrian Christians approached me at my head-quarters in the Green Zone. Their question to me was typical of what I had been hearing from Iraq's religious and ethnic minorities: "How do we fit into the future Iraq?" (As of this printing, this question has yet to be answered.)

The men then presented me with a handwritten letter they had found in the Fedayeen's Baghdad headquarters. It was from Saddam to a military aid by the name of Lt. Col. Rakan Abdul-Ghafour, explaining how to deal with the phenomena of desertion. Saddam ordered the aid to telephone a subordinate military commander and direct him on how to deal with deserters. Upon the first offense, amputate one ear; second offense, amputate the other ear; third offense—capital punishment. Saddam felt that once the word was out about the decree, ". . . [the deserters] will contact concerned authorities to give themselves up."

The men then presented me with a Fedayeen execution sword. It had a pewter handle and a steel blade. They explained that the blade would be heated to cauterize the amputation. The blade looked as if it had been heated over and over—I wondered just how many times.

Although numerous individuals from all over Iraq had shared with me their horror stories about the former regime's atrocities, this was the first time I had actually seen the psychopathic mentality of Saddam Hussein outlined in writing. I wondered if the deserters we captured during the war knew about the punishment that awaited them, and whether they were running *to* us or *from* Saddam.

A member of my Iraqi staff translated the memo for me. Once I understood its content, I passed the memo over to the Human Rights Commission to include in its file on the atrocities of Saddam's regime. While we rightfully object to the human rights abuses at Abu Ghraib, we should also consider the atrocities exemplified by this letter in evaluating our role in Iraq. Clearly, Saddam and his regime needed to go, and we were the only ones who could make it happen.

بسم الله الرحمن الرحيم

رئاسة الجمهورية
الرئيس

المقدّم/ وكامل عبد الغفور

إن القصد من قرارنا بوقف الاداء القتالي "وقف الحرب" مع
أذ أنه المها هو الدرع لتنفيذ القضا
على ظاهرة الحرب، وتنظيم الإجراءات
الرادع على مرتكبيه، ولأن المغبنين
في الحرب لم يبقى واع بوجوه
بغير مقصوديه كما يجب مناقشة طويلة
فأنا أوضح بأنه ما أن ليجعوا بتفيذ
هذه القصفم على من طبقت عليهما
يصبح لديه يحضروا إلى الكامت واعطاء
المرّد ليسلموا أنفسهم او

بسم الله الرحمن الرحيم

رئاسة الجمهورية
الرئيس

من قد يستفيد من ١١١١١ الرحمة صرامة
إضافية .... 
يبلغ الرفيقة حميد زمام هاتفيا

بما يلي .... ينفذ قرارنا المبلغ اليه بواحد
من كل خمسة طلقة القى القبض
عليهم ويكون ذلك ١ ......
؟ ما بعد هرب الطرب أربعم
يوفر القطاء لديه ليوفره مجموع ٣٠
الا تفذ ؟ بالخذمة لمهرتو؟
ويجلد ١١١١١ الآخرون لكل واحد
منهم خمسه جلد ٥ ٢١١١١١

بسم الله الرحمن الرحيم

رئاسة الجمهورية
الرئيس

طلقة رصاص لن يبلوا
لهم أن ينفسهم للخدمة العربية
وتتفق مع صول ...
يمول الذين لم يلقى ا
القبض عليهم قبل ساعة
اجتماع منظماتهم ابلاغ الرسمية
مهد من قبله طرة اسبوع)
اي بوقف القاهر القبض عليهم
طلة اسبوع واجرفتظ
من هذا الاجج يعقد
الحزب نعت جماهيره

بسم الله الرحمن الرحيم

(٣)

رئاسة الجمهورية

الرئيس

أود بنشاط بالطريقة التي
يراها الرفيق محمد لابلاغ الجميع
بقرار قطع الأذن والأذنين
في حالة العودة، وتطبيق قرار
الاعدام على من يتخلف هاربا
من الخدمة العسكرية لقد
جرى ذلك ليكون الجميع
بينة [illegible] إذ قررنا
هذا، وبانتهاء الحرب
في الجنوب حملات لالقاء القبض
على من يتخلف هاربا من الخدمة

بسم الله الرحمن الرحيم

رئاسة الجمهورية
الرئيس

المـــكرية ؟ ومنطلقاً
عن إ د اشباع دقة التعليمات
المبلغة الى الرصفة محمد .
بعد انتي و صمولة البجم
ايام ؟ .

١٩٩٤/٨/١٩

The Republic Presidency
The President

Lt. Col.Rakan Abdul-Ghafour

The purpose of our decree is to cut one ear, and then two ears for the one who deserts again as a deterrent to eradicate the phenomena of deserting and magnify deterrent measures upon its desertion. And since deserters have never been seriously prosecuted in the past, I expect that as soon as they hear about this punishment already executed on some, they will contact concerned authorities to give themselves up. This may give ones who benefit from the grace period another chance.

Comrade Mohammed Zeman should be informed by telephone of the following:

1. Our decree passed to him should be executed in one for every five arrested and he should select from among the worst, either by number of deserting or if he has no acceptable reason for not committing himself to military service regulations other should be flogged fifty times each and be released so that they submit themselves to military service voluntarily.

2. A grace period of one week should be given to all those who are not caught yet until Comrade Mohammed is informed by you, i.e., catching them should be suspended for only a week. During this week, the party may mass symposia or be active in any fashion appropriate to Comrade Mohammed to inform all of the decision of amputating one ear and then two for return to

deserting. Capital punishment should be carried out upon those who had both their ears amputated so that all will be fully aware of our above decree. That party should start in the south with his campaign to arrest those who remain deserted from military service or still late for joining the service, and in accordance to instructions relayed to Comrade Mohammed after the seven days are over.

Signed

Saddam Hussein
19-8-1994

# Appendix B

أيها المواطنون العراقيون!

نحن هنا لأزالة صدام و نظامه من السلطة.

نحن ملتزمون تماما بهذه المهمة، مهما

طال الزمن، وأيضا نحن هنا لأ عادة السلام

والأزدهار الى العراق.

نحن نراعي عاداتكم و معتقداتكم بدرجة

عالية من الأحترام. وأننا سنعمل كل جهدنا

لعدم حصول أي مضايقة. نحن نعتذر عن أي

أنزعاج يحصل لكم ولعوائلكم عندما نساعد

بأرجاع العراق الى مواطنيها.

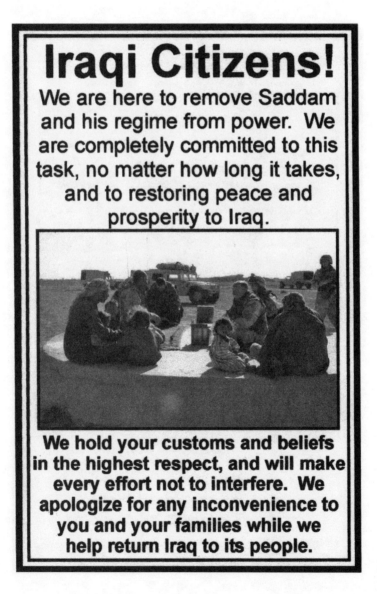

# Iraqi Citizens!

We are here to remove Saddam and his regime from power. We are completely committed to this task, no matter how long it takes, and to restoring peace and prosperity to Iraq.

We hold your customs and beliefs in the highest respect, and will make every effort not to interfere. We apologize for any inconvenience to you and your families while we help return Iraq to its people.

قوات التحالف تقوم بعمليات

عسكرية خطيرة في هذه المناطق

لسلامتكم أتبعوا مايلي:

أبتعدوا عن كافة الطرق.

أبقوا في بيوتكم قدر الأمكان.

تقربوا من نقاط السيطرات العسكرية

ببطء و بدون طريقة تهديدية.

أحموا أنفسكم و عوائلكم و ذلك

بتعاونكم مع كافة تعليمات قوات التحالف.

لا تتدخل أو تضايق قوات التحالف!

**Coalition Forces are conducting dangerous military operations.**

**FOR YOUR SAFETY**

- Stay off of the roads.

- Stay in your homes as much as possible.

- Approach military checkpoints slowly and in a nonthreatening way.

- Protect yourself and your families by cooperating with all Coalition Force instructions.

**Do not interfere with Coalition Forces!**

# Iraqi Citizens!

Coalition Forces are working around the clock to restore security, medical, electrical and water services

## Please be patient during this process

You can help Coalition Forces by identifying yourself if you possess special skills that will help restore Iraq to a nation of great prominence.

Medical professionals, power, water, and sewage engineers are in great need.
If you possess these skills, please approach Coalition Forces.

# Index

**R. Alan King** is a consultant for Consequence Management, Inc. He is a recognized authority in Middle Eastern affairs and security, with extensive specialized experience in Iraq. He served in Iraq for sixteen months, first as a civil affairs battalion commander and then as the deputy director of the Office of Provincial Outreach, Coalition Provisional Authority. In Iraq, King was credited with leading the Coalition's tribal affairs and Sunni outreach programs, meeting more than three thousand sheiks and clerics.

Dubbed "Alan of Arabia" by the press, the trust he formed with Iraq's tribal sheiks enabled him to help capture many of the former elites from Saddam's regime, including Mizban Khadr Hadi, number 23 on the most wanted Iraqis list (and the infamous "nine of hearts" in the U.S. government–issued deck of cards featuring the most wanted former regime officials); Sa'd Abdul-Majid Al-Faisal Al-Tikriti, number 55/three of spades; Muhammad Saeed al-Sahaf (a.k.a. "Baghdad Bob"), former minister of information; the former chairman of the Iraqi Atomic Energy; and countless former ambassadors, general officers, former cabinet ministers, parliament members, and other deposed elites.

King is among the most-decorated veterans of the Iraqi conflict, having been awarded two Bronze Stars for Valor, two Bronze Stars for achievement, and the Combat Action Badge. Wounded during combat operations in Iraq, King spent sixteen months in rehabilitation at Fort Bragg, North Carolina, following his return to the United States on July 4, 2004 King holds two Master of Art degrees and a Bachelor of Science degree, and is a graduate of the U.S. Air Force Air War College and the Army Command and General Staff College. As a military spokesperson, King has appeared on *NBC Nightly News*, CNN, CNN International, and Fox News Channel, among others. His work has been profiled by NBC, MSNBC, National Public Radio, *Harper's Magazine*, *Newsday*, *U.S. News & World Report*, the *Christian Science Monitor*, *New York Times*, *Washington Times*, *Washington Post*, *Wall Street Journal*, and other publications. *Twice Armed* is King's first book.